The Resurrection of Jesus

The Resurrection of Jesus

JOHN DOMINIC CROSSAN AND N. T. WRIGHT IN DIALOGUE

Robert B. Stewart, editor

FORTRESS PRESS
Minneapolis

THE RESURRECTION OF JESUS
John Dominic Crossan and N. T. Wright in Dialogue

Cover image: © Werner H. Müller/CORBIS
Cover design: Diana Running
Book design: James Korsmo

ISBN 0-8006-3785-2

The paper used in this publication meets the minimum requirements of American
National Standard for Information Sciences — Permanence of Paper for Printed
Library Materials, ANSI Z329.48-1984.

Manufactured in the U.S.A.

10   09   08   07   06   1   2   3   4   5   6   7   8   9   10

For
Bill and Carolyn
&
Tom and Dom
Without whom this would not be

— Contents —

Contents

– Contributors –

WILLIAM LANE CRAIG is Research Professor at Talbot School of Theology in La Mirada, California. He earned a doctorate in philosophy at the University of Birmingham, England, before taking a doctorate in theology from the Ludwig Maximilians Universität-München, Germany, at which institution he was for two years a fellow of the Alexander von Humboldt-Stiftung, writing on the historicity of the resurrection of Jesus. He spent seven years at the Katholike Universiteit Leuven, Belgium, before taking his post at Talbot in 1994. He has authored or edited over thirty books, including *Assessing the New Testament Evidence for the Historicity of the Resurrection of Jesus: Will the Real Jesus Please Stand Up?* (with John Dominic Crossan), and *Jesus' Resurrection: Fact or Figment?* (with Gerd Lüdemann), as well as numerous articles in professional journals such as *New Testament Studies, Journal for the Study of the New Testament, Expository Times*, and *Kerygma und Dogma*. He currently lives in Atlanta with his wife, Jan; they have two children, Charity and John.

JOHN DOMINIC CROSSAN is Emeritus Professor of Religious Studies at DePaul University in Chicago, Illinois. His most important books are *The Historical Jesus: The Life of a Mediterranean Jewish Peasant* (1991), *The Birth of Christianity* (1998), and *In Search of Paul: How Jesus' Apostle Opposed Rome's Empire with God's Kingdom*, coauthored with archaeologist Jonathan Reed of LaVerne University (2004). His work has been translated into ten foreign languages, including Korean, Chinese, and Japanese, and he has lectured to lay and scholarly audiences across the United States as well as in Ireland and England, Finland, Australia, New Zealand, and South Africa.

CRAIG A. EVANS is Payzant Distinguished Professor of New Testament at Acadia Divinity College in Nova Scotia. He received his Ph.D. from Claremont Graduate University. Professor Evans is author and editor of some fifty books. Among his authored books are *To See and Not Perceive: Isaiah 6.9–10 in Early Jewish and Christian Interpretation* (1989), *Luke* (1990), *Jesus* (1992), *Noncanonical Writings and New Testament Interpretation* (1992), *Word and Glory: On the Exegetical and Theological Background of John's Prologue* (1993), *Luke and Scripture: The Function of Sacred Tradition in Luke-Acts* (1993), *Jesus and His Contemporaries: Comparative Studies* (1995), *Jesus in Context: Temple, Purity, and Restoration* (1997), *Mark* (2001), *The Bible Knowledge Background Commentary: Matthew–Luke* (2003), and *Jesus and the Ossuaries* (2003). Professor Evans has also authored more than two hundred articles and reviews. He was also editor of the *Bulletin for Biblical Research* (1995–2004) and the *Dictionary of New Testament Background* (2000).

R. DOUGLAS GEIVETT is Professor of Philosophy at the Talbot Department of Philosophy, Biola University, in La Mirada, California. He is a graduate of Dallas Theological Seminary (M.A. 1985), Gonzaga University (M.A. 1985), and the University of Southern California (Ph. D. 1991). In addition to contributing numerous articles to various philosophical and theological journals, he is the author of *Evil and the Evidence for God* (1993) and coeditor of *Contemporary Perspectives on Religious Epistemology* (1992) and *In Defense of Miracles: A Comprehensive Case for God's Action in History* (1997). His interests range over the philosophy of religion, epistemology, and the history of modern philosophy.

GARY HABERMAS is Research Distinguished Professor and Chair of the Department of Philosophy and Theology at Liberty University. He received his Ph.D. from Michigan State University. He has authored or coauthored twenty-six books (thirteen on the subject of Jesus' resurrection), including *The Risen Jesus and Future Hope* and the coauthored volumes *Did Jesus Rise from the Dead? The Resurrection Debate* (with Antony Flew and Terry Miethe), *Resurrected: An Atheist and Theist Dialogue* (also with Antony Flew), and *The Case for the Resurrection of Jesus* (with Michael Licona) and has contributed chapters or articles to eighteen additional books. He has also written well over one hundred articles of various sorts in journals such as *Faith and Philosophy*, *The Journal for the Study of the Historical Jesus*, and *Religious Studies*. He has frequently been a visiting or adjunct professor, teaching some three dozen courses at more than a dozen graduate schools and seminaries during the last ten years.

TED PETERS is Professor of Systematic Theology at Pacific Lutheran Theological Seminary and the Graduate Theological Union in Berkeley, California. He is editor of *Dialog* and coeditor of *Theology and Science*. He is author of many important works in theology and ethics, including *God—The World's Future* (Fortress, 2nd ed., 2000), *Sin: Radical Evil in Soul and Society* (1993), and coeditor of *Resurrection: Scientific and Theological Perspectives* (2003).

CHARLES L. QUARLES is Vice-President for Integration of Faith and Learning, Associate Professor of Religion, and Chair of the Division of Religious Studies at Louisiana College in Pineville, Louisiana. He is a graduate of the University of Mississippi (B.A. 1986), and Mid-America Baptist Theological Seminary (M.Div. 1989; Ph.D. 1995). He is the author of *Midrash Criticism: Introduction and Appraisal*, and has published articles in scholarly journals such as *New Testament Studies*, *Novum Testamentum*, *Bulletin for Biblical Research*, and *Journal for the Study of the Historical Jesus*.

ALAN F. SEGAL is Professor of Religion and Ingeborg Rennert Professor of Jewish Studies at Barnard College, Columbia University, in Manhattan. He is a graduate of Amherst College (B.A. 1967), Brandeis University (M.A. 1969), Hebrew Union College–Jewish Institute of Religion (B.H.L. 1971) and Yale University (M.A. 1971, M.Phil. 1973, Ph.D. 1975). His studies included English Literature, Psychology, Anthropology, Comparative Religion, Judaica, Christian Origins, and Rabbinics. He has authored numerous books, including *Life after Death: A History of the Afterlife in Western Religion* (2004); *Two Powers in Heaven: Early Rabbinic Reports about Christianity and Gnosticism* (2002); and *Rebecca's Children: Judaism and Christianity in the Roman World* (1986).

Contributors

ROBERT B. STEWART is Associate Professor of Philosophy and Theology at the New Orleans Baptist Theological Seminary, where he occupies the Greer-Heard Chair of Faith and Culture. He is a graduate of Cameron University (B.A.) and Southwestern Baptist Theological Seminary (M.Div.B.L. and Ph.D.) He is author of *The Quest of the Hermeneutical Jesus: The Impact of Hermeneutics on the Jesus Research of John Dominic Crossan and N. T. Wright* (2006). He has published articles and book reviews in a number of theological dictionaries and journals, such as the *Revised Holman Bible Dictionary, Journal of the Evangelical Theological Society, The Southern Baptist Journal of Theology, Churchman: A Journal of Anglican Theology,* and *Southwest Journal of Theology.* He is also a contributor to the *Apologetics Study Bible* and the *Baker Dictionary of Cults and Sects.*

N. T. WRIGHT is Bishop of Durham (Church of England) and was formerly Canon Theologian of Westminster Abbey and dean of Lichfield Cathedral. A graduate of Oxford University, he previously taught at Cambridge, McGill, and Oxford Universities. Wright's *The New Testament and the People of God* (1992), *Jesus and the Victory of God* (1996), and *The Resurrection and the Son of God* (2003) are the first three volumes of his projected six-volume series entitled Christian Origins and the Question of God (SPCK/Fortress Press). Among his many other published works are *The Original Jesus* (1996), *What Saint Paul Really Said* (1997), and *The Climax of the Covenant* (1992). He is author of the For Everyone commentary series.

– Preface –

On Friday night, March 11, 2005, nearly one thousand people filled the Leavell Chapel on the campus of New Orleans Baptist Theological Seminary for the inaugural Greer-Heard Point-Counterpoint Forum. The forum is a five-year pilot program made possible by a gracious gift from William L. Heard Jr. and his wife, Carolyn. This program provides a forum for an evangelical scholar and a nonevangelical scholar to come together for a night of dialogue on a particular issue of religious or cultural significance. The forum is not exactly a debate, although by design the speakers necessarily differ in their opinions. Instead, the intention is to provide a model for civil discourse on important topics and an environment in which to discuss differences—without abandoning one's convictions—and to make a case for one perspective over against another.

The inaugural event featured two of the best-known Jesus scholars on the contemporary scene: John Dominic Crossan and N. T. Wright. The dialogue topic for the evening was "The Resurrection: Historical Event or Theological Explanation?" Wright, a former Oxford and Cambridge professor and the current bishop of Durham (Church of England), is the author of a seven-hundred-page tome on the resurrection entitled *The Resurrection of the Son of God*,[1] which is the third volume in his projected six-volume series, Christian Origins and the Question of God. Concerning this work, Craig Blomberg comments:

> My overall response to a volume like this is a combination of astonishment, awe, admiration (and not a little bit of jealousy at Wright's gifts and brilliance!), but most of all profound gratitude for his commitments to both scholarship and the church. . . . Doubtless many studies of resurrection will continue to be written; it seems inconceivable that any will prove nearly as important and convincing for a long, long time.[1]

Crossan shines in his own right. Professor emeritus at DePaul University and cochair of the Jesus Seminar, he is widely regarded as one of the most creative and knowledgeable Jesus scholars writing today. His book *The Historical Jesus: The Life of a Mediterranean Jewish Peasant* is a landmark in current research on the historical Jesus. He is respected not only for his knowledge but also for his irenic spirit. Concerning Crossan, Wright remarks:

> Crossan towers above the rest of the renewed "New Quest", in just the same way as Schweitzer and Bultmann tower above most of twentieth-century scholarship, and for much the same reasons. He, like them, has had the courage to see the whole picture, to think his hypothesis through to the end, to try out radically new ideas, to write it all up in a highly engaging manner, and to debate it publicly without acrimony. With foes like this, who needs friends?[2]

Expectations were thus justifiably high when the two men took the stage for their dialogue. And Crossan and Wright did not disappoint. Their exchanges were always respectful and cordial. They found several points on which to agree, and even to sharpen their own positions—and they insisted on retaining several points of difference as well. All this was done at a high scholarly level but for the most part in language that the ordinary layperson, interested in learning more of what history has to say about Jesus, could understand and appreciate. Humor, coupled with genuine respect and affection for each other, was evident throughout the evening. Though they disagreed on several significant points, they wholeheartedly agreed that the resurrection was very important and that it should make a difference in this world! The evening was a wonderful time of dialogue. All who were fortunate enough to attend came away the richer for it.

The format for the evening was decided over breakfast in San Antonio during the 2004 Society of Biblical Literature annual meeting: Tom and Dom would each present a brief synopsis of his position concerning the resurrection, and then they would genuinely dialogue, that is, talk *to* one another rather than alternately talking *about* each other. Each presenter was free to question the other, to agree with the other, to argue certain points of difference with the other—and to joke and provide commentary throughout the next forty-five minutes. This model for scholarly interaction is truly novel, so far as the three of us know. Nobody really knew how it would work or what to expect. We hoped that this format would allow two scholar friends to discuss their differences in a way that wasn't just one more debate. By all accounts, this new model was a smashing success.

In his opening comments Tom Wright summarized the major points of his book, *The Resurrection of the Son of God*, and explained to the audience what he intended to accomplish through the work. A number had already read the book but many others, perhaps most of those attending, had not read through the seven-hundred-page tome. Dom Crossan, on the other hand, briefly discussed a few of his major points in an unpublished paper entitled "Mode and Meaning in Bodily-Resurrection Faith" that he had distributed to the other presenters prior to the conference. That paper in its entirety became the appendix to this volume. The dialogue itself has the feel of an evening of informal speeches and conversation rather than dueling publications. We have endeavored to present the dialogue in a readable form, rather than a bare transcription, without losing the spontaneous feel of the evening.

The next day featured a series of six papers on topics related to the resurrection or to the work of Crossan and Wright or to both. The presenters represented several disciplines: Craig Evans and Chuck Quarles, New Testament studies; William Lane Craig, R. Douglas Geivett, and Gary Habermas, philosophy; and Ted Peters, theology. After each paper, Crossan and Wright briefly replied and in some cases posed questions to the presenters. Alan Segal was originally scheduled to take part in the conference but was unable to do so due to weather and travel concerns. We are very pleased that he nevertheless has provided an essay for this volume.

We trust that there will be many more such Greer-Heard events in the years to come. It is with great pleasure that we offer these essays to you. We hope that you will be further stimulated, challenged, and enriched by them.

‒ Acknowledgments ‒

Because projects like this require a lot from many people, one always feels a certain apprehension when acknowledging those who have helped to ensure the project's success. Inevitably, one or more deserving individuals will be left out. Nevertheless, many deserve to be thanked, and even praised, so one must go on.

Thanks are due first and foremost to William (Bill) and Carolyn Greer Heard. Without their gracious gift to the New Orleans Baptist Theological Seminary (NOBTS), the event from which this book was birthed never would have taken place. The Heards are people of great conviction, willing to try something new. Their passion for this sort of informed and balanced dialogue will surely bless not only the seminary and its students but also interested laypersons and scholars of religion for some time.

N. T. (Tom) Wright and John Dominic (Dom) Crossan must also be thanked. I owe them a personal debt as well. Nearly five and a half years ago, I wrote a dissertation on these two men and their work. Both were kind enough to read their respective chapters and to make helpful comments, and even compliment a few parts. Both are among the most gracious men I know, always willing to help a student. They share a concern to see Jesus understood better as a figure in history, and to see that what we learn of the historical Jesus makes a difference in our world.

In addition, all the presenters and writers deserve thanks. They are all highly respected in their fields. I would be grateful to work with any one of them—to work with them all was an unexpected pleasure.

The administration and staff at NOBTS must be applauded. The school's president, Chuck Kelley, led the way in bringing the Point-Counterpoint Forum before the trustees for their approval. Dr. Kelley understands that conservative theological beliefs and academic excellence are not dichotomous, that truth and determined enquiry are never enemies of the gospel, and that civility toward those with whom you disagree is not capitulation.

I will be forever grateful to Dr. Charles Harvey, vice-president of development at NOBTS, who took the idea of a forum seriously enough to promote the idea to philanthropists such as Bill Heard. Without Charlie's tireless efforts, there would be no Greer-Heard Forum.

Numerous staff people and seminary students assisted in significant ways. Jeff Audirsch's artistic genius is evident to anybody who saw any of the promotional materials for the event. The rest of the public relations staff did an outstanding job as well. Bart Box and Jason Sampler worked hours on the Web site. Kathy Lee and the staff at Providence Learning Center, including Sara Beth Glorioso and Darrell Lindsay, labored long hours leading up to and during the conference. Registering nearly one thousand people online, through the mail, and in person is no easy task. Neither is providing conference materials, refreshments, and meeting space for them to meet for academic activities. Sheila Taylor and the food services staff served more people in less time than I thought possible. Vanee Daure and the NOBTS media staff did a fantastic job of recording the event. My assistant, Adam Beach, was always willing to do anything at any time to help me. Countless other students worked as ushers, drivers, servers, guides, and so forth. Thank you all.

Similarly, my NOBTS colleague Ken Keathley, program chair for the Southwest Regional Meeting of the Evangelical Theological Society, and his assistant, Astasha Baker, spent many long hours working out the logistics of how two conferences could run concurrently in the same location—and each help the other. Drs. Rick Morton and Archie England provided much-needed support through the Student Enlistment Office and the Baptist College Partnership Program, respectively.

Dr. Steve Lemke, NOBTS provost, was always willing to provide advice and helpful insights, especially on how to help and be helped by other school offices and programs. His administrative assistant, Marilyn Stewart, who is also my wife, perhaps worked harder than anyone in making sure that all the various offices involved were properly informed as to what was about to take place. It is not easy working for

Acknowledgments

one philosopher and being married to another, but Marilyn handles it all with dignity and grace.

I am extremely grateful to Michael West, editor in chief at Fortress Press, for his interest in this project. Thanks also go to Kristine Anderson of Fortress, who first mentioned my proposal to people there, and Abby Hartman and James Korsmo for their efforts on behalf of the book.

Finally, I must express my gratitude to my wife, Marilyn, who transcribed the greater part of the dialogue, and to Kelly Salmon, with his keen eye and training as an English major. Kelly is one of the most gifted and humble young men I know; my affection for him is great.

I know I must have forgotten some other important people. Please bear in mind that I am an absentminded professor.

‒ INTRODUCTION ‒

Robert B. Stewart

*Now if Christ is preached, that He has been raised from the dead,
how do some among you say that there is no resurrection of the dead?
But if there is no resurrection of the dead, not even Christ has been
raised; and if Christ has not been raised, then our preaching is vain,
your faith also is vain.*
1 Corinthians 15:12-14 (NASB)

The resurrection of Jesus is a central tenet of historic Christian belief and, for that reason alone, a matter of great historical significance. Virtually no biblical scholar, early church historian, or theologian disputes this point. However, a great deal of disagreement follows from that initial agreement. John Dominic Crossan and N. T. Wright agree and disagree on the issue. They agree that it is a crucial theological issue that has enormous social significance but disagree as to whether or not "resurrection" refers to an actual event in history, that is, whether or not the dead Jesus was raised to embodied life by his God.

Crossan believes that following his crucifixion Jesus was probably never properly buried, given that he was a Jewish peasant. Victims of crucifixion were typically either left on the cross to be eaten by wild animals or buried in shallow graves, in which case the result was certain to be the same.[1] Part of the terror of crucifixion was the certain knowledge that one would not receive a decent burial and thus one's body would almost certainly be devoured.[2] He concludes, "With regard to the body of Jesus, by Easter Sunday morning, those who cared did not know where it was, and those who knew did not care."[3] Crossan sees a progression in the tradition "from burial by enemies to burial by friends, from inadequate and hurried burial to full, complete, and even regal embalming."[4] Simply stated, according to Crossan, the Passion Narratives do not relay accurate historical information concerning either Jesus' death or his burial, but rather reflect "the struggle of Jesus' followers to make sense of both his death and their continuing experience of empowerment by him."[5] If the Gospels are incorrect about his burial, then they are also likely wrong about his resurrection.

On the other hand, Wright insists that one cannot separate the resurrection from the birth of early Christianity. It is the resurrection that makes sense of what follows—the establishment of the Christian community with its own distinctive story, praxis, and symbols.[6] Given that Jesus was not the first or the last to lead a messianic movement, and that such self-proclaimed messiahs were routinely put to death, Wright asks, Why did his movement live on without replacing him as leader? The best explanation, he concludes, is the resurrection.[7]

In *The Resurrection of the Son of God* Wright devotes over five hundred pages to demonstrating how the afterlife was understood and talked about, *and what the relevant terms meant*, in ancient pagan writings, the Old Testament, post-biblical Judaism, and various Christian writings (letters of Paul, the Gospels, Acts, Hebrews, General Letters, Revelation—and non-canonical early Christian texts).[8] He follows this historical and literary tour de force by arguing that while neither the empty tomb nor the subsequent sightings of the risen Jesus by themselves constitute a sufficient cause for resurrection belief, both taken together do.[9] Although Wright holds his position with humility, as a committed critical realist should, he also clings to it with great passion.

In many ways the differing positions of Crossan and Wright represent a divergence of opinion that has existed in serious historical study of Jesus for over two hundred years concerning the historical reliability of the four canonical Gospels. During much of this time most scholars have leaned to the skeptical side of the ledger concerning this question. No Gospel stories, save, perhaps, the virgin birth narratives, have been as critically scrutinized as those concerning the resurrection. As a result, in the minds of many, the resurrection of Jesus, which undoubtedly lay at the heart of the earliest Christian confession of Jesus as Lord, is often either removed from the picture altogether or moved to one margin or another.

INTRODUCTION

Such skepticism is largely the result of methodological presuppositions founded upon enlightenment thinking. Although many of those whose work was responsible for this sea change were not outright enemies of Christian faith or practice, the law of unintended consequences applies to historians as much as it does to those in other professions, and their skepticism had the effect of either reducing the importance of resurrection in Christian theology or redefining the meaning of resurrection. The dialogue that follows in this book is thus best understood against a backdrop of roughly two hundred years of historical scholarship concerning Jesus and his resurrection.

Albert Schweitzer dates the beginning of the quest of the historical Jesus to 1778, when G. E. Lessing's edition of Hermann Samuel Reimarus's essay "On the Aims of Jesus and His Disciples" was published.[10] Prior to Reimarus, many harmonies of the Gospels existed, but there had been no scholarly attempt to study the Gospels as historical documents.[11] All that changed with Lessing's posthumous publication of Reimarus's work in a series Lessing named *Fragmente eines Ungenannten* (Fragments from an Unnamed Author), commonly referred to today as the Wolfenbüttel Fragments.[12]

Reimarus was born in Hamburg in 1694 and taught in Wittenburg and Wismar before spending 1720–1721 in Holland and England, where he became acquainted with deism.[13] The influence of deism may be seen in his attempt to ground understanding of the historical Jesus in deistic reason (*Vernunft*). Reimarus concludes that the preaching of Jesus was separate from the writings of the apostles. He thus argues that the Gospels, written by the evangelists (that is, historians)—not the New Testament epistles, written by the apostles (that is, theologians)—are where one finds the historical Jesus. Reimarus writes:

> However, I find great cause to separate completely what the apostles say in their own writing from that which Jesus himself actually said and taught, for the apostles were themselves teachers and consequently present their own views; indeed, they never claim that Jesus himself said and taught in his lifetime all the things that they have written. On the other hand, the four evangelists represent themselves only as historians who have reported the most important things that Jesus said as well as

did. If now we wish to know what Jesus' teaching actually was, what he said and preached, that is a *res facti*—a matter of something that actually occurred; hence this is to be derived from the reports of the historians. . . . Everyone will grant, then, that in my investigation of the intention of Jesus' teaching I have sufficient reason to limit myself exclusively to the reports of the four evangelists who offer the proper and true record. I shall not bring in those things that the apostles taught or intended on their own, since the latter are not historians of their master's teaching but present themselves as teachers. Later, when once we have discovered the actual teaching and intention of Jesus from the four documents of the historians, we shall be able to judge reliably whether the apostles expressed the same teaching and intention as their master.[14]

Interestingly enough, Reimarus defines the essence of religion as "the doctrine of the salvation and immortality of the soul."[15] No wonder, then, that he has no room for resurrection.

Reimarus posits that Jesus became sidetracked by embracing a political position, sought to force God's hand, and that he died alone, deserted by his disciples. What began as a call for repentance ended up as a misguided attempt to usher in the earthly, political kingdom of God.[16] After Jesus' failure and death, his disciples stole his body and declared his resurrection in order to maintain their financial security and ensure themselves some standing.[17] Peter Gay holds that this sort of conspiracy theory is typical of deism: "Even the sane among the deists had a paranoid view of history and politics: they saw conspiracies everywhere."[18] Reimarus maintains, correctly in my opinion, that Jesus' mind-set was essentially eschatological in nature. He also correctly discerns that the historical Jesus is never to be found in a non-Jewish setting, but he wrongly sees Christianity as discontinuous with Judaism. Unfortunately, he fails to grasp that resurrection was part of the Jewish hope in Jesus' day. Despite his concern to free Jesus from theology, Reimarus's Jesus was not free from the grave.

David Friedrich Strauss, influenced by Hegel's philosophy, pioneered an approach to understanding the Gospels in which Jesus' resurrection was understood to be a myth. Jesus understood mythically is the synthesis of the thesis of supernaturalism and the antithesis of rationalism. As a committed Hegelian, Strauss maintains that the inner nucleus of Christian faith is not touched by the mythical approach. In his (first) *The Life of Jesus Critically Examined*, Strauss declares:

> The author is aware that the essence of the Christian faith is perfectly independent of his criticism. The supernatural birth of Christ, his miracles, his resurrection and ascension, remain eternal truths, whatever doubts may be cast on their reality as historical facts. The certainty of this alone can give calmness or dignity to our criticism, and distinguish it from the naturalistic criticism of the last century, the design of which was, with the historical fact, to subvert also the religious truth, and which thus necessarily became frivolous. A dissertation at the close of the work will show that the dogmatic significance of the life of Jesus remains inviolate: in the meantime let the calmness and *sang-froid* with which in the course of it, criticism undertakes apparently dangerous operations, be explained solely by the security of the author's conviction that no injury is threatened to the Christian faith.[19]

Strauss emphasizes not the *events* (miracles) in the Gospels (although the book is structured as an analysis of Jesus' miracles) but the *nature* of the Gospels. Unlike Reimarus, he is not interested in explaining (away) how events in the Gospels took place. Neither is he interested in uncovering the sequence in which the Gospels were produced. His interest lies in revealing the nature of the Gospels as literature. By focusing on their literary nature, he anticipates several crucial issues in twentieth-century New Testament studies.

Strauss represents a paradigm shift in Gospel studies. Whereas Reimarus had proposed two possibilities—natural or supernatural—Strauss proposes two different categories for interpreting the Gospels: mythic or historical. Unlike Reimarus, Strauss attributes the nonhistorical not to deliberate deception on the part of the apostles but to their unconscious mythic imagination.[20] Strauss maintains that the biblical narratives were written well after they occurred and were embellished through years of oral retelling and religious reflection.[21] Strauss thus insists that the key to understanding Jesus historically is being fully aware of the differences between then and now.[22] The biblical myths, according to Strauss, are poetic in form, not historical or philosophical.[23] In his second book on Jesus, *Das Leben Jesu: für das deutsche Volk*,

Strauss abandons Hegelian categories for moral categories.[24] Eventually, Strauss repudiates entirely any attachment to Christianity. David Strauss died a committed materialist.[25]

Beginning about the middle of the nineteenth century, Jesus research was consumed with answering the question of sources: in what order were the Gospels written? Stephen Neill writes concerning the Synoptic problem: "The first scholar to approach the correct solution of the problem on the basis of careful observation of the facts seems to have been Karl Lachmann."[26] In 1835, Lachmann wrote an article proposing that Mark was the earliest of the four canonical Gospels.[27] The philosopher Christian Hermann Weisse soon echoed Lachmann's opinion on the matter.[28] Yet both Lachmann and Weisse were approaching the matter apart from a clearly stated and justified methodology.

It was left to Heinrich Julius Holtzmann to treat the matter systematically. Contra Strauss, Holtzmann is adamant that to understand Jesus historically one must first undergo a thorough investigation of the Synoptic Gospels. Holtzmann understands the primary problem in historical-Jesus research to be the order of sources. Therefore, the primary task is solving the Synoptic problem. In *Die Synoptischen Evangelien: Ihr Ursprung und geschichtlicher Charakter,* Holtzmann proposes two written sources containing sayings of Jesus that were available to the evangelists. He refers to these sources as *Urmarcus* and *Urmatthäus.*[29]

To the degree that Holtzmann shared the basic presuppositions of nineteenth-century German liberalism, he represents the mainstream of the First Quest. Behind the fascination with sources lay the liberal presupposition that the theological elements in the Gospels were later accretions from the early church. It was assumed, therefore, that the further back one goes the less theological and the more historical the picture of Jesus becomes. Behind this expectation lay the liberal presupposition that Jesus preached a timeless ethic.[30] They fully expected to find that Jesus was a teacher of moral truths who had a unique awareness of God working through him. They also thought that, by determining the order of the earliest sources, they could discern a noticeable shift in the personality of Jesus.[31] It is not going too far to say that the First Quest, the liberal quest, was based in large part on an unwarranted optimism concerning how much historical knowledge of Jesus one could acquire from the proper application of source criticism. The result of these presuppositions and concerns is that the resurrection, which is theologically significant if it is anything, was again excluded from the realm of historical investigation.

Albrecht Ritschl and Adolf von Harnack mark another significant bend in the road. Both men understood Jesus primarily as a great moral teacher whose life and teachings had a decisive impact on the psyche of the early church. According to Ritschl, the proper object of study is the *observable experience* of the church, because the statements in Scripture become "completely intelligible only when we see how they are reflected in the consciousness of those who believe in Him."[32] He also taught not only that the kingdom of God and the message of Jesus were ethical in nature but also that Jesus was the bearer of God's ethical lordship over humanity.[33] Ritschl's moralizing theology focused on Jesus' death, not his resurrection. For von Harnack, Jesus' message of the kingdom emphasized (1) the kingdom of God and its coming, (2) God the Father and the infinite value of the human soul, and (3) the higher righteousness and the commandment of love.[34] In other words, Ritschl and von Harnack combine ethics with psychology in an effort to understand the historical Jesus.

Ben Meyer comments that most Jesus scholars of that day coupled the liberal emphasis on ethics with an equally liberal "hermeneutic of empathy."[35] In turn, a host of imaginative theses were put forward in an effort to understand more fully Jesus' religious experience by tracing out the psychological development of Jesus' messianic awareness.[36] This was very attractive in that it allowed the authors to write something akin to a *biography* of Jesus.[37] The weakness of this approach lay in the fact that it depended more on imagination than on historical method. Again, the resurrection is moved to the background as the light is focused on Jesus' psyche and the effect his teachings had on the early church.

William Wrede responded to such ideas by insisting that the nineteenth-century psychological theories of Jesus' work were derived from somewhere other than the text. Wrede declares:

And this is the malady to which we must here allude—let us not dignify it with the euphemism "historical imagination." *The Scientific study of the life of Jesus is suffering from psychological "suppositionitis" which* amounts to a sort of historical guesswork. For this reason interpretations to suit every taste proliferate. The number of arbitrary psychological interpretations at the same time form the basis for important structures of thought; and how often do people think that the task of criticism has already been discharged by playing tuneful psychological variations on a given factual theme![38]

Wrede's chief concern was with the messianic secret. He believed that the early church understood historically that Jesus *was made* Messiah at his resurrection, not that he *was revealed* as Messiah through the resurrection.[39] The idea that Jesus was the Messiah before his resurrection was merely the result of the early church's theological reflection on his then-evident messiahship.[40] Simply put, the messianic secret was Mark's attempt to harmonize history with theology.[41]

According to Wrede, one must distinguish between historical and literary-critical questions, and literary-critical questions should be dealt with before historical ones. In this way, Wrede was able to point to messianic passages in the Gospels as support for his hypothesis, and problematic texts were thus neatly excised in the interest of historical tidiness. The result was predictable: truncated Gospels resulted in a truncated picture of Jesus. Wrede's Jesus lacked both messianic consciousness and theological creativity. While Wrede allowed that the messianic secret grew out of resurrection belief, his focus was consistently on the effect of resurrection belief rather than on the basis for belief in the resurrection.

Wrede's conclusions have been influential in both form and redaction criticism. Consistent with the emphasis of the history-of-religions school, of which Wrede is a representative, the result of Wrede's work was to shift the focus from Jesus onto the communities the evangelists represent. Discerning the nature of the tradition behind a text thus became the focus of biblical interpretation for a generation of scholars to follow.

On the same day in 1901 that Wrede published his book on the messianic secret, Albert Schweitzer published his work *The Mystery of the Kingdom of God: The Secret of Jesus' Messiahship and Passion.*[42] Schweitzer pictured Jesus as thoroughly conscious of his messianic role. In fact, it was this messianic consciousness that motivated Jesus to do all that he did. In contrast to Wrede, Schweitzer understood Jesus as a messianic hero, along the lines of Nietzsche's cult of the hero (*Übermensch*).[43] Schweitzer's Jesus is a heroic figure, seeking to usher in the kingdom through his decisive sacrifice of himself. Schweitzer saw the messianic themes, which Wrede understood to be later creations, as central to any understanding of Jesus. According to Schweitzer, one could not begin to understand Jesus without correctly perceiving that his messianic consciousness drove him to do all that he did—including going to the cross.[44] Tragically, although the idea of resurrection is clearly in the mind of Schweitzer's Jesus, Schweitzer's summary concludes: "On the afternoon of the fourteenth of Nissan, as they ate the Paschal lamb at even, he uttered a loud cry and died."[45] Related to the resurrection, Schweitzer contributed no more than any nineteenth-century liberal Jesus scholar.

Schweitzer's first offering was not overly well received.[46] This prompted him to write *The Quest of the Historical Jesus: A Critical Study of Its Progress from Reimarus to Wrede* in 1906.[47] Eventually, this work became the standard by which all other histories of life-of-Jesus research are measured.

Schweitzer is often cited as one who advocated the end of historical-Jesus research. Such is not the case, however. Schweitzer intended not to end the quest but to redirect it. Although Schweitzer did maintain that one could not use history to write a biography of Jesus, he believed that historical research could destroy false constructs of Jesus, including the most monstrous one of all—Jesus as a modern man. For Schweitzer, Jesus was the product of first-century Jewish apocalyptic expectation, not Enlightenment rationalism. In short, although Schweitzer believed that knowledge of the historical Jesus could not afford one a foundation upon which to ground Christian faith, he saw historical-Jesus research as useful in destroying the fictional platforms that had been built by ecclesiastical dogma or enlightenment historicism. The value of historical knowledge of Jesus was to be found in the recognition of one's inability to know him through investigation. Instead, Jesus is known most fully in decisive individual commitment. Again the voice of Nietzsche is heard in the conclusion of the *Quest*:

> He comes to us as One unknown, without a name, as of old, by the lake-side, He came to those men who knew Him not. He speaks to us the same word: "Follow thou me!" and sets us to the tasks which He has to fulfil for our time. He commands. And to those who obey Him, whether they be wise or simple, He will reveal Himself in the toils, the conflicts, the sufferings which they shall pass through in His fellowship, and, as an ineffable mystery, they shall learn in their own experience Who He is.[48]

To claim that Schweitzer's *Quest* ended the first phase of historical-Jesus research, but such a position is simplistic. While it is true that Schweitzer offered up a devastating critique of the liberal quest, it was left to others to provide a positive diversion from liberal historical-Jesus research. Several factors contributed to bringing the First Quest to an end.

In 1896, Martin Kähler published *The So-Called Historical Jesus and the Historic Biblical Christ*, in which he regarded "the entire Life-of-Jesus movement as a blind alley" because the necessary sources were not available.[49] His basic premise was that the certainty of faith could not rest on the unavoidable uncertainties of history. He declared that the accuracy of Scripture cannot be based "on the success or failure of the inquiries of historical research; for these are always limited and only provisionally valid, that is, their validity endures only until new sources of knowledge appear on the horizon."[50] Instead of searching for the *historical* Jesus, one should seek the *historic* Jesus, the one who has molded history and contributed to it.[51]

Also in addition to Schweitzer's critique of the liberal historical Jesus project was the influence of the history-of-religions school. Two names commonly associated with the history-of-religions school are Ernst Troeltsch and Wilhelm Bousset. Troeltsch served as the philosopher for the movement. He insisted that Christianity was not historically unique. Rather, like all religions, it was a historical phenomenon within its own time. Consequently, Jesus was no different than any other figure in history. To insist, like Kähler, that faith in Jesus is not subject to historical critique is simply naive, according to Troeltsch.[52]

INTRODUCTION

The historian is bound to explain movements in terms of causal events in the natural world.[53] Therefore, the historian's role in relation to Christian origins is simply to explain how Christianity came to be, not to answer theological or metaphysical questions concerning Jesus. Troeltsch's commitment to naturalistic explanations, à la his criterion of analogy, effectively rendered any critical judgment concerning the historicity of Jesus' resurrection moot.

In *Kyrios Christos,* Bousset maintained that the church came to deify Jesus through a historical process of transformation as a result of its encounter with Hellenism, in which alien ideas were grafted into Christianity. He maintained that the earliest traditions concerning Jesus contained nothing miraculous and did not proclaim Jesus to be divine.[54] Clearly, Jesus was not raised from the dead in any way that the average person considers historically meaningful.

The shadow of Rudolf Bultmann falls over any attempt to understand New Testament theology in the twentieth century. Along with K. L. Schmidt and Martin Dibelius, he pioneered New Testament form criticism.[55] Understanding the Gospels as collections of fragments edited together to address particular needs of the early church, not as single documents chronicling the life of Jesus, Bultmann saw the primary purpose of form criticism to be discovering the origin of the particular units of oral tradition that lay behind the written pericopae of the Gospels, not simply identifying different forms of Gospel sayings.[56] In *Jesus and the Word,* he declares: "I do indeed think that we can now know almost nothing concerning the life and personality of Jesus, since the early Christian sources show no interest in either, are moreover fragmentary and often legendary; and other sources about Jesus do not exist."[57] Bultmann posits that the early church was filled with controversy and infighting between Hellenistic Jewish believers and Palestinian Jewish believers, resulting in a situation where sayings are attributed to Jesus that he did not utter. This leads Bultmann to declare: "One can only emphasize the uncertainty of our knowledge of the person and work of the historical Jesus and likewise of the origin of Christianity."[58] The result was not only that form criticism, like the history-of-religions school, focused on something other than Jesus—that is, the "setting in life" of the early church—but also that its foremost proponent announced that historical-Jesus research could not succeed.

Bultmann's objections to historical-Jesus research were not only methodological but also philosophical and theological. Bultmann was influenced by Kierkegaard and Heidegger, as well as by the early Barth.[59] As a result, he thought that historical knowledge of Jesus' personhood (*Persönlichkeit*) was secondary in importance to existential knowledge of Jesus' word.[60] Bultmann's approach is, first, to recognize that the New Testament is mythological in nature, and second, to demythologize the New Testament myths. Bultmann openly draws on Heidegger's categories of existence and being to interpret the New Testament. But what often is missed in his method is that he adopts these categories because he believes that the New Testament demands to be demythologized—that such was the intention of the authors.[61] Regardless of motive, the result was that resurrection, that is, the bodily resurrection of Jesus from the dead, was at least unnecessary for Christian faith and perhaps even impossible.

A brief ray of hope shone through in a movement commonly called the "New Quest of the Historical Jesus," which began in 1953 with a speech by Ernst Käsemann to a group of Bultmann's former students.[62] Käsemann agreed with Bultmann that the primary interest of the primitive church was not historical verification of facts concerning Jesus but, rather, the proclamation of the kerygma. He held that the primitive church sought to rescue historical facts from obscurity through appeal to the reality of their present experience of Jesus as Lord. And Käsemann concluded that this not only was the experience of the primitive church but also is the task of Christians today.[63] But, he insists, to disregard Jesus entirely as a historical figure is to lapse into docetism.[64] Käsemann thus argues for a new type of historical inquiry concerning Jesus, one that recognizes that mere history apart from hermeneutics is insignificant. Käsemann's solution is to focus on the language of Jesus by separating the authentic from the inauthentic in the preaching of Jesus by applying the criterion of dissimilarity to his preaching.[65]

Although Käsemann was the initiator of the New Quest, James M. Robinson was the popularizer and historian of the movement. His 1959 book, *A New Quest of the Historical Jesus and Other Essays*, gave the phrase "New Quest" intelligibility in the vocabulary of contemporary historical-Jesus research.[66] Robinson was primarily concerned with answering how Jesus the proclaimer became Jesus Christ the proclaimed.[67]

Redaction criticism was primarily developed by Günther Bornkamm and Hans Conzelmann.[68] Although redaction criticism presupposes the results of source and form criticism, it also differs in several respects. It focuses on whole Gospels as well as the individual pericopae. It stresses the role of the evangelist before that of the community or tradition. In doing so, it seeks to answer the question, "What is the theology of this gospel?"[69] The hermeneutical effect of redaction criticism has been to focus on how the Gospel stories relate to one another, which has led to reading the Gospels as whole stories, not just as disparate fragments. This has resulted in renewed interest in theology among biblical scholars. But, as seen before with form criticism and the history-of-religions school, the focus is still not on Jesus or the resurrection but on the theology of the editors of the Gospels.

The effect of the New Quest of the historical Jesus was to focus on the message of Jesus and the theological intentions of those who edited his message for later readers. Through it all, the New Quest still maintained Bultmann's existential concerns and was relatively short-lived, in large part because it was perceived to be much the same in nature as the Bultmannian "no quest."

In the last part of his *Quest*, Schweitzer concluded that there were only two live options for those wishing to find the historical Jesus: Wrede's thoroughgoing skepticism or his own thoroughgoing eschatology.[70] Wrede's approach led to historical skepticism and non-Jewish, modernist conclusions concerning Jesus, based largely on his willingness to treat messianic texts as inventions of the evangelists. Schweitzer's approach, on the other hand, led to wholly eschatological, Jewish conclusions concerning Jesus, primarily for his refusal to assign messianic statements to the early church.

N. T. Wright holds that Schweitzer's words, written at the beginning of the twentieth century, have proven prophetic in that most who are seeking the historical Jesus may be understood as traveling different roads: those who have followed Wrede and are characterized by their thoroughgoing skepticism are traveling the "Wredebahn," while those who have followed Schweitzer and are in general agreement with his thoroughgoing eschatology prefer to take the "Schweitzerbahn." In recognizing these two distinct groups, Wright distinguishes between the Third Quest and the Renewed New Quest.[71] The Renewed New Quest has adopted the thoroughgoing skepticism of Wrede concerning the traditional Gospels as sources and has thus tended to discover a non-Jewish Jesus. The Third Quest has sought to ground Jesus within the Judaism of the first century and has been far less skeptical than the Renewed New Quest concerning the value of the canonical Gospels as sources for the life of Jesus.

The most obvious expression of the Renewed New Quest is the Jesus Seminar of Robert Funk. Prominent advocates of the Third Quest include Wright, E. P. Sanders, John P. Meier, Ben Witherington, and the late Ben F. Meyer. This does not mean, of course, that all contemporary parties in historical-Jesus research fit neatly into one of these two categories. But such recognition that these two overarching categories are not perfect does not render them useless.

Simply stated, we are living in one of the most exciting and fruitful periods in the convoluted history of Jesus research. One very exciting aspect of historical-Jesus research today is the renewed awareness that whatever else the historical Jesus was, he was, at least, Jewish. On this point, N. T. Wright and John Dominic Crossan agree, although they differ on several particulars of first-century Judaism. Related to this, the advent of serious interdisciplinary study of the ancient Middle Eastern world is a boon.[72] Crossan, in particular, has been a leader in this regard.

More and more, awareness is increasing among Jesus scholars that the time-tested methods of source, form, and redaction criticism, apart from some other methodological ingredient, are not up to the task. Both Wright and Crossan have proposed their own methodological corrections and additions at this point. These two men are clearly on the cutting edge of their field.

Finally, Wright and Crossan agree on one additional point. They both insist that one must do more than simply provide an answer as to whether one should think of the resurrection as an actual historical event that took place in time (first century) and space (Jerusalem). Both insist that one must not stop at that point. Instead, one must consider the significance of the resurrection for individuals, the church, and the world, however one answers the first question.

INTRODUCTION

It is a great pleasure for us to present the readers of this volume a transcript of an important recent dialogue between N. T. Wright and John Dominic Crossan on the topic of the resurrection. We are also pleased to offer our readers eight additional essays on the resurrection and the work of Wright and Crossan from an interdisciplinary team of scholars, most of whom took part in the March 11–12, 2005, Greer-Heard Point-Counterpoint Forum, "The Resurrection: Historical Event or Theological Explanation?"[73] If there is anything that all the scholars involved in this project agree on, it is that the resurrection of Jesus is an important topic. We hope that you also agree and find these offerings to be important contributions to an ongoing conversation.

THE RESURRECTION
Historical Event or Theological Explanation?
A Dialogue

N. T. Wright and John Dominic Crossan

Opening Statement
N. T. Wright

Thank you all for being here this evening and for coming to this extraordinary weekend. I am very grateful to the seminary and to Bob Stewart, who, as he said, has been after me for five years to do this, and for the chance to participate in this first Greer-Heard Point-Counterpoint Forum and, of course, as we have already said, to the sponsors themselves. I am grateful, too, to Dom Crossan for his willingness to go once more round the tracks in this debate. Dom and I have had several enjoyable and, I hope, fruitful discussions over the last decade and more, and my respect and affection for Dom have steadily increased through that. I have been fascinated to see the ways in which our thinking has converged at some points while remaining firmly divergent at others.

So my primary task in this session this evening, as I understand it, is to outline briefly the argument which I have set out in my book *The Resurrection of the Son of God*, which was published nearly two years ago. The book has, of course, a positive role, but one of its main tasks, if I can put it like this, was to negate the negative—that is, to show that the normal historical proposals about the rise of resurrection faith in the early church, the normal proposals that try to explain things without the actual bodily resurrection of Jesus, simply won't work historically.

I see what I was doing as primarily a ground-clearing task, sweeping away the rubble and debris behind which bad arguments had been hiding. Thus, for instance, I have shown against Gerd Lüdemann that the idea of resurrection is not something which ancient people could accept easily because they didn't know the laws of nature, whereas we moderns, with post-Enlightenment science, have now discovered that resurrection can't be true. That is simply absurd. From Plato to Homer, from Aeschylus to Pliny, the ancients knew perfectly well that dead people didn't rise. We didn't need modern science to tell us that. I've shown against Greg Riley that ancient pagan stories about people eating with the dead, or seeing the dead in realistic visions and so on, are completely different from the idea of resurrection, and that the same ancient pagans who knew all about visions and the like continued to reject resurrection with some scorn. I've shown against Kathleen Corley that the Hellenistic novels which feature stories of empty graves and so on cannot provide an explanatory context for the rise of Christian belief. And I've shown against many writers that in Judaism as in paganism, the word *resurrection* was not a general term for life after death, as it is often used today, to our shame in some Christian circles. Rather, the word *resurrection* always denoted the second stage in a two-stage process of what happens after death: the first stage being nonbodily and the second being a renewed bodily existence, what I have often called life *after* "life after death." Likewise, I've shown conclusively that Paul really did believe in the bodily resurrection, despite generations of critics going back as far as the second century who tried to make out that he didn't.

I have, I think, demolished the central thesis of the influential 1981 SBL [Society of Biblical Literature] presidential address by James Robinson—namely, that the early Christian experience of the risen Jesus was an experience of some kind of luminosity which could be interpreted as what we would call an essentially private religious experience rather than evidence for an occurrence in the public world and which developed rather slowly into a belief in bodily resurrection, on the one hand, and into gnostic theology, on the other. I've shown that we can't account for early Christian faith by suggesting that stories about appearances and stories about an empty tomb have nothing whatever to do with one another. I have shown that the idea of resurrection faith being generated by some kind of cognitive dissonance simply doesn't work. And I believe I've shown against Dom and others that the early Christian belief in the resurrection of Jesus could not have been generated from the combination of their previous knowledge of Jesus and their study of particular biblical texts, however much both of those things contributed to their interpretation of the event once it had happened.

Now the point to all this negative exercise, I stress, is not first and foremost to prove the resurrection by modernist or supposedly neutral or naturalistic historiography. The point is rather to force the question back where it ought to be rather than allowing yet another generation of students to be taught that the Easter stories and the Gospels are simply mythical back projections of early Christian consciousness rather than accounts of something exceedingly strange and unprecedented in the real world. Now I appreciate that in some circles this task may seem otiose. So, say people who have never taken history particularly seriously, why should you worry what historical critics and exegetes are saying and thinking? But for the seminarian in college and the parishioner in the pew, it matters a great deal. Enormous forces in our culture are determined to deny Jesus was raised from the dead. And, over and over again, they use arguments which can be shown to be invalid, and they propose alternative scenarios about the rise of Christianity which can be shown to be impossible. And that, I think, is an important exercise in itself.

But my book is, I think, more than merely negative. Let me spell out its main positive argument. Perhaps the most original aspect of the book—I'm honestly not sure now, my head was so full of it—is its compilation of six Christian mutations within first-century Jewish resurrection belief. My case here is that we can track with considerable precision and over a wide range of early evidence a phenomenon so striking and remarkable that it demands a serious and well-grounded historical explanation. Early Christian belief in resurrection is clearly not something derived from any form of paganism; it is a mutation from within Judaism, or rather six mutations.

First, belief in resurrection has moved from being a peripheral item of belief, as it is in Judaism, to the center. Second, the meaning of resurrection has been sharpened up. Jewish sources leave it vague as to what form the new body will take, but the early Christian sources, again and again, indicate that the body will be transformed into a new type of immortal physicality.

Third, there is no spectrum of belief in early Christianity on what happens after death, as there is in both Judaism and paganism; there were many different opinions out there. But from Paul through to Tertullian, there is development and reflection about what precisely resurrection would mean, and how to argue it before a skeptical audience. But they all, except the Gnostics and the semi-Gnostics, believe in resurrection. No Christians known to us retain signs of the other main beliefs of the period.

Fourth, resurrection as an event has split into two. Those first-century Jews who expected the resurrection saw it as a single event, the raising to new bodily life of all at the very end. But it is central to Paul and, after him, to all other early Christian writers that the resurrection is now a two-stage event—or better, a single event taking place in two moments, as Paul puts it: Christ the first fruits, and then at his coming, those who belong to Him.

Fifth, resurrection functions in a newly metaphorical way. Resurrection, the word or the concept, could be used in Judaism, as in Ezekiel 37, as a metaphor for the return from exile. That has disappeared in early Christianity. Instead, we find the term *resurrection*, still possessing its literal, bodily meaning, also functioning metaphorically, as in Romans 6 or Colossians 2 and 3 with reference to baptism and holiness.

Sixth, nobody expected the Messiah to be raised from the dead, for the simple reason that nobody in Judaism at the time expected a Messiah who would die, especially one who would die shamefully and violently. But not only did the early Christians believe that the Messiah had been raised from the dead, they made the resurrection a key element in their demonstration that he was the Messiah, developing several brand-new exegetical arguments to make the point, particularly from the Psalms and Isaiah, as in Romans 1, Romans 15, Acts 2, and so forth.

These six mutations, which I have tracked in considerable detail across the book, lend weight to the pressing historical question, "What caused these mutations within Judaism, and why, and how?" And it isn't difficult, then, to show that all the early Christians for whom we have evidence, and I have even argued that this would include Q people, supposing such people ever existed, would have given the answer that they really did believe that Jesus of Nazareth really had been bodily raised from the dead and that what they knew of the resurrection had precipitated these mutations.

Only when I have tracked all this in the book do I allow the reader to get into the resurrection narratives themselves. I sent a copy of this book, as I send everything that I write, to my parents. My father is in his middle eighties now, and he reads everything I write, bless him. He's not a trained historian or theologian. And a few days later, I got a phone call from him saying, "I have just finished the book," which is some feat within a week, seven hundred pages. He said, "I started to enjoy it about page six hundred." The reason was he finally had been given permission to think about the resurrection narratives themselves, which was what he thought we were going to be doing all along. This delay in presenting the final chapters of the four Gospels, not to mention the so-called *Gospel of Peter*, was quite deliberate, and I conceived it as a way of outflanking the begging of the question that has often taken place when people have assumed that they knew what resurrection might mean to early Christians and then projected that onto the narratives.

I eschew, to the dismay of some, any attempt at a tradition-history of the stories, since trying to write a tradition-history of the resurrection narratives presupposes that we know which elements in such stories must be early, whereas, in fact, we can only know such a thing with the help of an a priori belief about the development of resurrection belief in the early church. And such attempts, in my experience, routinely make the mistake of starting with the assumption of one or another of the revisionist schemes, whose foundations, as I have shown, are built upon quicksand. Instead, I draw attention to several features of the stories which demonstrate that they must be very early indeed even though they have been shaped and edited by the evangelists in their eventual writing down. Noting that even when they are telling the exact same story, the evangelists manage to use remarkably different words, making any theory of literary borrowing in the resurrection narratives very difficult. I point out that the stories, first, are remarkably free of scriptural quotation, illusion, and echo, and, second, that they give the women an extraordinarily prominent place, which has already disappeared by the time Paul writes 1 Corinthians 15. Third, they do not mention the future Christian hope, unlike almost all passages about Jesus' resurrection elsewhere in early Christianity. Those of you who are going to preach on Easter Sunday, please note that the resurrection stories in the Gospels do not say Jesus is raised, therefore we're going to heaven or therefore we're going to be raised. They say Jesus is raised, therefore God's new creation has begun and we've got a job to do. Very interesting. And, fourth, these stories convey, across all four accounts, a picture of Jesus himself which is neither that of a resuscitated corpse nor that of someone shining like a star—as in Daniel 12, which is the main biblical passage referred to in many Jewish discussions of resurrection—nor that of a ghost or a disembodied spirit, nor simply that of someone with the same kind of body that he had before. The same stories which speak of Jesus breaking bread, eating broiled fish, and inviting the disciples to touch him are those which also speak of his appearing and disappearing through locked doors, not being recognized instantly, and, finally, disappearing into God's space, that is, heaven. Each of these features is extraordinary in itself, and it is all the more remarkable that all four of these features—no scriptural quotation, the place of the women, no mention of the future hope, and this very odd picture of Jesus—are sustained across the four Gospels despite their very different language and the obvious apparent surface inconsistencies. None of these four features can be explained, I've argued, if the stories are as late in origin even as the fifties, let alone as the seventies, eighties, or nineties, as some have persisted in arguing.

This analysis of the stories, then, sits alongside my analysis of the early Christian resurrection belief, and together they press the historical question "How can we best account for all these extraordinary phenomena?" From this point on, I conclude the book with an argument, which still seems to me rock solid, that the empty tomb and the appearances of Jesus together constitute a sufficient condition for the rise of early Christian faith as we have studied it—that is to say, if Jesus did rise bodily and was seen not only having left an empty tomb but appearing in the garden and elsewhere, then this would offer a complete explanation of why the early Christians not only believed in his resurrection but told the stories the way they did and modified dramatically the basic Jewish resurrection belief.

I then go on to the more difficult argument that the empty tomb and the appearances constitute the necessary conditions for these phenomena. And here I appreciate that, if you take the phrase "necessary condition" in quite a strong sense, I do seem to be offering what some would call a "proof," in some sense, of the resurrection. I perhaps should have made it clearer that I mean it in a somewhat weaker sense, namely, that having examined as many of the alternative explanations as I could find, and having shown them all to be completely inadequate, the one that we are left with, however unlikely, must press itself upon us as being true.

One last thing about the book, something which forms a bridge to the concerns which I know Dom Crossan and I both share: I've hinted throughout the book that resurrection was a politically revolutionary doctrine and that it remains so for the early Christians. I use as an epigraph for the last section of the book the lovely quotation from Oscar Wilde's play *Salome* in which Herod Antipas hears by messengers about Jesus going around healing people, doing extraordinary things, and even raising the dead. It's a wonderful moment in which Wilde has caught exactly the politically subversive nature of resurrection. Herod hears that Jesus is doing these extraordinary things, and he is quite happy to have somebody going around healing people, but then, "He raises the dead?" And the servant says, "Yes, sir, he raises the dead." And Herod goes into bluster, "I do not wish Him to do that. I forbid Him to do that. I allow no man to raise the dead. This Man must be found and told that I forbid Him to raise the dead." The tyrant knows that death is the last weapon he possesses, and if someone is raising the dead, everything is going to be turned upside down.

Now it is because Jesus had been raised from the dead that he was Messiah and Lord, the true King of the Jews and the true Lord of this world. However, resurrection has often been co-opted within post-Enlightenment conservative Christianity into becoming part of a demonstration of the conservative modernist claim about supernaturalism over against the naturalism of the liberal modernist. I regard this as deeply misleading, not least because it has led those liberals who badly needed the resurrection as the ground for their proper social concern to reject it because it seems to them to be about mere pie in the sky. It is, in fact, (and I've hinted this throughout the book and have developed it in some of my other writings) only with the bodily resurrection of Jesus, demonstrating that his death dealt the decisive blow to evil, that we can find the proper ground for working to call the kingdoms of the earth to submit to the kingdom of God. That, I think, is the real reason for modernism's shrill rejection of bodily resurrection, exactly like the Sadducees, actually. Not that science has disproved Easter, but that Easter challenges the social and political pretensions of modernism, both right wing and left wing, and modernism knows it. Perhaps the most important thing then about the resurrection is also the most deeply countercultural in our own day—that a deeply orthodox theology about the resurrection, and a good deal else besides, is the proper seedbed of radical politics. And having thus kept you awake for my statutory twenty minutes, I shall allow room for Dom to take over. Thank you.

Opening Statement
John Dominic Crossan

It is a very special honor to be part of this first Greer-Heard Point-Counterpoint Forum, especially with Carolyn Greer and Bill Heard in the audience. It is also a privilege to speak on the subject of the resurrection of Christ. And, it is also an honor to be on the same podium as Tom. But Tom is now a bishop, and the last time, thirty-six years ago, I got into an argument with a bishop I was a priest and a monk and the bishop was the Cardinal Archbishop of Chicago. And, when the argument was over, I was an ex-priest and an ex-monk. It has never been clear to me who won that argument.

What I will be doing is talking through, not seven hundred pages, as Tom did, but a paper that Tom and other conference speakers already have. The title of the paper is "Mode and Meaning in Bodily Resurrection Faith" (see Appendix). And, to explain what I mean by "mode" and then by "meaning," I am going to quote from Tom. It's a little bit tongue in cheek.[1]

Tom, from his book *The Resurrection of the Son of God*:

To speak of someone going up to heaven by no means implied that the person concerned had (a) become a primitive space traveler and (b) arrived by that means at a different location within the present space-time universe. We should not allow the vivid, indeed, lurid language of the Middle Ages, or our many hymns and prayers which we use the term "heaven" to denote, it seems a far-off location within the cosmos we presently inhabit to make us imagine that first-century Jews thought literalistically in this way, too. Some, indeed, may have done so. There is no telling what things people will believe. But we should not imagine that the early Christians writers thought like that.[1]

Now, this is a good way of introducing my terms *mode* and *meaning*. By *mode*, I mean the difference between something which is literal and something which is metaphorical (Jesus is a peasant, Jesus is the lamb of God), or between something which is actual or factual and something which is fictional or parabolic (the Good Samaritan, for example). That's what I mean by *mode*. Is something literal or is something metaphorical? By *meaning*, which applies to both the literal and the metaphorical, I mean, "What are the implications of this for your life? What are they? What does this do for your life or for the world?" So, mode and meaning.

My first major point, and in a lot of this, I think, I am in very great agreement with Tom, is called "The Origin and Claim of Bodily Resurrection Faith in Jewish Tradition, in Christian Tradition." My first point concerns cosmic transformation. If your faith tells you that God is just and the world belongs to God, and your experience dreadfully tells you that you're a small, battered people, then eschatology is probably inevitable, and don't let us scholars mystify you on it. Eschatology means if the world belongs to God, and is patently unjust, God must clean up the mess of the world. Eschatology is the Great, Divine Clean-Up of the world.

Furthermore, if you have an *apocalypsis*, a special revelation, about that eschatology, it has come to mean, but does not necessarily mean, the imminence of that eschatology. It could be about anything to do with it. So, apocalyptic eschatology, in itself, means simply that you are claiming to have some special revelation about this Great Divine Clean-Up. That's always capital *G*, capital *D*, capital *C*, and capital *U*. Now this apocalyptic eschatology is the absolute—I was going to say background, foreground, matrix, everything to understand resurrection; without it, we're not even talking about the same thing. I must caution you: please never say, and cross out when any scholar you find, including myself, has ever said, that this is the "end of the world." We can dream of the end of the world because we can do it. We can do it atomically, biologically, chemically, demographically, ecologically—and we're only up to *e*! No first-century Jew or Christian would think about the end of the world, because that would mean that God had annulled creation, which God would never do. God had created the world and said and stamped every day of it as good, good, very good. The end of the world is not what we are talking about. We're talking about cosmic transformation of this world from a world of evil and injustice and impurity and violence into a world of justice and peace and purity and holiness.

Second major point, and I'm presuming cosmic transformation: bodily resurrection. Why would something so counterintuitive be involved? A general reason and a special reason. The general reason: if you are going to have a cosmic transformation of this world and not its evacuation into heaven, then you have to have, to use Tom's word, *transformed* physicality. How else can you have a transformed world? But the specific reason—and I think Tom agrees with this— is the martyrs at the time of the Maccabean revolt and persecution. Where is the justice of God when you're looking at the tortured *bodies* of martyrs? Bodies of martyrs. All of that is already in the Jewish tradition. And, as Tom has insisted, it's in the Pharisaic subdivision of that.

Now, concerning Christian tradition, I like very much Tom's word *mutation*. We are dealing with a mutation. What we must realize is how profoundly different everything is after a mutation, even though the people who are involved in it will probably try to think of it as not quite so great. What is the mutation? This is it: the Christian mutation, that which is most creatively, profoundly new about the Christian claim—this doesn't prove it right, but this is at least what is new—is that the general bodily resurrection was not just imminent but had already begun. I suppose if you had asked a Pharisee about it, he would have said, "Well, it will be a blinding flash of light in the future." Now the unbelievably creative mutation is that, no, it will have a beginning and it will have an end. And, of course, they console themselves by saying that there won't be much time in between. Mutations are hard to live with. It will have a beginning, it will have an end, and nobody has said that before. Tom's way of putting that is a question of how you explain that. How does somebody come up with something like this? I think that he is absolutely right that it requires a historical explanation. It's a historical question. Where did they come up with it? As he has just told us, his own view is that two things are the necessary and sufficient causes: the finding of the empty tomb and the apparitions and visions of the risen Lord. Put together, those things explain it historically.

My disagreement with this is rather profound. That could get you to exaltation; it could get you to the conclusion that Jesus has been exalted, maybe even to the right hand of God. (By the way, remember, if Jesus is at the right hand of God, then God is to the left of Jesus.) My point is not to debate either the empty tomb or the apparitions, but to say I think something else is absolutely needed to make that leap of faith, if you will. It is that the historical Jesus, that Jesus himself, had already said the same thing in different language, namely, that the kingdom of God was not just future, nor even imminent, but had already started. So I see the *language of Jesus* about the kingdom and the *language of Paul* about the resurrection, as exactly isomorphic. They fit upon one another. So, for me, it is important that Jesus had already said that the kingdom has begun. Without that, I do not see how to get to resurrection—exaltation, yes; resurrection, no—because, precisely as Tom has argued, it is such a huge mutation.

But there is a second equally important mutation. As soon as you say, "it has begun," and there is a span of time, even if you think it is a short period—and we know it's at least two thousand years and counting—there is a second thing. Jesus said, and I think that Paul takes for granted, that we're dealing with what I'm going to call a *collaborative eschaton*. And nobody had ever suggested that either. If you are going to have eschatology as a blinding flash of divine light, then it would be silly to say, "Please, what's my job?" Your job is to be very quiet, stay very holy, and pray—and wait. If you have, now, this period in between the beginning and the end, the first fruits and the harvest—the full harvest—then you have a job to do. And that is inevitable. So I want very much to watch what is in between that we are called to participate in—eschatology. And nobody had ever said that before. I take very seriously, for example, when Paul talks about unveiled faces seeing the glory of God, being transformed. Something is happening in between. It's not as if you had two magnificent, transcendental bookends: one, the resurrection of Jesus; the other, the resurrection of everyone; and in between you have no books.

My second major point is mode and meaning. I want to draw attention to something which is, I think, necessary. If you are coming out of Pharisaic understanding of general resurrection, if you are coming out of that matrix, then you would have to have something like what we call the harrowing or robbing of hell. In scholarship we can get into an argument whether that comes in early or late. I can't see how it could not be early, almost even if there's no evidence of it, because how could you think of the general resurrection beginning only with Jesus? Where are the Maccabean martyrs? Where is the justice of God for the backlog? If your claim is that God has begun the Great Clean-Up of the world, then the first thing God has to pay attention to is the backlog of injustice. Jesus was not the first Jew to die on a Roman cross, nor would he be the last. There was a backlog. So, for me, I think the harrowing of hell has to be given much, much, much more attention than Tom does. But—I will actually admit this—it is very much the harrowing of hell, that is, Jesus going down into Hades to liberate, not to give a sermon, not to preach, but to proclaim, "We're out of here!"; to proclaim to all those who had died before him their liberation from bondage, that I have great trouble seeing literally. Let me admit it. If I take that literally, that means that I think that the people who said it were literal. Then there would be hundreds of empty tombs around Jerusalem. It wouldn't be a matter of checking out one on Easter Sunday, but seeing how many empty ones. So I will concede that maybe I like the harrowing of hell, at least I place a lot of emphasis on it, and Tom does not, in the book at least. If you take the harrowing of hell, I think it will push you toward the metaphorical. If you don't talk about it, you might just be talking about Jesus' raising, and that is much easier to take literally.

Why is it important for me to speak of the metaphorical? Is it the Enlightenment? No, it really isn't—because I am in a pre-Enlightenment age when I am reading this. It really is this: if you look at the world in which Jesus and Paul lived, the world in which Caesar, Caesar Augustus, was divine, was Son of God, was God, was God from God—at least in Egypt—was Lord, was savior of the world, was redeemer, was liberator, and you ask yourself, or make the mistake of asking a classicist, "Did those millions of people who saw, who read those texts, who could read, saw those inscriptions, looked at those images, saw those structures, did they all take it literally or did they take it metaphorically?" The honest answer must be, "I do not have the faintest idea, nor does anyone else." But I do know that they took it operationally, they took it functionally, they took it programmatically. To say I believe in the divinity of Caesar meant I am getting with the program, I'm supporting Roman imperialism. If I were certain that all of that was taken literally, no question, then I might be more certain about how to read Christian, anti-Caesarian theology. That is the issue for me. How do we know, know enough to demand of our people, in the name of faith, that everything must be taken literally as distinct from metaphorically? What I am suggesting is that whether you take it literally or whether you take it metaphorically, you must take it programmatically. And that means you must be able to spell out in detail what is the program of the divine Christ as distinct in great detail from the program of the divine Caesar. That is the first-century question. The first-century question is not "Do you think Jesus is Lord?" It is "Do you think Caesar or Jesus is Lord?" And when you say, "Jesus is Lord," you have just committed high treason. I would even want to spell out the program a little bit. The Roman program, if you think about it as a bumper sticker on their chariots, would be, "First victory, then peace." First victory, then peace. Or piety, then war, then victory, then peace, to give it a fuller bumper sticker. I think the opposite program coming from Jesus, Paul, and the New Testament is "First justice, then peace." Or better: "Covenant, nonviolence, justice, and peace."

My conclusion: I see now two routes before us. We can argue about mode: Is the resurrection to be taken literally or figuratively? Is it maybe, as Tom has suggested, a literal resurrection for Jesus, metaphorical for Christians, literal again for everyone? Or might it be metaphorical for Jesus, literal now for everyone who is a Christian, again metaphorical at the end? We can go on debating that. It seems to me that we have been debating it for two hundred years, and we have reached an impasse; nobody is persuading anyone else about it that I can see. So, I want to make this suggestion tonight: if you want to debate mode, what has to be taken literally, what has to be taken metaphorically, it is a perfectly valid debate. But there is something else: *the question of meaning*. I would like to ask anyone who says "literally" to spell out exactly what is the meaning of that? That is, what are the implications, how does it work out, how does it change the world, how do we participate in a new creation? Tell me that from your literal reading. I would try, and anyone who takes it metaphorically, to spell out the implications from a metaphorical reading. I'm not saying that whether you take the resurrection literally or metaphorically is not important. I'm not even saying bracket it. I'm saying give me the meaning that comes from a literal reading of this. Give me a reading that comes from a metaphorical reading of this. Could it be that we might overlap tremendously in the field of meaning, where we will not agree at all in the field of mode? My point is not that mode is not important, that it doesn't make any difference what you believe but how you act. That is not what I am saying. I'm saying that I don't want any longer just to argue about the beginning and the end, the past and the future. I want to think about the present. I want really to know how we are going to take back God's world from the thugs. Thank you.

Dialogue
N. T. Wright and John Dominic Crossan

Wright: Dom and I have had this conversation before, but I think it is important that we have it as part of this discussion here: these blessed words *literal* and *metaphorical*. *Literal* and *metaphorical* are words which describe the way words refer to things. Often, we use *literal* and *metaphorical* when actually we mean "concrete" and "abstract." I think we are in danger in talking about mode if we use the words *literal* and *metaphorical* when actually we mean "concrete" and "abstract," something that happens which is concrete and definite and solid and something which is abstract like an idea or a feeling. Because, just to pull it around to the end, I do think that it makes the most enormous difference if you say that what happened on Easter day was not a concrete event because the meaning of that for the real world would be that we must have a lot of other nonconcrete events, maybe in our hearts or our heads—nice ideas, good thoughts, prayers—whereas you're appealing for action in the real world to change the real world. And it is precisely because of that, if you want to start at that end, which you do, that I think we have to go with *concrete*. And I would be glad if we could drop *literal* and *metaphorical,* at least for the moment.

Crossan: We can't, for me, because I don't equate those things. A literal statement and a metaphorical statement can both apply to exactly the same concrete event. A current example, if I may use one: Two people are talking in the last election. One says, "Well, President Bush is my president." The other says, "President Bush is my eagle." One's literal; the other's metaphorical. They both mean the same concrete thing. They both mean, "we approve of the program, we approve of the policies, we're going to fight for this, we're going to vote for this." Those two things are like vectors, saying, for me, exactly the same thing. That's what I mean by *literal* and *metaphorical.* They can point to the same meaning. They may not, too.

Wright: I'm perfectly happy with that. My point, then, is in fact that's the sort of point that I was expecting to make. I have to say, listening to Dom and then maybe him listening to me, I'm not sure if we're actually crossing as we meet. My point, then, is that whether you refer to that concrete event in literal language—"He was bodily raised from the dead"—or whether you refer to that concrete event in some metaphorical language—but the resurrection language I'm stressing there was used by the early Christians literally and was meant to be taken as denoting a concrete event—if you don't go that route, you're left with saying that whatever happened, whether you refer to it literally or metaphorically, was an abstract event, was a nonconcrete, nonbodily thing, which then leaves you without the groundwork for dealing with the bodily realities of martyrdom, Caesar's world, and all the rest of it. In other words, is not your political agenda going to push you ultimately to saying that there really was an empty tomb on Easter morning? I didn't intend that we should get there so soon, but since we have . . .

Crossan: No, it wouldn't, but let me put it this way: if all Christians in the world today were perfectly happy with a literal empty tomb and everything literal, a body coming out which you could see, everything like that, I don't think I'd care enough to even raise the issue. It is that I know thousands of Christians for whom the bodily resurrection is equated with the resurrection. They've—how would I put it—reduced it to "Do you or do you not believe that Jesus came bodily out of the tomb?" and then that means that a camera could have picked up Jesus, as it were. And that's all they want to talk about. If they take resurrection to mean just that, then they say I can't be a Christian. I think that is awful. I am ready to say that if you are a Christian then you must believe in the resurrection. If they ask literally or metaphorically? I would say, tell me what you mean by "literally"; tell me what you mean by "metaphorically." That's the language I would use. I wouldn't speak of concrete or abstract. I really wouldn't, Tom. Because it does point to something concrete in the world—changing the world, not just changing me subjectively.

Wright: It's very interesting that we have shifted already to arguing from the way we want the world to be to statements about what we think ought to have happened or might have happened in the past. Can I just proceed with another question and then you can come back to me with some questions of your own, but can we go back to the historical ones because I'm not sure that in our various dialogues in the last year or two we have gotten very far with this? I'm fascinated by that extra mutation, and I think if I were rewriting the book, that I would want to add a seventh mutation, the one that you insisted on, the collaborative eschatology, which seems to me exactly right, and that's exactly what Paul is talking about again and again. So, thank you for that; you'll get the footnote in the second edition, at least. Actually, I think that is very important. We might come back to it again. But

how, then, do you explain all those mutations? I think you agree mutations took place. You've highlighted one which I highlighted as well,
the splitting of the event into two. And then you've introduced this
new one, collaborative eschatology. What precipitated those? And, if I
can just sharpen that up, what people believe about what happens at
or after death goes very deep in any culture. People may change some
beliefs about some things, but when it comes to burying Mom or Dad,
they want to do it the way the family has always done it. So, something
happened which caused all those Christians from very different back-
grounds to transform the beliefs that their cultures had given them
into this remarkable new shape. How do you explain that?

Crossan: Okay. Your explanation is, empty tomb necessary and
sufficient, right?

Wright: No, we've got another stage in between. My explanation
is they all really did believe that Jesus was bodily raised from the dead.
That's the explanation of the mutations. Then we have to ask, "Why
did they believe that?" And then . . . but we can't short-circuit that.

Crossan: No, no. I'm following your argument. I think it is perfectly valid. I did notice you used the term *really* rather than *literally*—
but, I'm not quibbling. I'm not quibbling, because if you ask me, "Do
I think something *really* happened?" Yes! Yes! If you confuse—I'm not
saying you're doing this—if one confuses literal and real, then one has
succumbed to the Enlightenment, as far as I'm concerned.

Wright: The word *real* is one of the slipperiest ones in modern
English, but . . .

Crossan: And it's fair enough because it is a slippery one. To answer
your question, though—if I'm looking at this as a historian and I'm
saying, "How can they come up with this?"—the first half of your book
shows that this is an extraordinary mutation; it's not just some nice
evolution, and the next step, and anyone would have gotten there. No,
it's an extraordinary mutation. I think you are absolutely right there. I

think, for me, it's very, very important that the announcement of the historical Jesus—the Jesus of the Gospels, let's put it that way—as I understand his announcement, is not that the kingdom is imminent, it is that the kingdom has already begun. And when he sends people out, he's telling them to cooperate; he's already in a cooperative eschatology. Now I think these people have experienced that; they have experienced the power of the kingdom. Then there's the terrible shock of the crucifixion. Now what has to happen next is that *plus* the risen apparitions. I am convinced as a fact that they had apparitions. How you explain that is a separate issue, but it happened; they are not making it up; it's not hallucinations. My statement is that the stories in the Gospels, as I've argued, are primarily interested in who's in charge and had an apparition. But that presumes an apparition, even if I claim, as I would, that Mark's tomb story is made up. I think I'm with you, apparitions happened. But I think, apparitions plus the experience of "the kingdom is already here"; that's my explanation of those two things. With regard to the empty tomb, honestly I would say, plus or minus, it's not worth it. I don't mind. Historically, I'm not sure about it because I think Mark created it, but it's not something I would argue. I concede it.

Wright: Okay, this is extremely interesting, because I agree with you that Jesus' proclamation of the kingdom and their awareness of the power of God through the work and preaching of Jesus is one of the preconditions for the eventual overall interpretation at which they arrived. I don't myself think that those by themselves would be sufficient to generate anyone saying he's been raised from the dead when he hadn't been. I mean, I've explored elsewhere an imaginary scenario supposing in 70 c.e. at Titus's triumph in Jerusalem when Simon Bar-Giora was brought into the forum and then killed the way they did (they killed the enemy king at the end of the great triumph).[2] Supposing, three or four days later, some lucky Jew who managed to escape with some friends and be hiding out somewhere saying, "You know, I think Simon really was the Messiah. You know, we felt God's power at work when he was leading us. I really think he was and is God's Anointed One." His friends would say, "You must be crazy. The Romans caught him; they killed him, just like they always do. You know perfectly well what that means. It means he couldn't possibly be the Messiah, because we all know that when the pagans execute somebody—celebrating their triumph over him—that shows that he couldn't have been the Messiah." So, without something happening next, all of that stuff goes down the tubes. I think that scene in Luke 24, whatever you say about the overall historicity of it, is absolutely spot-on in terms of first-century Jewish perceptions: "We had hoped that he would be the One to redeem Israel," but the implication is, we know that the fact that they killed him shows that he can't have been. Without something to reverse that, they would say, "We've just been living in a wonderful dream, but now it's all over and we've woken up to the normal imperial reality."

Crossan: But the something that I'm insisting on, at that point, is that they did have visions. I am, I really am. Otherwise I would not be able to understand it. I don't know how you make the jump without that. Whether it's possible to have taken Jesus' proclamation that the kingdom had already started and bypass the resurrection, I don't know. I don't know. But, as far as I'm concerned, incarnation comes first.

Wright: Yes, I've heard you say that before, and in a sense, theologically, I agree with you, though I don't think myself that the disciples believed in the incarnation, as later Christian theology has seen it, until they put the whole package together after the resurrection, though they were puzzled by some things. But I don't see them actually making some kind of an implicit, trinitarian or proto-trinitarian statement. That would be a wonderful solution, wouldn't it? Headlines in the newspaper next week: "Crossan believes that the incarnation was there even during the period of Jesus' lifetime." That would be wonderfully revolutionary.

Crossan: Let me probe the counterfactual for a moment. I think you would agree Jesus' proclamation is not "the kingdom is coming soon," and then comes the resurrection, and, "Ah, it started!" That's not what I am saying, at least. I think Jesus is saying, "In my life and in your cooperation with it, the kingdom has already started." And I'm quite willing to leave it as possible that it's going to be over very soon. I'm not going to get into that one. Well, giant mutations are hard to swallow. But let's imagine that's what's happening in Galilee. The kingdom has already started. What reason would there be that that might not have continued? I know it's counterfactual, but just to make us think of it.

Wright: What reason would there be that the kingdom wouldn't have just continued? Because, I think, the kingdom for them, as we see from Josephus again, from his account of the rebellions around the time of Jesus' birth, the "kingdom of God" was bound up with actual events in saying, "We don't want Caesar ruling over us; we don't want Herod ruling over us; we don't want Caiaphas and his crew ruling over us, either. We want only God to be King." And, if the Romans kill your Messiah, it's evidence that God just hasn't done it yet, however good it felt when you were walking around with Jesus, healing the sick and sharing open commensality and so on. So, I really think the crucifixion is the denial of that, without something else.

Let me press you on the apparitions, you see, because I don't know if you've changed your view, but in one of your books, at least, and I've heard you say it as well, you say that we are actually all hard-wired to have visions of people after they die. And I've heard you there to be aligning yourself with the argument that Gerd Lüdemann has put out, that in fact, and this is a well-known phenomenon in the ancient and in the modern world, that after someone you love has died, sometimes even before you know they have died, you can actually see them in the room with you and it's very real and very clear. Now, first I want to know, is that your argument, because if so, presumably plenty of other people in the ancient world had visions of people after they died, and that doesn't mean they're alive again—it means they're dead. That's the point. The ancient pagan writers were very clear about that. That's one of the reasons that you have these meals with the dead at the tomb, not to bring them back again, but actually as a way of making sure that Uncle Joe ain't coming back again. That's how those things function. So that you wouldn't then say—this is why Greg Riley is completely wrong in *Resurrection Reconsidered*—you wouldn't then say, well, this is basically the same thing as somebody being alive again. That's precisely what it isn't. So let's get to that one first.

Crossan: If I could imagine all sorts of modern medical technology on a person having a vision of the risen Lord, and somebody having a vision of a beloved person who has, say, died tragically, suddenly—I would imagine a horrible thing, you go to work on 9-11 and are never heard of again—I would think those visions are exactly the same in terms of what I might call "psychological anthropology." *But,* it is what is there before and what has come afterwards that's going to make all the difference, if what is there before is your experience of Jesus. Or even if your knowledge of Jesus is bad enough that you want to persecute the followers, like Paul, you already know enough that's going to change it. And the result afterwards will change it. For example, everyone in the early church had a magnificent vision of Jesus, and they all said, "Oh, good! Ah-h, it's all right," and then went back to fishing, for example.

Wright: Which they did, according to John 21.

Crossan: Right. That would not be the same vision. In other words, the difference, for me, is in the preparation, if you will, and the result.

Wright: Yes, but . . .

Crossan: That does make a difference.

Wright: Yes, but my problem then is, if people having visions of recently dead people was as well-known as you and others have suggested, then they would simply have said that he's with God, that he's alive in some other sense. They would have said what Wisdom of Solomon 3 says about the martyrs: the souls of the righteous are in the hands of God. Or what they said about the Maccabean martyrs, as you know: they are great martyrs, and we honor them, and we respect their memory, and we will visit their graves and pay respect to their graves, but they haven't been raised from the dead yet; they *will* be raised from the dead in the future. Indeed, Steve Patterson, in his book on

Jesus, argued that it began with people saying Jesus, like a martyr, will be raised from the dead and that they gradually transposed that into He's already been raised from the dead.[3] You're not saying that, but I wonder how, then, the argument sticks, because you see it with Acts 12 when Peter gets out of jail, surprisingly, and comes and knocks on the door and this wonderful scene with the little maid, Rhoda, who hears Peter's voice and forgets to open the door because she's so excited and comes and tells them. And *they* say, "It must be his angel." Now that's regular Jewish language for, "We are having one of those postmortem visitations."

Crossan: Right.

Wright: And that doesn't mean, "Wow, Peter is alive again from the dead." It means, "They've just killed Peter and presumably tomorrow we will go to the prison, get his body, and bury it."

Crossan: All right. But . . . if, for example, they had said—let us say they had apparitions, let's say they were unique, ontologically unique, they're not like anything that had ever happened in the whole history of the world—I can only get from that to exaltation, to the Philippians hymn, maybe, that Jesus now is with God, Jesus sits at the right hand of God, Jesus is lord of the universe, but you haven't yet got to resurrection, because resurrection means a *whole new* mutation.

Wright: But if you simply have apparitions without an empty tomb, they would say, "he's with God," he maybe even in some sense is exalted, though only in the same way as the martyrs are. If you have an empty tomb and something's happened to the body, and then if the apparitions actually are not just apparitions, such as one has if somebody you love has just died, but actually involve some extraordinary physical things. You know, according to Luke 24, there must be a broken loaf lying on the table somewhere which they didn't break—somebody did that—and so it's not just eating broiled fish. There's a bunch of physical phenomena going on, and this is where the stories are so odd, as well as these kind of paraphysical phenomena—I don't think anyone could have made up these stories, actually, I think they're so bizarre—and that's part of the point. Those are the sorts of things that, when coupled with the apparitions, the physical evidences, of which the empty tomb is the first example, make me say and, I think, made them say, this isn't just an ordinary apparition, and it isn't just exaltation; it really is resurrection. And, obviously, they weren't expecting resurrection. That's the key thing.

Crossan: I can't see it, Tom. And it's not necessarily that for any reason I would resist it. I can't see that the empty tomb alone—and let's not imagine anyone stealing [the body] or anything like that—and risen apparitions, risen visions: I can see that getting them to exaltation, I really can (I think it is almost inevitable), but I cannot see it getting to resurrection. Let me put it this way: I think the two halves of your book magnificently strain against one another; the more you insist on the extraordinary nature of this mutation—which I'm with you all the way on that—the more you need a bigger explanation than even empty tomb or apparitions, no matter how literally you take them. It gets you to exaltation without resurrection.

Wright: Well, I don't understand why you can't get to resurrection if you have an empty tomb and somebody is clearly there, palpably alive again, inviting you to touch him, and eating broiled fish.

Crossan: Can I focus on that to be clear? But, you see, if everyone was expecting the resurrection to split into a one and a many, then it would be perfectly clear, "This is the one we've been waiting for." But you've proved conclusively in your book that the Pharisaic expectation was of a general resurrection, maybe even tomorrow. But now the leap that says this is the beginning of the resurrection happens, which means that now we must think of the resurrection involving a time span.

Wright: I think I can get a razor blade here between what you think I'm thinking and what I think I'm thinking. Take the example of one of the brigands crucified alongside Jesus: What if he had, two or three days later, been found walking around again, appearing to people, and his tomb was found to be empty? I think that people certainly would have said the world is an extremely strange place, we haven't a clue what is going on. Let's put it like this: they wouldn't have said, "He's the second person of the Trinity, he's the Son of God, he's the Messiah," because of what they knew about his former life, and that's what makes the difference in the interpretation of the event. I think what I'm saying is this—and it's kind of a linguistic slipperiness, between saying *the* resurrection, which from that point of view is an interpretation of the event, and saying what I think I'm wanting to say—they see that here is somebody who was genuinely dead, and was dead for a short period, at least, and is now in phase two of a postmortem existence. And that phase two is a new embodiment that has used up the old body in some way or other. Now I think that is the conclusion that they came to. Then, if you like, and here I'm trying to find a way of agreeing with what I hear you saying, then calling that *the Resurrection*, with a capital *R*, is an interpretative leap. But what I want to hold out for and what I would press you back to is, would they not think that this person has had happen to him that of which those Jewish traditions spoke, which spoke of a two-stage postmortem existence of which the second stage is a newly transformed embodiment? Could they not have reached *that* conclusion from empty tomb plus appearances—they couldn't have reached it from appearances alone, and they wouldn't have reached it from empty tomb alone. I think they would have just concluded grave robbery; there were plenty of examples of that. It's the two together that makes them say this odd event, a two-stage postmortem existence of which the second stage is re-embodiment, has happened. Then I agree with you because of what they know about Jesus and because of the Jewish world they're living in, they call it *the Resurrection*, with a capital *R*. Does that make sense?

Crossan: It does, but what I suppose I don't understand is why it would not be simpler, honestly, to say that it would involve three things. Don't give an inch on the empty tomb, if you want, and the risen apparitions as unique. Why not, also, the life of Jesus? That is what I didn't understand in your book. I thought it would not at all weaken your argument. I thought it would strengthen your argument.

Wright: It could have strengthened the argument. You know the "setting in life" of my book was that it started out life as the last chapter of *Jesus and the Victory of God*, and that it sort of grew, so it had to have a book to itself. So, I was kind of presupposing all that and that it is precisely the aliveness after a period of being dead of *this* man who had announced the kingdom, feasted with sinners, healed the lepers, and so on, and had been crucified as a Messiah—in other words, had been deemed to be a failed Messiah. So, it's the aliveness after a period of being dead of *this* man who did these things and said these things. I've no problem with that. I just didn't say it in this book because I had said quite a lot about it in the previous one.

Crossan: I'm pressing harder on that. It's not simply of this man that we knew all about. It's of this man who had already said, and who had helped us experience that, the kingdom—that's Jesus' language—had already started. So, they were already primed to understand that it's not just the great clean-up that's in the future, imminently in the future. It has begun. Now they know that already. So, it's the language of Jesus that I really find isomorphic with the language of resurrection.

Wright: I don't find them isomorphic. And I think we have to recognize that there are other Jewish groups in roughly the same period, give or take two hundred years, who also have inaugurated eschatologies about the kingdom having really begun, secretly with them or whatever, and whose hopes then get shattered. Qumran had an inaugurated eschatology. It wasn't a resurrection eschatology because nobody thought the Teacher of Righteousness had been raised from the dead, at least I don't think they did. But they did believe that God had reestablished the covenant with them. And then, my favorite example, when Bar-Kochba in 132 announced his rebellion with the backing of Rabbi Akiba, they even struck coins with the year 1 on them. It's like the French revolutionaries: they restarted the calendar. And there is, very interestingly, a three-year period, 132 to 135, when they mint coins, year 1, year 2, year 3. They really believe that the kingdom has arrived. They've still got to fight the decisive battle, they've still got to rebuild the temple, so Bar-Kochba has the temple on his coins as a sign of what he intends to do. And then, 135, Rome comes—game over.

And nobody says, in 136, "Actually, we experienced the kingdom with Bar-Kochba and we're now carrying it on." Instead, you have a rabbi saying, "It's time to give up all this kingdom language because it just gets you into trouble." Which it does. And it should.

Crossan: To be fair to the counterfactuals of history, if in that time in the middle of the Bar-Kochba revolt, the Celts—let's give it to the Celts—had decided to invade on all fronts, and if Rome finally gave back and said, you can have your own country, just send back a little taxation; run your own country again. Then he probably would then have been proclaimed the Messiah. But I don't want to go into that. Let me put it this way . . .

Wright: An Irish Messiah who saved the world.

Crossan: Well, yes; people are weird about their messiahs. . . . Let me put it as a slightly different question. Is there any way that, using the metaphor used before, we could leave the bookends and talk about the library? How do we take seriously the duty of Christians? Because as I would understand Paul talking to, for example, an open-minded, pre-Enlightenment pagan who says, "Well, Paul, you're a nice guy, I'm willing to believe your word that Jesus is bodily up there. Julius Caesar is up there in spirit, Jesus is up there bodily—that surprises me—but that's OK now." You would have to concede that could be possible, not for Arian-like Platonists, but for the ordinary popular person who lives in the pre-Enlightenment culture. Their question is going to be, "So what, Paul?" or "What's going on?" And Paul is going to say, "Come and see how we live." That's what I wanted to get to. How do you persuade—persuade, not prove—an open-minded pagan who is not going to get into your post-Enlightenment, "Well, I don't think that could happen" mindset? I agree with you that most philosophers are not going to think up bodily resurrection. I think that in popular culture—I taught undergraduates for twenty-six years—the Enlightenment never "took." It's a lovely idea; it just didn't work. So, I'm trying to imagine, now, the pre-Enlightenment; I really would like to try and get back to what's our responsibility for a new creation. Collaborative eschaton?

Wright: I'm totally with you on what I think you're driving at there. Let me just challenge one of the premises, when you talk about Jesus being "bodily up there" and Caesar being "spiritually up there." Part of the point of the resurrection in the New Testament, as I understand it, is not that Jesus died and was bodily raised to heaven. I heard a priest say that in a sermon the other day, and I shuddered. That's precisely *not* what's going on. The collapsing of resurrection and ascension into one another in a lot of popular New Testament scholarship, I think, just misses the point entirely. You can't actually do that with Philippians 2 and so on. Paul sometimes makes one point, sometimes the other, sometimes both, but he knows the difference. As incidentally, despite a whole chorus of scholarship, does John. Otherwise, why in John 20 do you have that very strange thing of the risen Christ saying, "Don't touch me because I have not yet ascended"? In other words, John knows perfectly well that there's a difference between resurrection and ascension, and you can't simply collapse it with the Johannine language of glory, as people often do. So, I'm a little worried about that. But yes, for me, the key text is 1 Corinthians 15:58, where, at the end of Paul's great chapter on the resurrection, he does not say, therefore, sit back and relax because there's this wonderful future ahead of you. He says, "Therefore, be steadfast, immoveable, always abounding in the work of the Lord, because you know that in the Lord your labor is not in vain." And it took me a long time before I realized why that logically goes with the chapter on resurrection. It means precisely because if there is bodily resurrection, if there is the renewal of the cosmos of the creation, à la Romans 8, à la Revelation 21 and 22, it means that what we do in the present by way of justice and mercy and grace and forgiveness and healing and liberation and all the rest of it, all that is done in the name of Christ and in the power of the Spirit, will not be lost but will be part of the eventual kingdom that God will make. In other words, there is continuity as well as discontinuity. And it is precisely that continuity which I see as modeled, paradigmed—my goodness, I am using a noun as a verb; that's a very American thing to do— in the bodily resurrection of Jesus, where you have continuity, not just the discontinuity of a body moldering in a tomb with the soul going marching on. So it is precisely because I share that that I love the phrase, *collaborative eschatology*. You know, Oscar Wilde said to somebody, "I wish I had said that," and the answer was, "You will, Oscar; you will."

Crossan: He was Irish. Let me raise this as almost a pastoral problem. As a bishop, you must have Christians for whom the resurrection has been reduced to "Do you or do you not believe that Jesus came bodily out of the tomb, in the crudest sense of the word?" Period. And, for whom, the answer is, "No, or I'm not sure I'm a Christian because I can't believe that." Is there any way of getting past that? I mean, I meant what I said if everyone took it for granted that, of course, this was all literal, I would say, let's get on with what we are supposed to be doing then.

Wright: I take the point. I have to say I wish Anglican Christians in the Church of England were as concerned about the question of the bodily resurrection as you and I are, from one way or another. But that's a whole other problem. I agree that a lot of Christians have shrunk the meaning of Easter to, "Do you or don't you believe that God did this particular, spectacular miracle?"—as one example, albeit, the supreme one, of God the great, supernatural intervener. And I hope you know from my writings that I simply don't see the world and God and Jesus like that. I don't like that language of intervention because I think it buys into a deistic framework of a God outside the process who occasionally reaches in and does things. And, likewise, I don't think that resurrection must be believed because it is the supreme example of believing something in the Bible even when it tells you some extraordinary things. Resurrection is, if it's anything, and must be, the center of the Christian worldview, and the center of a Christian epistemology. We may come back to that tomorrow. But let me say, I think you can get to the results you want by taking more seriously than I think you do the early Christian, particularly the Pauline, language of Jesus as the incorporative Messiah, the king who sums up his people in himself, so that what happens to the king happens to them. It is by that means that I can bring on board all of that incorporative thing.

Calvin said, Jesus Christ did not ascend into heaven in a private capacity. That's a good piece of reformed theology. He goes there with his people. And all those Greek Orthodox icons. . . . I went into an icon shop on one of the Greek islands once, and said, "I want an icon of the resurrection." And all the icons of the resurrection, as you well know, are of Jesus leading up Adam and Eve out of the tomb. Now that is the incorporative Messiahship which I see there, and I agree with what you implicitly said that that's probably underneath that very odd passage in Matthew 27, though I still don't claim to know exactly what that's about. So, I think you can get that "harrowing of hell," and I think Paul already has it by implication. I didn't use that phrase, but I think it's there within the incorporative Messiahship, that when God vindicates Jesus, that is the vindication of all God's people. The model for that in the Old Testament is David fighting Goliath. Here you've got the Israelites, here you've got the Philistines, here is one man fighting one man, but when David defeats Goliath, that actually means that Israel has defeated the Philistines. They have to do the mopping up operations afterwards, but it's basically "game over." That's the image of the king, the Davidic king, in whom God's people are summed up. And when God vindicates *him*, it isn't just a pat on the back for this one man for a job well done, and now that's over. It's rather, and this is why I said at the beginning, certainly in John 20, but I think in the other Gospels as well, the point of Easter in the Gospels is that new creation has begun and we've got a job to do. And I actually think that you and I are now on the same page on that. It's just that I think what you want to say would be much better grounded theologically and actually if God literally, concretely, really, in that sense, actually did it.

Crossan: Well, a couple of things. First of all, when you say, "the world I want," it's the world they want. It happens to be also the world I want. It's the world that Jesus wants. It's the world that Paul wants.

Secondly, I don't know when I go back into a pre-Enlightenment world, this is really what's rock bottom for me; it's not post-Enlightenment, because, well, I'm Irish; we never had an Enlightenment. We skipped that.

Wright: You said it.

THE RESURRECTION: A DIALOGUE

Crossan: Well, we didn't. We were busy with other things, as you know. I tease Tom that we had the British and we found them most enlightening.

Wright: You weren't the only people who did.

Crossan: But my point is, when you go back into a pre-Enlightenment world, where wonders, even the bodily resurrection of one person, at least, I think, in popular culture in the Roman world, that would be a possible wonder, but with no implications unless you . . .

Wright: Toward the end of the book I envisaged a Roman soldier hearing in the mid-60s a plausible-sounding story: "Hey, there's lots of us who really believed this and who saw him," and so on. The categories that that Roman soldier might have would be totally un-Jewish. He wouldn't know about *the* resurrection. What he might think would be like what some of them thought in the early 70s about a Nero Redivivus. He was such a great guy; maybe he didn't actually die; maybe he'll be back someday. And that owed nothing, as far as we know, to any ideas about Judaism or Christianity. It was simply, Nero made such an impact on the troops that they really thought he might be back. So, I can easily imagine that somebody might hear it in that way. That presumably is why, from very, very early on, the early apostolic creed, if you like, 1 Corinthians 15:3 and following, says, Christ died for our sins in accordance with the scriptures and was raised on the third day, in accordance with scripture. In other words, these are the most bizarre events that have ever happened in the history of the world. If you want to know what they mean, go and read the Bible. But I don't think you can do it the other way and say that it's simply because they started reading the Bible that they then came up with this, "Hey, maybe he's been raised from the dead." Because my point is, had they done that, the resurrection narratives would have been so fused with scripture, like the crucifixion narratives are. And, they would have done it quite differently, because with Daniel 12 in their heads, they would certainly have had the risen Jesus shining like a star, which he doesn't.

Crossan: We're not disagreeing on that. To make it clear, I do not think you can get anywhere without "It began with Jesus." I get a bit nervous if somebody says the new creation began at the resurrection. I think, no, the new creation began with Jesus saying, if you will, but more importantly living out "the kingdom of God has arrived." I think that's when it began. Now I don't find that in any contradiction with Paul saying, somebody saying, it has begun with the resurrection. But that's why you say "isomorphic."

Wright: I'm happy with that. That there's an early inauguration and then there's kind of a middle inauguration. That's not a problem.

Crossan: That's a different theological way of explaining what happened. What I'm trying to imagine is the ordinary people of the Roman empire, when they saw all this stuff about a divine Caesar, and all the rest of it. And I think it's shocking to a lot of people to know that before Jesus ever existed, the titles that we think are peculiarly Christian, that we kind of invented, were the popular discourse to the Roman Empire.

Wright: They're on coins.

Crossan: They are on all the coins. It was the only mass medium of antiquity. I'm trying to imagine, let's say, some people took that 100 percent literally. Some other people, I'm sure, took it metaphorically. Some other people, who might have been planning an assassination, if they got a chance, didn't believe in it. Now if I take that spectrum, from 100 percent literal to 100 percent metaphorical, and I want to say, OK, with Jesus, let us say 100 percent metaphorical or 100 percent literal. Wherever you take it, if you take the Jesus 100 percent literal and the Caesar, any way you take it you are committing high treason. That's what I want to insist on, rather than getting into an argument of is it literal or is it metaphorical? I can do that argument. We've spent most of our time, actually, doing it. That's what scares me a little bit, because we've been doing it for two hundred years. I don't see much evidence of it changing people. And, it seems to me that it's the great magnificent cop-out. Let's discuss that and not get into trouble by putting it into practice, because you can get yourself crucified doing that stuff. So, I think I'm not saying that invalidates it, but at least could we spend as much time, not talking to anyone in particular, could we spend as much time talking about putting the resurrection of Jesus, the general resurrection, into practice as at least equal time for in between, because now it's stretching.

Wright: I'm totally with you on that. It's just that, to repeat, I do think that because God made a good world, and I'm totally with you on this business of God saying, "Good, good, good, very good," that is the foundation of all Jewish and Christian theology and therefore God cannot in the end, if he is a just God, and if he cares about this good world that he's made, just throw it in the trash and rescue everyone off to a different place entirely. I think we're completely on the same page there and together, over against a great many people in various different Christian traditions around the place. But, for me, it is that entire picture which then sustains me from the other end, from the history, if you like, in believing that God actually did precisely that for Jesus and did not leave his body in the tomb to suffer corruption. And because I believe that Jesus, as Messiah, was representing his people and through that representation was, as it were, the focal point of the entire cosmos, and there I'm with Paul in Colossians 1, and so on, then I believe that in his Easter moment, the whole cosmos in a sense, a shock wave ran through it. Paul says in Colossians 1:23 that this gospel has already been preached to every creature under heaven. Now you could say that's like a sort of "harrowing of hell," but with Easter, something has happened to the cosmos. Now, if it actually happened, then a door has been opened through which we can go towards that kingdom of God which is over against the kingdom of Caesar. I totally agree with you that the Enlightenment, both the right-wing Enlightenment and the left-wing Enlightenment, has ignored that open door and used the resurrection quite spuriously, in my view, as a way of saying, "Therefore, there is a heaven and that's what matters rather than earth." And I think there we are actually in full agreement.

Crossan: Yes. Thank you.

– 2 –

IN APPRECIATION OF THE DOMINICAL AND THOMISTIC TRADITIONS
The Contribution of J. D. Crossan and N. T. Wright to Jesus Research

Craig A. Evans

It is ironic that I find myself taking part in a project focused on the resurrection of Jesus and the contributions that Professor J. D. Crossan and Bishop N. T. Wright have made to it. My first academic publication, which appeared nearly three decades ago, was in response to a chapter that Professor Crossan wrote on the empty tomb story in the Gospel of Mark.[1] I had no idea at that time how much the stimulating and innovative work of this Irish American would engage my attention and take up my energies for so many years to come!

It is a pleasure for me to offer an assessment of the contribution that Crossan and Wright have made to Jesus research. The focus of the present book is on the resurrection, and all of the other chapters speak to this topic. I shall say a few things about it too, but the focus of my

---

My impish title is inspired by the delightful and satirical review essay by N. T. Wright, "Taking the Text with Her Pleasure: A Post-Post-Modernist Response to J. Dominic Crossan, *The Historical Jesus: The Life of a Mediterranean Jewish Peasant* (T. & T. Clark/HarperSanFrancisco, 1991)," *Theology* 96 (1993): 303–10, esp. 305. Wright facetiously calls attention to the irony that John *Dominic* Crossan emphasizes the *Thomistic* tradition (that is, the *Gospel of Thomas*) at the expense of the dominical tradition (that is, the New Testament Gospels), while N. *Thomas* Wright emphasizes the *dominical* tradition, eschewing the Thomistic tradition.

paper is broader and is intended to provide a fuller context in which discussing the resurrection is a part.

I divide the balance of my remarks into three parts: (1) Crossan's and Wright's general contribution to Jesus and Gospel studies, (2) Crossan's distinctive contribution, and (3) Wright's distinctive contribution. I will conclude with a brief postscript on the resurrection of Jesus and why his followers understood it in terms of resurrection and not in other terms.

Crossan's and Wright's General Contributions to Gospel Studies

The discussion of the resurrection at the Greer-Heard Forum was significantly shaped by the lectures and publications of Professor Crossan and Bishop Wright. Both scholars have given us full-scale treatments of the historical Jesus and his resurrection.

Dom Crossan's *The Historical Jesus: The Life of a Mediterranean Jewish Peasant*, published in 1991, represents some two decades of research and writing.[2] This book, like all of Professor Crossan's publications, is well written, provocative, and engaging. It makes a serious attempt to situate Jesus in the eastern Mediterranean world in full context. I believe this is that book's great strength, and I shall return to this feature shortly. The book gained notoriety for suggesting that the teaching and behavior of Jesus should be viewed as a form of Jewish cynicism, suggesting that while growing up Jesus may have been influenced by Cynics in the nearby city of Sepphoris.

Crossan again gained notoriety with his book *Who Killed Jesus?* (published in 1995), which suggested that Jesus may not have been taken down from the cross and buried properly, according to Jewish custom; or that, if his body had been taken down, it may have been thrown into a ditch, covered with lime, and left as carrion for animals.[3] As did Crossan's earlier book *The Historical Jesus*, his *Who Killed Jesus?* concluded with some thoughts on the resurrection.[4] Crossan returned to this theme in *The Birth of Christianity* (published in 1998), in an essay published in 1999, and in another essay published in 2003.[5] In these essays, Professor Crossan restated his view that the empty tomb story of Mark, which is followed by the other evangelists, was a creation of the Markan evangelist for social and theological reasons. The empty tomb is not history, but the resurrection is real, even if only visionary.

In addition to these works, Professor Crossan has published a series of books and articles on the Gospels inside the New Testament as well as on the Gospels that were not included in the New Testament. His work is marked by exploration, exegetical detail, fresh hypotheses, and sometimes daring conclusions, a few of which will be looked at shortly.

Bishop Wright has also published several major works. His *The New Testament and the People of God*, which appeared in 1992, provides a rich context for his massive sequel, *Jesus and the Victory of God*, which appeared in 1996.[6] The first book reviews the problems related to sources and the writing of history, an understanding of first-century Judaism in the Greco-Roman world, and an understanding of the emergence of the Christian faith. The second volume focuses on Jesus, who announced Yahweh's return to Zion and who by his ministry, death, and redemption made possible all that the Scriptures of Israel had promised. I am impressed by Bishop Wright's learning, by his erudition, and especially by his nuanced appreciation of the scriptural and ideological traditions—both Jewish and non-Jewish—in circulation in late antiquity.

Bishop Wright has also given us an extensive treatment of the resurrection of Jesus.[7] He engages all of the major players, including Professor Crossan, coming to conclusions that in broad outline may be regarded as "orthodox" but which at points are hardly conventional or traditional. Again, I am impressed by the bishop's grasp of the primary literature and how it impinges on this important topic.[8] Frequently, he offers fresh insights and vigorous argument. It is the kind of meat that academics love to chew.

Everyone contributing to the present volume knows that Professor Crossan and Bishop Wright disagree profoundly on many points, not least on the resurrection. But what should not be lost in the arguments and counterarguments is how much progress their work represents, and how at points it is mutually supportive. This progress is especially apparent when their work is compared to some of the most influential scholarship produced a generation or two ago. As I pondered this point, I picked up a few of my old books by Rudolf Bultmann. In his heyday Professor Bultmann was as influential as anyone could be; even his critics conceded his greatness. And although his influence has waned considerably in the past few decades, it has not completely disappeared, surviving in a somewhat mutated form in the Jesus Seminar.[9]

I looked at Bultmann's chapter on background in his famous book titled simply *Jesus*, published in 1926.[10] In this chapter, Bultmann discusses the "Jewish religion" and "messianic movements."[11] He tells us that the Jewish people "had no intellectual or spiritual life in the sense of cultural achievements."[12] Elsewhere, he reduces Jewish religion and faith to "legalism."[13] Throughout, Bultmann speaks in the abstract; he is acquainted with some of the literature, such as Josephus, and some of the apocalyptic literature, but he gives evidence of almost no acquaintance with the land of Israel (which, by the way, he never visited) or its geography, topography, archaeology, or material culture. What Bultmann called "background" would not pass muster by today's standards.

In marked contrast, Crossan and Wright provide readers with rich discussions of the setting and background of Jesus and his movement. No one can read their writings and come away without a deepened knowledge of the land of Israel, the Mediterranean world, Jewish customs and traditions, and the dangers that Jews and Christians faced in a world very different from our own.

As a matter of fact, Crossan and Wright challenge Rudolf Bultmann at two key points: Crossan calls into question Bultmann's hasty and categorical dismissal of the extracanonical Gospels as having no value. Bultmann states that the Synoptic Gospels "are completely subordinate to Christian faith and worship. And what we know of the Apocryphal gospels does nothing to change the picture; they are but legendary adaptations and expansions."[14] Crossan's painstaking, detailed study of the extracanonical Gospels may show that there is a little more to them than simply "legendary adaptations and expansions." Wright challenges Bultmann's deficient interest in the Judaic setting of Jesus, on the one hand, and, on the other hand, the simplistic distortions that often surface when the Judaic components are mentioned.

Craig A. Evans

Crossan's Distinctive Contribution

In my opinion, Professor Crossan has made three important contributions to the study of Jesus: (1) his redaction-critical assessment of the Passion story, (2) his openness to the extracanonical sources and what they might tell us about Jesus and how they might shed light on the nature of the tradition preserved in the canonical sources, and (3) his imaginative and creative exploration of and application of Jesus' environment and how it may give us new insight. Let us review them in this order.

First, Crossan's insightful redaction-critical study of the empty tomb story in Mark raises important questions and opens up new interpretive possibilities in our attempts to understand the purpose this evangelist had in writing his Gospel. Put simply, Crossan takes nothing for granted. Story after story, even detail after detail, is subjected to careful, critical scrutiny. Is it history, or is it confession based on something in Scripture or in culture? Was Jesus buried? Was there a tomb? Was there a man named Joseph of Arimathea who supervised Jesus' burial? Did women go to the tomb and find it empty? Did Jesus appear to his disciples, revealing the marks of nails in his hands? Did he appear to them and eat food? No detail goes unexamined, and no traditional explanation is accepted without critical assessment. In short, Professor Crossan has done his homework, and whether or not we agree with his conclusions, we are the richer for considering his arguments and the data he has assembled.

Second, Crossan's critical and exegetical treatments of the extracanonical gospels are masterful and constitute important steps forward in gospel research, whatever one's views are regarding his conclusions. Crossan investigates these writings on their own terms, without assumptions regarding their literary relationship to other gospels, inside or outside the New Testament. He offers exegetical study, passage by passage, drawing conclusions about the meaning of these passages in their earliest form and function and in their extant contexts. In other words, Crossan has treated the extracanonical gospels with the academic respect with which most scholars treat the canonical Gospels. In this, Crossan's work is exemplary.

His work is succinctly presented in *Four Other Gospels: Shadows on the Contours of Canon*, published in 1985 and reissued in 1992.[15]

In this book, Crossan investigates passages from the *Gospel of Thomas*, the Egerton Papyrus (or Egerton Gospel), the Secret Gospel of Mark, and the *Gospel of Peter*. The latter—the *Gospel of Peter*—has been subjected to a detailed study in which Crossan concludes that an early Cross Gospel underlies Peter and that this Cross Gospel is the Passion source for Matthew, Mark, Luke, and John.[16] Indeed, Crossan argues that all four of these extracanonical Gospels contain materials that are independent of the canonical Gospels. They are independent, parallel, and in some instances perhaps earlier and even superior. When viewed as independent and possibly as prior, we may find a Jesus somewhat different from the one preserved in the New Testament Gospels.

Crossan's heavy reliance on the extracanonical gospels has generated as much controversy as any of his conclusions. Many think that all four of the extracanonical gospels that Crossan has identified as potentially independent, or at least containing early, independent materials, probably derive from the second century. For example, the Egerton Papyrus may well be an instance of the kind of conflation (in this case, conflating John and the Synoptics) seen in second-century Christian writers, such as Justin Martyr.[17] The *Gospel of Thomas* may also be secondary, for it appears to quote or allude to more than half of the New Testament writings and may also be acquainted with second-century Syriac traditions, including Tatian's *Diatessaron*.[18] Many have grave reservations about the alleged antiquity of the *Gospel of Peter*, with its fantastic details, errors regarding Jewish conventions and political realities, and gnostic touches.[19] And finally, there is the so-called *Secret Mark*, discovered by the late Morton Smith, two quotations of which have been found in a Clementine letter written in the back of a seventeenth-century edition of the letters of Ignatius.[20] It may in fact be a hoax, based on a remarkably parallel fictional story titled *The Mystery of Mar Saba*, published in 1940, one year before Smith says he was invited to visit the Mar Saba Monastery, where he too would eventually find a long lost document that could be embarrassing to the Church.[21] The parallels are so close that, taken together with the lack of proper testing and verification and the curious fact that Smith *signed his name* to the first extant page of the volume in which the Clementine letter was found, we should be very cautious about hypothesizing reconstructions of Gospel origins and relations on the basis of this "source."[22]

Third, I commend Professor Crossan for imaginatively exploring in what ways the environment may have shaped Jesus' thinking and behavior. Often, writing about Jesus seems to give hardly more than lip service to the question of social, cultural, political, and economic background and how this background qualifies our understanding of Jesus. About half of the aforementioned *The Historical Jesus* is devoted to the Roman Empire (the "Brokered Empire") and to Israel (the "Embattled Brokerage"). This reminds me of E. P. Sanders's magisterial work *Paul and Palestinian Judaism.* Just as Sanders begins his book with a lengthy discussion of Jewish thought before plunging into Paul's theology, so Crossan treats his readers to a lengthy and highly informative description of life in the Mediterranean world.[23] The result of this comparative work is the conclusion that the "historical Jesus was, then, a peasant Jewish Cynic. His village was close enough to a Greco-Roman city like Sepphoris that sight and knowledge of Cynicism are neither inexplicable nor unlikely."[24]

Although I and others cannot accept this conclusion—not least because ongoing archaeology at Sepphoris has demonstrated the strongly Judaic character of this city prior to 70—I appreciate the comparative work that Crossan has undertaken.[25] Historiography and exegetical precision are impossible without comparative study. The nuance of many of Jesus' sayings is sharpened by comparison with Cynic idiom, even if in the end we conclude that Jesus himself was not a Cynic.

Wright's Distinctive Contribution

In my view, Bishop Wright's most significant contribution to Jesus research is his unflagging exploration of the Judaic context of Jesus' life, death, and resurrection, and in what ways his life, death, and resurrection have continuity with the story of Israel. Bishop Wright has a way of seeing the big picture even while delving deeply into a myriad of details and complexities. His studies of Jesus and Paul, along with his commentaries on many of the writings of the New Testament, and the clarity and persuasiveness with which he articulates his views have placed Wright in center stage as the leading evangelical New Testament scholar.

I shall say less about Bishop Wright's work because I agree with it and often find myself following his lead and occasionally defending some of his ideas that strike some scholars as daring and novel. A case in point is his argument that Jesus and others viewed Israel as, in a sense, in a state of exile. Maurice Casey was quite indignant over this—and those who know Dr. Casey know that he cannot disagree any other way—claiming that Wright was quite wrong for, after all, Israel existed as a country and many, if not most, Jews lived in Israel.[26] In what sense can one say that Israel was "in exile"?[27]

Casey's failure to grasp this point indicated a failure also to appreciate the big picture that Bishop Wright was trying to help us see. Jesus was concerned with the rule of God and with the concomitant liberation of Israel from the rule of Satan. His proclamation of the forgiveness of sin, or "debt," with its jubilee connotations; his exorcisms, to which he pointed as evidence that the kingdom of God really had manifested itself; his healing of the bent woman, releasing her on the Sabbath—she whom Satan had cruelly bound for eighteen years (see Luke 13:16)—and of course the binding of Satan, the strong man (Mark 3:26–27), are part and parcel of the task of liberating Israel from the most damning exile and captivity of all—that of estrangement from God and from one another.

Another great strength in Wright's work is his appreciation of the contribution that Israel's sacred stories and scriptures made to the thought and activities of Jesus and his followers. In Jesus' ministry, the narrative of God's work in, for, and through Israel continues. For Wright, finding this continuity clarifies the intentions of Jesus and the meaning of his ministry.

Ironically, it is this very continuity between the Gospel narrative and Israel's scriptures that raises doubts in the mind of Crossan. Whereas Wright finds history looking for scriptural explanation and prophetic fulfillment, Crossan believes what we really have are scriptural promises generating historical narrative.[28]

In my view, the truth of the matter lies somewhere in the middle, for the evidence seems to cut both ways. We find appeals to Scripture ("in order that it be fulfilled") that may well have shaped the story (and I think the fourth Gospel has several instances of this), but we find other appeals where it looks more like history searching for scriptural clarification.[29] Of course, in some of these cases it is difficult to say which way the influence flows—from historical reminiscence to Scripture, or from Scripture to narrative.

I have no doubt that I have introduced some of my own perspectives here, but they arise largely in response to Bishop Wright's stimulating and provocative publications. The 2005 Greer-Heard Forum centered on the question of the resurrection. The conveners assembled an impressive array of theologians, philosophers, and biblical scholars. At the center of this array are two Christian thinkers— Dom Crossan and Tom Wright—whose work will no doubt stimulate fruitful dialogue and a deeper understanding of what lies at the very heart of Christian faith, the resurrection of Jesus.

A Postscript

I conclude with a postscript concerning the resurrection: I find very compelling the point of asking why Jesus' followers spoke of resurrection at all. Why not treat the Easter appearances of Jesus as "apparitions," as assurances that Jesus was in the blessed presence of God, and let it go at that? The Jewish people, like all peoples in the Mediterranean region of late antiquity, had their ghost stories. What was it that made the Jewish disciples of Jesus speak of *resurrection*?

The rumor, swiftly running through the ranks of Jesus' following, to the effect that some had seen Jesus, seemingly alive, would have been interpreted through the lens of Jewish and Mediterranean ideas of ghostly apparitions and perhaps even the transcendence of the soul, of the immaterial and immortal essence, over the physical. The proclamation that Jesus lives and that he is in heaven would not of necessity have led to the conclusion that Jesus had been resurrected. Indeed, the singularity of the event—that it was Jesus only[30]—would have argued against resurrection, because resurrection in the thinking of Jews who believed in such a thing was understood in terms of a *general* resurrection, that is, when *all* would be raised (as in Dan.

12:2). The widespread belief among Jesus' original followers that their master had in fact been raised from the dead strongly suggests that there was something about the Easter and post-Easter appearances that could not be explained in the more easily accepted terms of ghostly apparitions.[31]

− 3 −

THE HERMENEUTICS OF RESURRECTION
How N. T. Wright and John Dominic Crossan
Read the Resurrection Narratives

Robert B. Stewart

Few contemporary scholars have been as acclaimed and criticized as N. T. Wright and John Dominic Crossan. Too often, however, those reading their works try to cut to the chase, or the back of the book, to see what Wright or Crossan has concluded, rather than patiently reading the books through to see what each has intended to say. Both men are creative exegetes of Scripture who propose innovative ways of understanding texts and reading them for historical meaning. In the brief space allotted, I will pose three fundamental hermeneutical questions to Wright and Crossan: (1) What is a text? (2) How should texts be read? and (3) What is the relationship between history and hermeneutics? I will then summarize how the two men handle the resurrection narratives and assess how their answers to my herme-neutical questions are borne out in their readings of the resurrection narratives.[1]

What Is a Text?

Wright believes that texts are "best conceived as the articulation of worldviews, or, better still, *the telling of stories which bring worldviews into articulation.*"[2] All texts communicate an implied narrative—a story that at least conceivably may be discovered within the text.[3] Worldviews are expressed through (1) stories that order one's view of reality; (2) symbols (shorthand statements of stories); (3) answers to five ultimate questions (who are we? where are we? what is wrong? what is the solution? and what time is it?); and (4) praxis, a way of being in the world. Although through any of these the entire worldview can be glimpsed, stories contain the fullest expression of a worldview.[4] All worldviews have their own *story*; all texts relate to a worldview story. Worldviews provide the reader with a fundamental framework through which to discern the meaning of a text.

Texts do not put one directly in touch with the thoughts or feelings of an author. Yet they are not entirely removed from the author because they express the worldview of the author and the worldview in which the author is situated. For Wright, worldviews are never understood individually until they have first been understood corporately.[5] Worldviews thus present readers with a (narrative) grid upon which to perceive their meanings and from which those meanings arise.[6]

Texts may also contain or generate multiple meanings. In fact, *meaning* is a term subject to multiple meanings. Texts may inform readers of the intentionalities of the characters, the contemporary relevance or consequence of the events, or even the divine purpose of God.[7] Meaning may be understood either as "referent" or "implication," the latter referring to its significance within the wider world of human life and experience.[8]

Critical realism is a key component in how Wright understands texts. An approach to knowledge borrowed from philosophy of science, critical realism recognizes that all knowledge is sociohistorical in nature but rejects the claim that "religious language provides only a useful system of symbols that can be action-guiding and meaningful for the believer without being in any sense reality depicting in its cognitive claims."[9] Critical realism "acknowledges the *reality of the thing known, as something other than the knower* (hence 'realism'), while also fully acknowledging that the only access we have to this reality lies along the spiraling path *of appropriate dialogue or conversation between the knower and the thing known* (hence 'critical')."[10] Advocates of critical realism grant that all knowledge is provisional and, thus, subject to revision. Related to the efficacy of language, critical realists do not hold that texts are derivative of an objective world, but they do insist that the texts may represent and refer to an objective world.[11]

For Crossan, Jesus research has always been wrapped up in hermeneutics. In the preface of *In Parables,* he writes: "The term 'historical Jesus' really means the language of Jesus and most especially the parables themselves."[12] In the introduction to *In Fragments*, Crossan writes: "The problem of the historical Jesus thereby translates itself and transforms itself into the problem of the hermeneutical Jesus."[13] While Crossan's understanding of texts, indeed the nature of language in general, has changed somewhat through time, his emphasis on understanding Jesus' language as the key to discovering the historical Jesus has remained constant. In his earliest writings, he espouses something similar to the "New Hermeneutic," stressing that language, particularly the language of Jesus' parables, is always "world creating." Texts, in particular the parables of Jesus, are intended not to present the reader with *information* nor to illustrate a point that could be made apart from the metaphor, but rather to involve the reader in the world of the parable. One cannot hope to understand a poem (or a parable) until one has entered into its world.[14] Crossan focuses on the structure and the effect produced by Jesus' parables rather than on their content. The influence of the New Hermeneutic, with its emphasis on *language events,* is clear at this point.[15]

In *The Dark Interval,* Crossan begins to stress not the world-creating nature of language but the universality and limitations of language. Crossan declares that there is only language and that one cannot get out of language: "We live in language like fish in the sea."[16] Drawing on the early Wittgenstein as well as on Nietzsche, Dickenson, and Eliot, he stresses that language cannot tell us of the transcendent but instead takes us only to its edge, where by pushing the envelope of language, we can hope to experience transcendence. But, of course, we can never know objectively of transcendence (God) through language, or transcendence would not be transcendence. Crossan insists that what matters is not the content of a text but its structure and the effect that a text's structure produces. He declares of Jesus' parables: "They are stories which shatter the deep structure of our accepted world and thereby render clear and evident to us the relativity of story itself. They remove our defences and make us vulnerable to God. It is only in such experiences that God can touch us, and only in such moments does the kingdom of God arrive. My own term for this is transcendence."[17]

In his next two books, Crossan continues to stress language's inability to refer to a reality outside language (text) itself. In *Finding Is the First Act*, he has the parabolic declare: "I will tell you, it says, what the Kingdom of God is like. Watch carefully how and as I fail to do so and learn that it cannot be done. Have you seen my failure? If you have, then I have succeeded. And the more magnificent my failure, the greater my success."[18] In *Raid on the Articulate*, he begins to press on from structuralism to poststructuralism as he calls for the abandonment of eschatology and thus the end of interpretive closure. To this end, Crossan quotes Stanley Cavell:

> Suppose what Hamm sees is that salvation lies in the ending of endgames, the final renunciation of all final solutions. The greatest endgame is Eschatology, the idea that the last things of earth will have an order and a justification, a sense. That is what we hoped for, against hope, that was what salvation would look like. Now we are to know that salvation lies in reversing the story, in ending the story of the end, dismantling Eschatology, ending this world of order in order to reverse the curse of the world laid on it in its Judeo-Christian end.[19]

The full force of Crossan's poststructuralist tendencies becomes evident in *Cliffs of Fall*. He agrees with Paul Ricoeur that metaphorical language stands in binary opposition to literal language. But, contra Ricoeur, Crossan insists that metaphorical language does not grow out of literal language. Rather, it is the other way around—all language is essentially metaphorical and only becomes literal—that is, ordered—through time.[20] Crossan makes it clear that this ubiquitous and primordial metaphoricity is more akin to Derrida's "absence of meaning" than to Ricoeur's "surplus of meaning" when he states:

> It is precisely the absence of a fixed, literal, univocal, or univalent language that releases the inevitability and universality of metaphor itself. And this absence is the foundation and horizon of all language and of all thought. If Derrida is correct in this challenge, and I think that he is,

it would mean that metaphor or symbol does not so much have a "surplus of meaning," in Ricoeur's phrase (1976), as a *void of meaning* at its core.[21]

Though Crossan's understanding of texts has shifted and developed over time, throughout all these works runs an implicit commitment to structuralism/formalism, the theory that various types of writing have different characteristics, ends, and ways of functioning, and that discerning these structures or forms enables our understanding of them by focusing not on what texts say but on how texts communicate what they say. Whether he discusses parable or myth, apologue or satire, poetry or historical narrative, Crossan holds that certain types of language, and hence texts, produce certain effects. What matters in texts is not what they say but, rather, what effect they produce.[22]

One should not think that these ideas are found only in Crossan's early work or that his Jesus research is of an entirely different nature than his earlier hermeneutical writings. As recently as 2002, he affirmed his understanding of parables as producing multiple interpretive effects in the service of historical-Jesus research. In the journal *Interpretation,* he discusses parables *by* Jesus and parables *about* Jesus, the former representing the structure of Jesus' parables (*ipsissima structura*), although not his exact words (*ipsissma verba*).[23] Jesus' parables, at least as originally given, invariably produced a number of interpretations—and intentionally so. They are intended as vehicles of bottom-up self-education for his listeners by creating debate and dialogue as to their meaning.[24] Unlike parables *by* Jesus, parables *about* Jesus do not come from Jesus but nevertheless share a similar parabolic structure.[25] They were created for the purpose of involving the church in the process of making this world a place of justice. After analyzing the feeding of the multitude with five loaves and two fish, Crossan concludes:

> It suggests that when God in Jesus distributes food fairly, equitably, and justly what is there is more than enough food for all. It also suggests that the church (the disciples as leadership or as symbolic entirety?) wants no part of this functional destiny and must be pulled by Jesus (kicking and screaming, as it were) into the middle of that process: Jesus to disciples

to people. The disciples: "send them away." Jesus: "you give them food." No wonder we prefer to emphasize a miraculous multiplication which we want but cannot obtain rather than a just distribution which we can obtain but do not want.[26]

It thus becomes clear that for Crossan even narrative portions of the canonical Gospels, whether explicitly parabolic or not, are parabolic in nature.

Differences and similarities exist between Wright and Crossan concerning the nature of texts. Wright insists that texts carry within them implicit worldviews, or ways of seeing the world, within which texts mean what they mean. Crossan would probably agree on this point. Nevertheless, for Wright, texts generally refer to the world outside the text; content matters for Wright. Crossan, on the other hand, believes that texts create their own worlds, and he generally focuses on their effect rather than their content.

How Should Texts Be Read?

For Wright, texts should be read in light of their worldviews. To do this, Wright recommends paying particular attention to the story that a text is telling (or subverting). Narrative criticism is a useful tool for achieving this goal. To this end, he recommends reusing elements of A. J. Greimas's narrative structuralism.[27] Recognizing that Greimas's method is decidedly formalist, and thus antihistorical, Wright's intention is not so much to follow it slavishly but to reuse a particular aspect of it, namely actant analysis, in order to understand the structure and function of a text, particularly sayings of Jesus.[28]

Readers must make an effort to discern the aims and intentions of historical figures. Wright states, "History, I shall argue, is neither 'bare facts' nor 'subjective interpretations', but is rather *the meaningful narrative of events and intentions*."[29] He contends that one may reasonably grasp the intention of historical figures by evaluating their words and actions against the backdrop of their worldview.[30] Building on the work of Ben Meyer, he seeks to discern Jesus' intentions by evaluating his praxis (both verbal and visual) within the context of the worldview of Second Temple Judaism.[31] He then works from his worldview to uncover Jesus' basic beliefs, aims, consequent beliefs, and intentions.[32]

Wright insists that a legitimate reading of the Bible will also take seriously Scripture's historical, literary, and theological dimensions. If a reading does not allow for all three, it is incomplete. Reading a text simply for its (modern) historical meaning (what did it mean when written?) results in the loss of contemporary and personal relevance. But when a text is read simply for its (postmodern) literary effect (what does this mean to me?), it often is stripped of its public relevance.[33]

One must not be afraid to read texts for theological meaning. There is a necessarily theological component, either explicitly or implicitly, within the stories that is inherent in worldviews.[34] Asking theological questions of a text thus goes hand in hand with posing historical or literary questions. Wright believes it is hermeneutically inconsistent to treat statements that are theological (about God) any differently from statements that are political or sociological. Theological language is therefore "on the same footing as language about anything else," and as such one should "affirm the right of theological language to be regarded as an appropriate dimension of discourse about reality."[35]

Wright does not propose to bypass literary or historical concerns. Nor does he assume that theological language is gifted with a perspective that other language lacks. Consistent with critical realism, he sees theological language as *public*, that is, subject to critique and correction.[36] In this way he seeks a theological reading that will enhance both literary and historical dimensions.[37]

A theological reading must be part of a biblical hermeneutic, because a concern for theology brings out a dimension of worldviews that historical and literary criticism are not equipped (or intended) to address, specifically the dimension of the symbolic.[38] Furthermore, theology "suggests certain ways of telling the story, explores certain ways of answering the questions, offers particular interpretations of the symbols, and suggests and critiques certain forms of praxis."[39]

In conclusion, Wright insists that readers must give attention to the worldview of a text, particularly to its worldview story, and read with a mind to discerning the intentionality of historical characters. One must also allow a text to speak fully—to allow for historical, literary, and theological meaning in texts. To this end, worldview analysis, narrative criticism, and critical realism serve as useful tools.

Crossan, on the other hand, maintains that texts must not be read with the intent to arrive at one authoritative meaning. Crossan's treatment of the parable of the sower in *Raid on the Articulate* highlights his rejection of authoritative readings. He grants that the traditional interpretation is in "obvious harmony with the data of agricultural experience" and that "as *an* interpretation of the story one can hardly deny its cogency and its validity." But he insists that "as *the* interpretation precluding all others it domesticates permanently and thereby destroys completely the paradox of gain-in-loss and loss-in-gain which is at the heart of the story's abrupt juxtaposition of losses and gains, of sowing failure and harvest plenitude."[40] Crossan writes: "An allegorical parable will generate interpretations that are both *multiple* and *paradoxical*. While any given interpretation may maintain that it is the best, fullest, or most interesting reading, and while this can always be tolerated and argued as a phenomenon of human play (exegetes have a right to play just as much as artists), the paradox at the heart of the parable must never be omitted in any interpretation."[41] Readers must resist the temptation to read Jesus' parables as example stories because, when this is done, the paradox at their heart is lost and other perspectives are marginalized.[42] Readers should thus seek to allow the original plurality and paradox that have been suppressed through authoritative readings to reemerge. This goal is achieved when readers "give up" seeking the correct interpretation and simply acknowledge that "allegory allegorizes allegory. The story always has the last laugh."[43] As Crossan declares in *Cliffs of Fall*: "He who finds meaning loses it, he who loses it finds it."[44]

One should not suppose that the reader is free to ignore the findings of historical criticism. In fact, Crossan insists that one should build on the findings of source, form, and redaction criticism. In *Finding Is the First Act*, Crossan writes:

> I presume the basic validity of the most rigorously methodical and necessarily negative determination of what in the evangelical Jesus tradition actually stems with some security from the historical Jesus himself. My own work has always begun *after* and been based *upon* the corpus of Jesus material established by that historical scholarship which considers

the various titular confessions, for example, and especially the Son of Man complex, as interpretations of Jesus from the early communities but not at all as the original language of Jesus himself.[45]

But historical criticism serves only as the first step toward discerning meaning. Crossan writes that historical methods apart from literary criticism have "failed rather completely and even dismally in understanding and interpreting what they had so painstakingly reconstructed" primarily because "*historical* thinking was required for reconstructing the corpus but *literary* appreciation was required for interpreting its meaning."[46] Ultimately, then, historical-critical methods function as prerequisites for interpretation, not as the final or most important step in interpretation. Crossan insists that hearing and responding to the parabolic challenge is most important when he declares: "Historicity is always a valid question and there are times when it is an absolutely important one. But notice how, in parables *by* or especially *about* Jesus such questions about historical accuracy may be used and welcomed to avoid questions about parabolic challenge."[47]

A legitimate reading will therefore be one that embraces polyvalency and considers the perspectives of marginalized groups that have been shut out by the majority tradition. Legitimate readings promote justice. Crossan presumes interpretive plurality and even insists that "*that is original which best explains the multiplicity engendered in the tradition.*"[48] But no reading can be legitimate that does not truly address the parabolic challenge that Jesus presents to all he encounters.

What Is the Relationship between History and Hermeneutics?

Wright contends that the task of historical reconstruction is impossible if one fails to understand the interpreted nature of all historical inquiry. He does not deny either the reality of objective events in the past or that people often speak of history in this sense. He simply wants to disabuse his readers of the idea that there is such a thing as "mere history."[49] On the other hand, history is not created by hermeneutics in an ontological sense. History does not consist of either "bare facts" or "subjective interpretations."[50] Clearly then, interpretation (hermeneutics) is as much a part of writing history as it is of reading history. Wright attempts to write about history as interpretation in a way that does not exclude history as "real events in the past."[51] His understanding of the relationship of hermeneutics to history is consistent with critical realism: history tells about *objective events* in the past *through interpretation*, not apart from it.

The goal of the historian is to move from event to meaning.[52] To this end, Wright distinguishes between history as what actually happened—that is, history as event (History-E)—and history as what was written about what actually happened—that is, history as written (history-W).[53] Wright states of his work: "The task to which I gave myself, then, was that of studying 'history-W' with the intent of coming as close as I could to 'history-E.'"[54]

Consistent with critical realism, Wright suggests a model of historical research that is similar to—but different in ways that are appropriate for the historian's particular concerns and the unique, unrepeatable nature of history—the model employed by most sciences: *hypothesis followed by verification.* He suggests three criteria by which any historical claim must be evaluated. The first concerns the available data. Any hypothesis must include all known data concerning the subject.[55] The second involves the scope of the hypothesis. It must be no more complex than required by the coherent inclusion of all the data.[56] The third criterion is in many ways the ultimate test of any historical conclusion. The hypothesis must make better sense not only of the available data but also of other related fields, as well as life as one lives it, than all other available hypotheses.[57] This model is essentially what some philosophers have called *abduction,* a type of commonsense reasoning, most fully enunciated by C. S. Peirce, that borrows from induction and deduction but technically is neither.[58]

As with every other part of Wright's approach, this is all conditioned by critical realism's ongoing spiral of knowledge. Historians can know at least some things about the past, but historical knowledge, like all knowledge, is always knowledge under critique, knowledge constantly subject to potential revision.

Crossan agrees that there can be no history apart from interpretation. Even eyewitness observers of Jesus were forced to interpret both his words and his actions. In "The Historical Jesus," Crossan states:

> Imagine, for example, these responses from different observers all of whom have heard and seen exactly the same phenomena in the life of Jesus.
>
> > He's dumb, let's ignore him.
> > He's lost, let's leave him.
> > He's dangerous, let's fight him.
> > He's criminal, let's execute him.
> > He's divine, let's worship him.[59]

Again, Crossan affirms this interpretive plurality:

> The New Testament itself contains a spectrum of divergent theological interpretations, each of which focuses on different aspects or clusters of aspects concerning the historical Jesus, or better, different historical Jesuses. It may be, for example, only the sayings, or only the miracles, or only the death, that is of primary concern for a given tradition, but any of those emphases presumes divergent historical Jesuses who said something, did something, and died in a certain way. I think, therefore, that different visions of the historical Jesus present a certain dialectic with different theological interpretations and that the New Testament itself is an obvious expression of that plurality's inevitability.[60]

Crossan maintains that "there will always be different historical Jesuses" and "divergent Christs built upon them," but "the structure of a Christianity will always be: *this is how we see Jesus-then as Christ-now*. I am proposing that the dialectic between Jesuses and Christs (or Sons, or Lords, or Wisdoms, or . . .) is at the heart of both tradition and canon, that it is perfectly valid, has always been with us and probably always will be."[61] Crossan calls the dialectic between Jesus-then and Christ-now *interactivism*. Interactivism eschews quests for the historical Jesus, as if Jesus were something that could ever be found once and for all time. The historical Jesus is never found once and for all. He is reconstructed over and over again as past and present interact.[62] It is not simply that one cannot obtain objective knowledge of history (or of a text); it is that one should not. Crossan allows that one could force history (or a text) into a static, once-and-for-all form or interpretation, but that would be highly undesirable because it would make any new sources of knowledge irrelevant.[63] History must be much more meaningfully defined. He writes:

> This is my working definition of history: *History is the past reconstructed interactively by the present through argued evidence in public discourse.* There are times we can get only alternative perspectives on the same event. (There are *always* alternative perspectives, even when we do not hear them.) But history as argued reconstruction is necessary to reconstruct *our* past in order to project *our* future.[64]

Because history is by nature reconstructed through argued discourse, Crossan can write:

> But there is not in my work any presumption that the historical Jesus or earliest Christianity is something you get once and for all forever. And that is not because Jesus and Christianity are special or unique. No past of continuing importance can ever avoid repeated reconstruction. . . .
> . . . In every generation, the historical Jesus must be reconstructed anew, and that reconstruction must become by faith the face of God for here and now.[65]

There is, thus, no history apart from hermeneutics. Accordingly, Crossan's goal is to understand the interpretive process that was at work in writing and canonizing the Gospels.[66]

The historical Jesus scholar, therefore, should not seek objective conclusions or even probable conclusions. The best that one can hope for is critical self-evaluation and honesty. Crossan thus does not claim that his method is objective. He forthrightly declares: "I am concerned, not with an unattainable objectivity, but with an attainable honesty. My challenge to my colleagues is to accept those formal moves or, if they reject them, to replace them with better ones. They are, of course, only *formal* moves, which then demand a *material* investment."[67]

What then is there to keep the historical Jesus scholar honest? Crossan's answer:

> Method, method, and once again, method. Method will not guarantee us the truth, because nothing can do that. But method, as self-conscious and self-critical as we can make it, is our only discipline. It cannot ever take us out of our present skins and bodies, minds and hearts, societies and cultures. But it is our one best hope for honesty. It is the due process of history.[68]

Ultimately, Crossan is arguing for an understanding of the historical task in which one is open to multiple interpretations, as long as each interpretation can be supported by a clear and coherent methodology. In other words, history, like literature, is polyvalent.

In summary, historical investigation for Crossan is primarily a hermeneutical task. It carries no sense in which one should read history authoritatively. As the interpreter of a poetic text or a parable seeks to be sensitive to other readings of a text, the historian must be sensitive to other readings of historical events and persons. Attention to all the various readings concerning a historical person or event allows one to see how an authoritative tradition arose from the original pluralistic (polyvalent) setting. The ultimate task is to interpret history so that it becomes meaningful for today, which, in Crossan's view, is also the task of historical-Jesus research.

The Resurrection according to Wright and Crossan

According to Wright, one cannot separate the resurrection from early Christianity without distorting the Christian worldview. He writes: "They reconstructed their worldview, their aims and agendas, around this belief so that it became, not merely an extra oddity, bolted onto the outside of the worldview they already had, but the transforming principle, the string that had pulled back the curtain, revealing God's future as having already arrived in the present."[69]

For Wright, the early Christian worldview represents a "startling, fresh mutation within second-Temple Judaism."[70] But, he asks, "What caused this mutation?"[71] His answer is that the establishment of the Christian community, with its own distinctive story, praxis, symbols, and way of answering Jewish worldview questions, sprang from early Christian belief in the bodily resurrection of Jesus from the dead. This leads him to ask what caused early Christian belief in the resurrection. His answer is twofold: the empty tomb and the resurrection appearances.

Wright considers the fact that Jesus was not the first or the last to lead a messianic movement and that such self-proclaimed messiahs were routinely put to death. Asking why Jesus' movement lived on without replacing him as leader, Wright concludes:

> If nothing happened to the body of Jesus, I cannot see why any of his explicit or implicit claims should be regarded as true. What is more, I cannot, as a historian, see why anyone would have continued to belong to his movement and to regard him as its Messiah. There were several other Messianic or quasi-Messianic movements within a hundred years either side of Jesus. Routinely, they ended with the leader's being killed by the authorities, or by a rival group. If your Messiah is killed, you conclude that he was not the Messiah. Some of those movements continued to exist; where they did, they took a new leader from the same family. (But note: Nobody ever said that James, the brother of Jesus, was the Messiah.) Such groups did not go around saying that their Messiah had been raised from the dead. The early Christians did believe that Jesus had been raised bodily from the dead. What is more, I cannot make sense of the whole picture, historically or theologically, unless they were telling the truth.[72]

How extensively the early Christians reshaped their worldview is evident when one considers that they maintained their commitment to Jewish monotheism while at the same time beginning to worship Jesus.[73] Wright's point is that although the resurrection *alone* would not account for such a radical praxis on the part of the (Jewish) early church, it is inconceivable that worship of Jesus could take place as it did apart from a literal resurrection of Jesus.[74]

In *The Resurrection of the Son of God*, Wright asks two overarching questions concerning resurrection: "What did the early Christians think had happened to Jesus, and what can we say about the plausibility of those beliefs?"[75] The second question clearly concerns historical method and epistemology. The first, however, implies hermeneutics. Indeed, a significant portion of Wright's tome on the resurrection is devoted to answering a *hermeneutical* question: "When the early Christians said 'The Messiah was raised from the dead on the third day' what might they have been heard to be saying?" Wright calls this the question of *meaning*.[76] He devotes more than five hundred pages to discussing how the afterlife was understood and talked about, *and what the relevant terms meant*, in ancient pagan writings, the Old Testament, postbiblical Judaism, and various Christian writings (Letters of Paul, the Gospels, Acts, Hebrews, General Letters, and Revelation as well as noncanonical early Christian texts). Wright insists that only when we understand the context for such statements can we grasp their meaning, understand their significance, and correctly assess them.

After assessing numerous traditions and their texts, concepts, and categories, Wright concludes that statements about Jesus' resurrection in the canonical Gospels "belong with the Jewish view over against the pagan one and, within the Jewish view, with the Pharisees . . . over against the various other options."[77] His conclusion concerning the question of meaning is clear:

> The evangelists themselves, and the sources to which they had access, . . . really did intend to refer to actual events which took place on the third day after Jesus' execution. . . . Each of them, in their very different ways, believed that they were writing about events that actually took place. Their stories can be used to refer metaphorically or allegorically to all sorts of other things, and they probably (certainly in the case of Luke and John) intended it to be so. But the stories they told, and the deliberate and climactic rounding-off of their whole accounts, indicates that for reasons of narrative grammar as well as theology they must have intended to convey to their readers the sense that the Easter events were real, not fantasy; historical as well as historic.[78]

Concerning the plausibility of those beliefs, Wright insists that the empty tomb and the resurrection appearances, both individually necessary conditions for such beliefs to arise, taken together constitute a sufficient condition for such beliefs to be birthed.[79] That Jesus was raised bodily is the most likely explanation for such belief. It makes the most sense of the data in light of the Second Temple Jewish worldview, and moreover, it is historically highly probable.[80]

Not content to rest at this point, Wright sees yet another hermeneutical issue to consider. Most of *The Resurrection of the Son of God* deals with meaning as *referent*, but one must not neglect meaning as *implication*. The meaning of "God raised Jesus on the third day" *as referent* was that whether one affirmed or denied the statement, one was referring to bodily resurrection. The question of meaning *as implication*, on the other hand, asks what worldviews were being affirmed or challenged when the early Christians said, "God has raised Jesus from the dead."[81] The implications of affirming Jesus as the resurrected Son of God (or son of god) were momentous. To affirm such a statement was to challenge both the Jewish religious leaders and the Roman emperor. To the Jewish leaders, it meant "the inauguration of the new covenant."[82] To the Romans, it was a challenge to Caesar's authority—Jesus, not Caesar, is "the true monarch of the Gentile world as well."[83] But the truly significant question is, what does affirming the resurrection say about God? Wright contends that when early Christians affirmed the resurrection, they "meant it in the sense that he was the personal embodiment and revelation *of* the one true god."[84] These are serious affirmations, and they have this-worldly implications: "This world is where the kingdom must come, on earth as it is in heaven. . . . No wonder the Herods, the Caesars and the Sadducees of the world, ancient and modern, were and are eager to rule out all possibility of actual resurrection. They are, after all, staking a counter-claim on the real world."[85]

Wright grounds his reading of the resurrection narratives in the worldview of Second Temple Judaism and early (first-century) Christianity. He makes sense of these stories by viewing them against the backdrop of Israel's larger story. And he sees clearly their religious and political implications as a result. As a critical realist, he deems resurrection as historically highly probable, not certain.

Crossan, on the other hand, insists that "Jesus' first followers knew almost nothing whatsoever about the details of Jesus' crucifixion, death, or burial. What we have now in those detailed Passion accounts is not *history remembered* but *prophecy historicized*."[86] Building on Martin Hengel's writing concerning crucifixion, Crossan maintains that, in all likelihood, Jesus was never properly buried.[87] Typically, victims of crucifixion were either left on the cross to be eaten by wild animals or buried in shallow graves (and thus almost certainly also eaten by wild animals).[88] Crossan notes that part of the terror of crucifixion was the certain knowledge that one would not receive a decent burial and that, thus, one's body would almost certainly be devoured.[89] He sees a procession in the tradition "from burial by enemies to burial by friends, from inadequate and hurried burial to full, complete, and even regal embalming."[90] Simply stated, the Passion Narratives, according to Crossan, do not relay accurate historical information concerning either Jesus' death or his burial. Their modus operandi was "Hide the prophecy, tell the narrative, and invent the history."[91]

One would suspect that given his denial of Jesus' burial, Crossan would also deny Jesus' resurrection. But technically, Crossan does not so much *deny* the resurrection as *redefine* it. Crossan understands resurrection as a metaphor for Jesus' continued presence in the Church. As such, he insists that the embodied life of Jesus "remains powerfully efficacious in this world."[92] He continues:

> Bodily resurrection has nothing to do with a resuscitated body coming out of its tomb. And neither is bodily resurrection just another term for Christian faith itself. Bodily resurrection means that the *embodied* life and death of the historical Jesus continues to be experienced, by believers, as powerfully efficacious and salvifically present in this world. That life continued, as it always had, to form communities of like lives.[93]

When asked what happened on Easter Sunday, Crossan concludes:

> In a nutshell, these are my conclusions: First, the Easter story is not about the events of a single day, but reflects the struggle of Jesus' followers to make sense of both his death and their continuing experience of empowerment by him. Second, stories of the resurrected Jesus appearing to various people are not really about "visions" at all, but are literary fiction prompted by struggles over leadership in the early Church. Third, resurrection is one—but only one—of the metaphors used to

express the sense of Jesus' continuing presence with his followers and friends.[94]

In other words, the resurrection is more hermeneutical than historical. Crossan maintains that "the ways in which the evangelists told and retold, adopted and adapted the parabolic stories *by* Jesus seem remarkably similar to the way they told and retold, adopted and adapted the resurrection stories *about* Jesus.[95] He understands "those resurrection stories as parables *about* Jesus, as utterly self-conscious creations by writers who knew exactly what they were doing."[96]

In a recent article entitled "The Resurrection of Jesus in Its Jewish Context," Crossan brackets certain valid historical questions concerning the burial of Jesus, the discovery of the empty tomb, the apparitions to Jesus' companions, and the purpose of those stories in their present Gospel contexts in order to raise more fundamental questions concerning how "resurrection" was understood by first-century Jews.[97] He notes: "Jesus not only lived and died as a Jew, he also rose as a Jew. In other words, the bodily resurrection of Jesus can only be understood correctly within the faith and theology about resurrection present in certain circles of his contemporary Judaism."[98] Concerning the former questions, Crossan asks: "Even if all of that happened as recorded, why did anyone call it 'resurrection'? Does empty tomb and risen vision ineluctably indicate 'resurrection' so that no other term, interpretation, or understanding is possible within that first-century Jewish context?"[99]

Crossan thinks it anachronistic to insist either that dead people do not return to life or that Jesus was uniquely raised from the dead. He views such contentions as the product of post-Enlightenment categories, which nobody in the first century entertained. In a pre-Enlightenment world, resurrections were generally accepted among those things that could and did take place. Instead, the crucial question was one of relevance: Why should anybody care if Jesus was raised bodily from the dead?[100]

First-century Jewish belief in resurrection was the end product of a theological transformation from a culture that actively *disbelieved* in life after death, which they associated with paganism, to one in which certain segments insisted on bodily resurrection.[101] This shift, which brought belief in an afterlife and in next-worldly sanctions into Judaism, resulted from Judaism's encounter with Hellenism and provided an answer to the death and bodily destruction of righteous martyrs.[102] Crossan insists: "Bodily resurrection is not about the survival of us but about the justice of God. . . . *Bodily* resurrection was not a philosophical vision of human destiny but a theological vision of divine character."[103] He further insists that a first-century Jew expected resurrection to be *general*, not *individual*, in nature. The Christian claim that Jesus was raised bodily from the dead was a startling innovation within Judaism, one indicating that the resurrection had begun—but was going to be a process rather than a single, instantaneous divine action. Such a claim would require evidence that the world was being transformed. Such evidence was found in the Christian community, which was making the world better by its inclusive lifestyle.[104]

This brings Crossan to his final, and most important, question: Is bodily resurrection to be understood as literal or metaphorical? Crossan allows that then, as now, the spectrum of understanding runs from 100 percent literal to 100 percent metaphorical.[105] At the end of the day, he seems to grant that one may take bodily resurrection either literally or metaphorically, as long as one takes it seriously as general resurrection and apocalyptic consummation already begun—that is, as long as one engages in making the world more just. Failure to do so is proof that our faith is vain, and thus that Christ has not been raised—exalted, perhaps, but certainly not resurrected.[106]

Assessment

Two aspects of Wright's method stand out in his reading of the resurrection narratives: worldview analysis and abduction. He understands the meaning of Christian resurrection language against the worldview of Second Temple Judaism. He also tests his reading's plausibility against other competing hypotheses and concludes that his makes the best sense of the data.[107]

Certain features of Crossan's hermeneutic stand out in his treatment of the resurrection stories as well. First, his commitment to structuralism/formalism is obvious when he declares that the resurrection narratives are parables *about* Jesus because of their similar structure to parables *by* Jesus. Second, his commitment to interpretive pluralism (polyvalency) is evident when he concludes that what matters is not how one understands the mode of resurrection (literally or metaphorically) but, rather, how one lives in light of one's beliefs about it.

Wright and Crossan agree that we cannot simply answer the question, "What happened to Jesus?" They also concur that we cannot simply ask, "What difference does it make to me?" They declare together that we must see the difference that resurrection makes for the world. They both deplore triumphalism and declare that God is concerned with justice. But Wright insists that what happened to Jesus—he was actually raised from the dead—provides the basis for repairing a distorted world. The resurrection of Jesus is why we, to say nothing of the early Christians, can live as though there is another king in this world—because there is, and he is setting things right. Both men must be applauded for insisting that the resurrection is not fully understood apart from a concern for justice in the world at large. This is a message that my own tradition (evangelicalism in general, Baptist in particular) has often overlooked—and must regain. But we must be careful not to deny the significance of a historical, literal resurrection of Jesus or to downplay the resulting theology of grace, atonement, faith, and redemption in recovering Jesus' concern for justice.

– 4 –

MAPPING THE RECENT TREND TOWARD THE BODILY RESURRECTION APPEARANCES OF JESUS IN LIGHT OF OTHER PROMINENT CRITICAL POSITIONS

Gary R. Habermas

Tracking theological trends can be a rewarding enterprise. Observing not only recent movements but the ebb and flow of subcurrents reveals much about the state of contemporary research. This essay will map recent developments in research on the resurrection appearances of Jesus.[1] Admittedly, such an attempt in so brief a space necessarily requires some broad sketching and sometimes sweeping statements.

Jesus' resurrection often occupies the center of Christian theology, whatever one's theological persuasion or inclination. For the careful observer, various tendencies and alignments are emerging. Over the past five years, I have tracked well over two thousand scholarly publications on the resurrection. Each source appeared between 1975 and the present, in German, French, or English, written by a wide range of critical scholars.

From this contemporary scene, I will outline four broad positions regarding the nature of Jesus' resurrection appearances. These distinct camps range from natural to supernatural positions, with some significant shifts between these views during the past few years. In this essay, I will attempt to categorize the four positions, including naming two alternative proposals that seem to have avoided such recognition.

Then I will identify where most current scholarship rests, though I will not attempt to explain these shifts.

The Crux of Resurrection Studies

The latest research on Jesus' resurrection appearances reveals several extraordinary developments. As firmly as ever, most contemporary scholars agree that, after Jesus' death, his early followers had experiences that they at least believed were appearances of their risen Lord. Further, this conviction was the chief motivation behind the early proclamation of the Christian gospel.

These basics are rarely questioned, even by more radical scholars. They are among the most widely established details from the entire New Testament. As such, to address the enigma of the appearances, these early Christian convictions need to be explained. Why are these concessions standard scholarly fare? An entire series of reasons lies behind this critical recognition, reasons that will be summarized only briefly here.[2]

For example, among the earliest New Testament writers, Paul states that he experienced personally one of these resurrection appearances (1 Cor. 9:1; 15:8). Further, soon after his conversion (Gal. 1:15-16), Paul traveled to Jerusalem and discussed the gospel message (which included the resurrection appearances, 1 Cor. 15:1-8) with two other apostles, Peter and James, the brother of Jesus (Gal. 1:18-24). Later, Paul returned to Jerusalem specifically to verify his gospel message with these two apostles plus John (Gal. 2:2), who confirmed it (2:9-10). Paul stated that he also knew what the other apostles were teaching concerning the resurrection appearances, which he said was the same message (1 Cor. 15:11). So it is widely recognized that Paul's testimony brings us very close to the earliest apostolic gospel message.

Moreover, the majority of recent scholars concede that James was an unbeliever until he experienced an appearance of the risen Jesus (1 Cor. 15:7). For the seeming majority of scholars who recognize early creedal passages in the Acts preaching, this adds to the potential testimony to the appearances.[3] Many of the apostles were willing to die specifically for this message, which differentiates their transformation from those, then or today, who are willing to die for an *ideology* that often is not linked to events, and for which the convert is not in a position to check out the nature of the claim. For the lesser number who think the tomb was empty (still the majority of scholars), this also favors some sort of experience.[4]

Now we must be careful here. It does not directly follow that, after his death, Jesus appeared to his followers. What most scholars grant is that some or all of these reasons indicate that Jesus' followers *thought* that Jesus was raised, and a number *claimed* that they had seen him, both individually and in groups. This has been a mainstay of critical thought since nineteenth-century German theology.

For instance, as Reginald Fuller remarked decades ago, that Jesus' disciples believed he was raised from the dead "is one of the indisputable facts of history." That they indeed experienced what they thought were Jesus' appearances "is a fact upon which both believer and unbeliever may agree."[5] Accordingly, Fuller concluded that these experiences must be adequately explained. This "requires that the historian postulate some other event over and above Good Friday, an event which is not itself the 'rise of the Easter faith' but the *cause* of the Easter faith."[6]

More recently, James D. G. Dunn agreed: "It is almost impossible to dispute that at the historical roots of Christianity lie some visionary experiences of the first Christians, who understood them as appearances of Jesus, raised by God from the dead." But Dunn cautions that these early believers were not merely relating an internal realization or conviction: "They clearly meant that something had happened to *Jesus* himself. God had raised *him*, not merely reassured *them*."[7]

Perhaps surprisingly, more skeptical scholars often still acknowledge the grounds for the appearances as well. Norman Perrin writes: "The more we study the tradition with regard to the appearances, the firmer the rock begins to appear upon which they are based."[8] Helmut Koester is even more positive: "We are on much firmer ground with respect to the appearances of the risen Jesus and their effect. . . . That Jesus also appeared to others (Peter, Mary Magdalene, James) cannot very well be questioned."[9]

The *crux* of the issue, then, is not *whether* there were real experiences, but *how we explain the nature* of these early experiences. What best accounts for the early Christian belief that Jesus had appeared after his death?

As Peter Carnley explains: "There is no doubt that the first disciples interpreted the Easter visions or appearances as signs of the heavenly presence of Christ. *Why* they should be minded to do this *with the degree of conviction that is so clearly reflected in the early testimony* is what we must seek to explain."[10] Along a similar line of thought, Bart Ehrman writes: "Historians, of course, have no difficulty whatsoever speaking about the belief in Jesus' resurrection, since this is a matter of public record. For it is a historical fact that some of Jesus' followers came to believe that he had been raised from the dead soon after his execution."[11] This early belief in the resurrection is the historical origin of Christianity.

Scholars widely agree that some of Jesus' early followers claimed to have seen him alive after his death. The main point of contention comes when we ask, with scholars like Fuller and Carnley, how these early Christian experiences are best explained. Historically, the major disagreement marking this broad range of explanations, of course, is between those scholars who hold that natural hypotheses can explain the historical and other data better than the supernatural thesis that Jesus appeared alive after his death.

I propose that these two broad explanations should each be subdivided once, with agnosticism occupying the ground between them. At the expense of oversimplifying, this will allow us to map the major critical reactions to the nature of the disciples' experiences into a total of five categories, four of which I will describe in some detail.[12] The purpose, again, is to ascertain the scholarly lay of the land as well as to note a few recent shifts across this terrain.

Let us begin with those who hold that natural hypotheses can best explain the data. Some of these scholars appeal to the internal, subjective states of the early Christians, arguing that this best unlocks the secret of the appearances. While agreeing with the likelihood of a natural explanation, other scholars prefer more external, objective solutions, involving events and conditions outside the early Christians. Both groups agree that Jesus did not rise from the dead and that the phenomena in question can best be explained another way. I will name these two perspectives the *natural internal* and the *natural external* theses, respectively.[13]

Many other scholars disagree, holding that reasons such as those outlined above indicate that the early believers' had actually witnessed appearances of the risen Jesus. With Dunn, they agree that something happened to Jesus and not just to his followers. But there is a secondary distinction here as well. Some of these scholars, emphasizing faith, prefer "luminous," often heavenly, manifestations of Jesus that did not involve Jesus' physical body, bolstered by several of the above reasons. Others, placing more emphasis on the evidence, hold that Jesus appeared in an external, bodily form. Both share the conviction that Jesus was raised from the dead and really appeared to his followers. I will name these positions the *supernatural internal* and the *supernatural external* theses, respectively.[14]

In between these two large categories is another view. While acknowledging perhaps even most of the reasons outlined above, scholars who hold this view conclude that they just are not sure how to best evaluate the data. Further, they often explain that it is not crucial to decide what probably happened—Christianity can survive just fine without giving an answer to this question. This is the agnostic position.

The crux of the issue, then, is that the early Christians fully believed in Jesus' resurrection. Some of Jesus' disciples taught that he had appeared to them after his death. This is at the center of several acknowledged facts regarding the end of Jesus' life and the beginning of the early church. While scholars explain this data in various ways, the appearances are the starting point.

I have argued elsewhere that, while they still hold a decidedly minority position among the total number of commentators, recent decades have revealed a slight increase in scholars who espouse naturalistic hypotheses to account for Jesus' resurrection.[15] Some of us had predicted this occurrence for years, so the increase was not a shock. Much more surprising, however, are the latest developments among those who believe that Jesus was raised from the dead in some sense.

Mapping Natural Theories

During the past two or three decades, a number of scholars have embraced various naturalistic alternatives to the New Testament report that Jesus was raised from the dead. After a lengthy lapse, and with-out new evidence emerging that favors these alternatives, it is difficult to account for this trend. With few exceptions, the theses parallel the nineteenth-century German lives of Jesus, along with some occasional new twists. Many of the suggestions have been published by scholars, although many others have been espoused in popular writings. Some have been developed in detail, while others have been mentioned only briefly. These natural hypotheses come in both internal and external varieties.

Natural Internal Theories

Scholars in this category hold that Jesus' appearances are best explained as a result of the *internal, subjective states* of the early Christians. As it was at the end of nineteenth-century German liberalism, as well as at the end of the twentieth century, probably the single most popu-lar alternative to Jesus' resurrection was the hallucination, or subjec-tive vision, theory. The disciples became convinced that they had seen Jesus alive, even though nothing had actually happened to him.

This option may have been largely prompted by the trends that we have already noted. The critical community has long acknowledged that the disciples *believed firmly* that Jesus had appeared to them after his death. While not the only theory in this category, the internal the-ses move to the heart of the issue—explaining the disciples' belief.

After a hiatus of many decades, arguably almost a century, the subjective vision theory has made a comeback. Hallucinations involve a mistaken perception that is not linked to the real world. They are defined as "false sensory perception not associated with real external stimuli."[16] German theologian Gerd Lüdemann has argued the most influential version of the subjective vision theory. Lüdemann appeals to "stimulus," "religious intoxication," and "enthusiasm" as the men-tal states leading to the visions seen by Peter and the others, but he is clear that nothing actually happened to Jesus.[17] There was a notable response, often an outcry, that was vociferous in its opposition.[18]

Another seemingly nameless internal thesis is what I have termed the *illumination* theory. In this theory, championed by Willi Marxsen, through some almost entirely nondescript internal process, Peter is the key to the other disciples becoming convinced that Jesus had been raised from the dead. Peter's insights provided the initial impetus, and his contagious enthusiasm persuaded his friends that Jesus was alive. Rarely are more specifics provided.[19] Strangely enough, in a later volume, Marxsen conceded that he was no longer sure whether Jesus' vision (or visions) was subjective or objective.[20]

Although not moving as far as what I have called the illumination thesis, Rudolf Pesch's early work typifies the view of a few scholars who thought that Jesus' precrucifixion authority, teachings, and influence were enough to cause his followers to survive the crucifixion with their faith intact.[21] However, Pesch later changed this view, recognizing that the appearances of the risen Jesus could be established by careful research.[22]

The hallucination, or subjective vision hypothesis, and the illumination thesis are the chief instances of internal naturalistic theories. Championing the power of inner faith and enthusiasm, they have sought to explain the disciples' subsequent experiences.

Natural External Theories

Various recent attempts have sought to explain the New Testament accounts of Jesus' appearances in terms of the *external states and conditions* of the early Christians. Some of these explanations are rather incredible and even fanciful.

One old standby, the *swoon or apparent death* theory, has even appeared in a few places recently, although it is seldom espoused by scholars. One scholarly exception is a very brief article by Margaret Lloyd Davies and Trevor Lloyd Davies that postulates that Jesus lost consciousness, leading bystanders to conclude that he was dead. When removed from the cross, however, Jesus revived and was treated. Quite surprisingly, according to this theory, the appearances apparently were caused not by Jesus actually being seen later but by some unspecified sort of "perceptions," raising once again the possibility of hallucinations.[23] Physicians reacted immediately against the Davies' stance, offering multiple demonstrations that Jesus really died by crucifixion.[24]

Overall, the swoon or apparent death theory has been rare ever since David Strauss's critique in 1835.[25] By the turn of the twentieth century, it was treated mainly as nothing more than a historical curiosity.[26]

Other scholars have questioned the Gospel accounts of the burial and empty tomb, sometimes by returning to hypotheses that reflect older German efforts. The best known is John Dominic Crossan's thesis that Jesus' dead body was either simply left on the cross or buried in a shallow grave. Either way, "the dogs were waiting."[27] Other-tomb theories have also been proposed.[28]

As at the end of the nineteenth century, various versions of the legend theory also existed at the end of the twentieth century. Of course, most critical scholars employ legendary *elements* without postulating full proposals of this sort. But others have stretched legendary accretion to a far greater extent. One of the best known and most radical is the view offered by G. A. Wells, who holds either that Jesus never lived or that he was an obscure, ancient individual who cannot be dated even to the first century C.E. Wells thinks that the Gospels are largely fabrication and explains the resurrection appearances as the growth of legend.[29]

A popular thesis at the close of the nineteenth century was that of the history-of-religions school, which attributed New Testament teachings to the ancient mystery religions. Evan Fales, a rare recent representative of these scholars, agrees with them that the best approach is to study Near Eastern mythical figures, such as Tammuz, Adonis, Isis, and Osiris.[30]

Another naturalistic hypothesis—what I will call the *illusion* theory, for lack of a recognized name—is often treated as a relative to hallucinations but needs to be cataloged differently. It is clearly an external alternative response because it is concerned particularly with perceptions in the objective world, although this is seldom recognized. As discussed earlier, hallucinations are subjective in nature. An illusion, however, is a mistaken substitute of one condition for its actual object—the "misperception or misinterpretation of real external sensory stimuli."[31] Unlike hallucinations, then, the illusion theory builds on situations where persons, either singly or in groups, mistake actual phenomena for something other than what they are in reality.

Michael Martin enumerates several illusions that he thinks parallel the early Christian belief in Jesus' resurrection appearances. His examples include some exceptionally curious cases—for example, UFOs, cattle mutilations, along with reports of witchcraft and related phenomena in colonial America.[32] G. A. Wells mistakenly refers to such illusional data as hallucinations.[33] Michael Goulder also employs some odd illusional incidents, concentrating especially on stories of Bigfoot![34]

I could provide other examples of naturalistic theories that have been suggested during the last few decades, but this demarcation should provide enough of a framework for observing the differences between internal and external natural alternatives. While they have made a bit of a comeback, these theories remain a minority of the scholarly views that have appeared during this time.

Each of the naturalistic theories was attacked piece by piece by the liberal scholars in the nineteenth century, as each criticized the others' approaches.[35] In the twentieth century, critical scholarship has largely rejected wholesale the naturalistic approaches to the resurrection. For example, while discussing these naturalistic approaches to the resurrection, Raymond Brown calls the attempts "gratuitous charges" and points out that they are at odds with the information we have on these subjects.[36] N. T. Wright treats a number of what he terms "false trails" and concludes that the problem with each attempt is that it runs up against "first-century history."[37] Similarly, James D. G. Dunn asserts that "alternative interpretations of the data fail to provide a more satisfactory explanation" than the New Testament message that God raised Jesus from the dead.[38]

Certain philosophers agree; for example, Steven T. Davis writes: "All of the alternative hypotheses with which I am familiar are historically weak; some are so weak that they collapse of their own weight once spelled out. . . . The alternative theories that have been proposed are not only weaker but far weaker at explaining the available historical evidence."[39] Richard Swinburne concludes the matter: "Alternative hypotheses have always seemed to me to give far less satisfactory accounts of the historical evidence than does the traditional account."[40]

Exhibiting an amazing amount of consensus, most researchers across a very wide conceptual spectrum have rejected naturalistic approaches as explanations for the earliest Christians' belief in the resurrection of Jesus. Even a small sample of these scholars over recent decades forms an impressive list.[41] Accordingly, the path of natural alternative theories is definitely a minority approach.

Mapping Supernatural Theories

Though nuanced, the theses that postulate that Jesus was raised from the dead in a supernatural manner vary less. What these views share is the belief that, after Jesus' death, something actually happened to him rather than merely to his followers. The theses differ in the way in which Jesus appeared—whether as a luminous (or other) vision or as a spiritual body.

Supernatural Subjective Theories

Toward the end of the era of nineteenth-century German liberalism, in his major work *Die Geschichte Jesu von Nazara* (The History of Jesus of Nazara), Theodor Keim challenged David Strauss's subjective vision theory. Convinced that Strauss's thesis was severely lacking, Keim first forcefully restated the hypothesis. He then followed with a multifaceted critique that is often credited as the chief refutation of Strauss.[42]

Keim postulated what came to be called the *objective vision* theory. This view proposed that although subjective visions ultimately fail, these appearances still must be explained because all the data indicate that the disciples still saw Jesus in some sense. Agreeing with Strauss and others, Keim rejected the Gospel accounts of the women's role on Easter Sunday morning and removed the appearances to Galilee in order to avoid having to explain the empty tomb. Turning to the appearances, or "visions," Keim concluded that they must be the "objective" work of God, who cooperated with the glorified Jesus himself. So Jesus was raised from the dead and appeared to his disciples in the form of heavenly "telegrams," revealing his glorified state and convincing them that he was alive and well. Keim realized that his theory was supernatural and involved a miracle.[43]

This general approach, minus a few of Keim's details, tremendously influenced critical theology in the second half of the twentieth century. Hans Grass's 1956 work *Ostergeschehen und Osterberichte* (Easter-event and Easter-reports) favored a similar proposal—that the empty tomb accounts are legendary but that Jesus did appear in Galilee in a noncorporeal but supernatural manner that cannot be explained in natural terms.[44] Grass's much-cited work influenced theology and brought conceptions of the resurrection like Keim's to the forefront of discussion.

Few scholars described this phenomenon more thoroughly than Reginald Fuller. Accepting the historicity of the empty tomb, contrary to Keim and Grass, Fuller defines the appearances as "visionary experiences of light, combined with a communication of meaning."[45] Fuller notes some similarities to Keim's position here, as well as some dissimilarities, such as his qualifying the use of the term *objective*.[46]

For a few decades after Grass, what I have termed the *supernatural subjective* characterization of the resurrection appearances grew in popularity, becoming at least the most influential, if not also the most popular, approach. Many major scholars took this position.[47] It was usually characterized by an emphasis on nonbodily visions, most likely from heaven, where the risen Jesus communicated his message to his disciples (perhaps by imparting meaning without literal words). While Jesus was actually raised as an act of God, it was usually said that this event cannot be historically demonstrated, although there may well be some decent arguments in its favor. But despite this position's popularity, another view had begun to gain influence by the end of the twentieth century.

Supernatural Objective Theories

Even before the publication of N. T. Wright's monumental volume *The Resurrection of the Son of God* in 2003, the tide had begun to turn toward the view that Jesus not only was raised miraculously from the dead but also appeared in a spiritual body.[48] So, the resurrection is an event that happened to Jesus, rather than either an internal experience or a natural occurrence. The risen Jesus featured both bodily continuity, including qualities that could be observed and perhaps even touched, as well as transformed discontinuity. Thus, Jesus appeared as far more than a vision of light from heaven. Further, it was usually held that firm historical evidence accompanied these appearances.[49]

Intriguingly, some commentators who still reject the facticity of Jesus' resurrection, such as Gerd Lüdemann, still acknowledge that the New Testament authors held this view, because of the manner in which Jesus appeared to his followers. For Lüdemann, even Paul thought that

Jesus appeared to him "in his transformed spiritual resurrection corporeality," signifying both bodily and transformed elements.[50] This is striking given the direction of recent conceptualizations of Paul's appearance that tend to favor the view described earlier as supernatural, glorified, or luminous visions.

Likewise, John Dominic Crossan and Jonathan Reed agree that, for Paul, Jesus' appearance to him was also bodily in nature. They state, "To take seriously Paul's claim to have *seen* the risen Jesus, we suggest that his inaugural vision was of Jesus' body simultaneously wounded *and* glorified." Regarding the Lukan claim of a luminous vision, Crossan and Reed propose that "we bracket that blinded-by-light sequence and imagine instead a vision in which Paul both *sees* and hears Jesus as the resurrected Christ, the risen Lord."[51] If such critical scholars as Lüdemann, Crossan, and Reed are correct, any position that takes seriously the early Christian teachings should at least address the nature of their claims.

Another particular effort that signals a change in this direction is the 2002 volume entitled *Resurrection*, edited by Ted Peters, Robert John Russell, and Michael Welker.[52] The eighteen contributors argue repeatedly that the resurrections of both Jesus and believers will be embodied, with most also holding some form of reconstitutionalism.[53]

N. T. Wright furthered the argument yet another step. For more than five hundred pages in his recent volume, he argues very persuasively that, among *both* pagans and Jews in the ancient Mediterranean world up until the second century C.E., the term ἀνάστασις almost uniformly meant that the *body* would be raised. So ἀνάστασις and its cognates (such as ἐξανάστασις) along with related words (such as ἐγείρω) almost without exception referred to bodily resurrection. Even the ancients who rejected the doctrine still used the relevant terms in this manner. Conversely, if they spoke about the soul or spirit being glorified or otherwise living after death, they used terms other than *resurrection*.[54] Moreover, even Paul, who is most often said to have taught otherwise, held strongly to Jesus' bodily resurrection, as did the rest of the New Testament authors.[55]

Not to be missed or glossed over lightly is that, on the two earlier occasions when Tom Wright and Dom Crossan dialogued on this subject, as well as here, Crossan noted his essential agreement with

Wright's major emphasis on the meaning of bodily resurrection, especially in a Jewish-Christian context.[56] As it turns out, Crossan "was already thinking along these same lines."[57]

Crossan and Reed are helpful here too. They agree that the early Christian hope, like the major Jewish interpretation, was bodily resurrection. Paul clearly takes the bodily position when addressing the Greek Platonists at Corinth, who opposed Paul's teaching of "the materiality of Christ's bodily resurrection." Paul countered the Greek arguments several ways, chiefly by teaching his concept of the spiritual body, whereby Jesus was raised in a real body that was still transformed by divine empowerment, as the beginning of the resurrection of the dead. Paul taught the same view to the Thessalonians.[58]

Thus, current theological trends at the close of the twentieth century and continuing into the twenty-first century may reflect some areas of general agreement. Especially given the current popularity (see below) of what I have termed the *supernatural external* view, it seems that fairly traditional views have again moved to the forefront of research and discussion. While sporting a few new wrinkles as well as some improvements, the view that Jesus was raised bodily is currently the predominant position, if judged in terms of scholarly support. Moreover, some scholars who reject this view still hold that it was at least the New Testament position, including Paul's own teaching.[59] This is a marked change from recent decades when Paul's view was often interpreted far differently.

Conclusion

As mentioned at the outset, this study has admittedly and necessarily been sketchy. It consists chiefly of a brief survey of recent trends on the subject of natural and supernatural theories designed to explain the resurrection appearances of Jesus. Even many scholars seem to have missed the distinctive history and especially the current distribution of these theses.

My chief goal was to map a wide range of stances and, particularly, to differentiate four categorical explanations—the natural internal and external theories, and the supernatural internal and external approaches. I also named and described two of the naturalistic theses—the illumination and illusion views—that are seldom, if ever, either identified or qualifiedly differentiated from other views.

Though the recent upturn toward opting for naturalistic alternatives has not been overly popular, and is still far from the most common option, the numbers are noteworthy. Not surprisingly, virtually none of these natural paths has been traveled by the scholarly pens of the most influential writers contributing to the Third Quest for the historical Jesus. On the other hand, recent years have shown a stronger migration to one of the supernatural camps.

How do current scholars line up? In my own survey of recent resurrection sources mentioned at the start of this chapter, less than one-quarter of critical scholars who addressed the historicity question offered naturalistic theories, of either the internal or external varieties. More surprisingly, only a few specifically identified themselves as agnostic on the issue, but one suspects that there are reasons for such a low number.[60] The almost three-quarters of remaining scholars hold either of the two views that Jesus was raised from the dead in some sense.

Further, if my survey of recent resurrection sources provides an accurate gauge, the subcategories may also be estimated, even if generally. Taken as a separate entity, the natural category was subdivided into the internal theories, such as hallucination (about a third of these particular scholars), and the objective theories, such as legend (about two-thirds). Among the supernatural positions, we have the further subdivisions of those who prefer more visionary views (less than one-quarter of these particular scholars) and those who take the position that Jesus was resurrected in a real, though still transformed, body (more than three-quarters).

Some intriguing trends have emerged. One may quibble or even disagree with the estimated percentages here, but certain broad movements seem clear.[61] On the natural side, the overall position is held by a distinct minority of scholars. Within this perspective, while hallucination theses are arguably the single most popular option, the external category as a whole is decidedly more popular (approximately two to one).

The supernatural view that Jesus rose from the dead in one of two senses is a distinct majority position over the natural option (almost three to one). Very surprisingly, while the supernatural internal category (the old "objective vision theory") was the most popular among scholars through the middle to late twentieth century, it has been relegated to a minority response in recent years, in favor of bodily appearances of the risen Jesus (more than three to one).

This essay concerns recent trends. Rather than demonstrating any particular view, it serves as a general indication of the current scholarly climate.

– 5 –

THE EPISTEMOLOGY
OF RESURRECTION BELIEF

R. Douglas Geivett

Is traditional Christian belief in the bodily resurrection of Jesus epistemically justified? I believe it is. But it's not my purpose here to make an argument for this claim. Instead, I wish to explore a nest of issues germane to assessing the epistemic status of resurrection belief. To narrow my reflections, I'll develop my topic in connection with the scholarship of N. T. Wright and John Dominic Crossan on the nature of the resurrection of Jesus and what it is rational to believe about it. I risk placing myself in the crosshairs of Crossan and on the wrong side of Wright. (This may be the sort of mistake New Testament scholars have come to expect from philosophers.)

I'm interested especially in the question, what counts as a plausible conception of the resurrection of Jesus, given the methods of investigation adopted by Crossan and Wright? Wright affirms a literal bodily resurrection of Jesus; Crossan denies this in favor of a metaphorical interpretation. Wright and Crossan have radically different conceptions of the resurrection. This may seem to indicate that the two are working with equally different methodologies. But I think their methods are quite similar, especially when it comes to direct engagement with each other on the nature of the evidence and its implications for resurrection belief. One especially important similarity is that both ground their verdicts about the resurrection on *historical evidence* that prescinds from any particular metaphysical perspective, conceptual framework, or worldview. I suggest that this general sort of approach (1) under-determines the divergent conclusions they reach and (2) should be supplemented by what else is known, or by what else there is good reason to believe, independently of what might be called "special histori-cal evidence." I distinguish between "special historical evidence" (that is, evidence turned up by historians in their role as historians) and other evidence that a responsible historian should not ignore when making historical judgments, even when the evidence in question derives from an inquiry that is not peculiar to the practice of history.

N. T. Wright affirms a bodily resurrection of Jesus in the quite lit-eral sense along traditional lines. Jesus was seen alive again for a period of days following his crucifixion and burial. John Dominic Crossan thinks of the resurrection of Jesus as the embodiment of the life of Jesus in a believing community.[1] Those who were most intimate with Jesus and who were most deeply grieved by his departure when he was crucified did not see Jesus alive again in any literal sense. What they experienced was an "apparition" of Jesus, much like the experience that normal people often have under similar circumstances. Crossan is not your garden-variety naturalist. He denies that the alleged eye-witnesses of the resurrection were delusional or hallucinating, as so many "anti-Christian secularists" have suggested.[2] Nevertheless, from Wright's point of view, Crossan's conception of the resurrection surely counts as a case of "sophisticated skepticism."[3] From Crossan's point of view, it would seem that Wright's perspective is a version of "Christian fundamentalism."[4] So an alternative title for my chapter here would be "'Sophisticated Skepticism' vs. 'Christian Fundamentalism': A Case Study of N. T. Wright and John Dominic Crossan on the Resurrection of Jesus—Surmounting the Impasse?"

Wright thinks the case for a bodily resurrection (of the traditional sort, not of the idiosyncratic sort suggested by Crossan) can be made on the historical evidence, prescinding from any particular worldview. This argument is made in his book *The Resurrection of the Son of God*.[5]

Speaking of "the case for a bodily resurrection" is ambiguous in many ways. Here are just four of the possibilities. The case for the res-urrection may be a case that:

1. the earliest Christians believed Jesus rose bodily from the dead;
2. Jesus actually did rise bodily from the dead;
3. the earliest Christians believed Jesus was *raised* bodily from the dead *by God*;
4. Jesus was actually *raised* bodily from the dead *by God*.

Compare these propositions. Propositions 1 and 2 differ: proposition 1 is about what the earliest Christians *believed* happened, whereas proposition 2 is about what *did* happen. Propositions 3 and 4 differ in this same respect: proposition 3 is about what the earliest Christians *believed* happened, whereas proposition 4 is about what *did* happen. But notice that propositions 1 and 2 are alike in that they both mention an *event* of bodily resurrection without referring to a *causal explanation*, whereas propositions 3 and 4 both refer to a causal explanation: "*raised* bodily from the dead *by God.*"

Now suppose we ask, does Wright argue for proposition 1, 2, 3, or 4? It seems clear to me that he argues directly for propositions 1, 3, and 2, in roughly that order. He reasons that we have good historical evidence (which I shall refer to as "special historical evidence") that the earliest Christians believed Jesus had risen bodily from the dead (proposition 1). They believed this on the grounds that the tomb where Jesus was buried following his crucifixion was found to be unoccupied shortly after his burial and that Jesus appeared alive again in a physical body to many who knew him. Moreover, in their attempt to make sense of this event, the earliest Christians believed Jesus was raised by God (proposition 3). The best explanation we have for the evidence that the earliest Christians believed these things is that Jesus actually did rise bodily from the dead (proposition 2).

I gather that this is about as far as we can go on the basis of historical evidence, according to Wright. As he says: "The question which must be faced is whether the explanation of the data which the early Christians themselves gave, that Jesus really was risen from the dead, 'explains the aggregate' of the evidence better than . . . sophisticated scepticisms. My claim is that it does."[6] Notice the conclusion here is that "Jesus really was risen from the dead." But Wright does not, it seems to me, press the claim in proposition 4, that Jesus was actually *raised* bodily from the dead *by God*. If I understand him correctly, he steers clear of making a case for proposition 4.

Why would he do that? Let's put it this way: if he were interested in arguing for proposition 4, how might he go about it? I don't think a historian, prescinding from worldview commitments, can make the inference to proposition 4. It may be that Wright agrees. A causal explanation for a bodily resurrection will not be discovered hidden in the special historical evidences at our disposal. It will have to be found elsewhere. But we might ask, what are the serious candidates? Certainly, God is one; God could easily bring it about that Jesus was raised from the dead. That much seems uncontroversial (as much as anything can be in philosophy, let's say).[7] But what else could explain the phenomenon of a bodily resurrection occurring in late antiquity (some two thousand years ago)? I can't think of a single other plausible explanation. So why not conclude that God did it?

Here's why. Suppose you don't believe in God. What's the likelihood that you would, however carefully you followed Wright's own historical method, conclude that Jesus had risen bodily from the dead (proposition 2)? I'd say, not likely at all. You might agree that good evidence exists for all sorts of things that, in principle, fall within the purview of historical investigation: many believed that Jesus had risen bodily (indeed, many believed that Jesus had been *raised* bodily from the dead *by God*), the tomb was found empty within a few hours of the burial of Jesus' body, Jesus was seen alive after these events by many people on various occasions, and so forth. But events are made more or less likely not only by circumstantial evidence susceptible of historical analysis but also by metaphysical possibilities that fall outside the special province of historical investigation. It falls outside the special province of historians to declare what are the metaphysical possibilities, and it also falls outside their province to set forth the criteria for rational belief that this or that causal explanation is the best one. This is because, in the present context, historians—as historians—have nothing to go on; no string of past bodily resurrections exists. If Jesus rose from the dead, and our historical evidence *indicates* that, then the event is a historical singularity, so far as historical evidence (or knowledge) is concerned.

Historians do seek causal explanations for events that come under their scrutiny. But the range of explanations made available within their domain as historians *and prescinding from worldview commitments* does not include divine agency, or, for that matter, extrahuman agency. None of this means that historians cannot make sense of the events they examine in terms of divine agency. It's just that when they do, they do so as historians who, for some reason or other, have what might be called a "providentialist perspective," which holds that God exists and is an agent in the human arena. A providentialist approach to history, let's say, also holds that God's action in the human arena is sometimes, at least in principle, identifiable. But a historian working in this manner is not prescinding from worldview commitments.

At any rate, I think the historian will not be inclined to entertain seriously a causal explanation that he has no disposition to accept otherwise. Of course, that "otherwise" is crucial, for independent grounds may exist for allowing more or less direct divine agency into the available range of possible explanations for events occurring in human history. But I'm suggesting that Wright's historical method prescinds from any worldview that recognizes that sort of possibility. *Why* he does so may have to do with his conception of proper historical practice or with a desire to search out the strength of the evidence and the available range of inferences on worldview-*neutral* grounds for the special purpose of engaging others on *common* ground. Or it may be because he sees little hope for grounding his own theistic worldview in evidence (for example, the evidence of natural theology).

Nevertheless, Wright thinks a bodily resurrection of Jesus is the best explanation of the available *historical* evidence. Yes, he allows that "historical argument alone cannot force anyone to believe that Jesus was raised from the dead."[8] But he goes on to say that "the proposal that Jesus was bodily raised from the dead possesses unrivalled power to explain the historical data at the heart of early Christianity."[9] From my knowledge of their work in Christian apologetics, I take it that Gary Habermas and William Lane Craig, among others, agree with Wright on this point. But I'm skeptical about this claim. Or at least, this suggestion needs to be qualified a certain way. Given that the data in question (that is, empty tomb, post-resurrection appearances, and so forth) are, as it were, eminently historically *investigateable*, there is substantial historical pressure to conclude that Jesus did rise bodily from the dead. But this pressure is counterbalanced by the limited range of available causal explanations for events that fall within the purview of historical examination—*when prescinding from worldview commitments.*

As I see it, the best causal explanation for a bodily resurrection is a *miracle*—an act of God. Thus, the data adduced by Wright in his impressive volume on the resurrection do provide some evidence for a theism of some sort. But is this evidence enough to clinch the case for theism? I don't think so, at least not for us at this historical remove from the events and states themselves. Wright himself says, "The historian *qua* historian cannot mount an argument from first principles and end up proving God."[10] Since, as I maintain, the worldview-neutral case from history is not sufficient to justify belief in theism, it is no more sufficient to justify belief in a bodily resurrection. I agree, however, that the historical evidence is provocative, as Wright suggests. But I think this is better understood as a stimulus to pay renewed attention to a fuller range of evidence confirming theism over the alternatives. In other words, we should repair to the evidences of natural theology and locate the data of history for the resurrection within a properly structured cumulative case for Christian theism.

Wright parts company with Habermas and Craig in one important respect. Wright (so I think) supposes that a historian may conclude that a bodily resurrection occurred (proposition 2 above), though he cannot envision this as a basis for inferring anything at all about God. Habermas and Craig, on the other hand, think that an inference to the existence of God is justified. Does it matter whether they think this inference is, in effect, a separate move made "on top of" the historical evidence? I don't think it matters. They make the inference with confidence; Wright demurs. Who's got it right? In one sense, neither conclusion is satisfactory, because both conclusions presume to ground belief in a bodily resurrection in the historical evidence *alone*. Since, I argue, historical evidence can't do that, Wright's historical argument for a bodily resurrection doesn't go through, and since the Habermas/Craig argument for theism depends on a historical argument for bodily resurrection that parallels Wright's (at least in broad outline), their argument doesn't go through, either. On the other hand, Habermas and Craig are right about this: a bodily resurrection set within the peculiar context of the life and teaching of Jesus implies divine action—that is, it implies this for us today. And Wright, as I understand him, doesn't allow this.

It might seem, then, that on the assumptions about historical method and evidence made by Wright (and Habermas and Craig)— again, prescinding from worldview convictions—I'm more sympathetic with Crossan's explanation of the data and his conclusion about the nature of "bodily resurrection." But that wouldn't be right, either. Set aside the fact that Crossan's method is, as he says, "interdisciplinary," taking into account the data of anthropology and archaeology (and, I think crucially, human psychology). Crossan's explanation of the data, all things considered so far as he goes, is still only one possible explanation. It's not clearly better than Wright's.

In fact, while Wright's and Crossan's explanations are, let's allow, both possible, neither is especially plausible. And why is that? First, as long as it's at least an open question whether the first Christians believed in a literal bodily resurrection of Jesus, the possibility of miracle is not out of the question. (Despite all that Crossan argues, I think the first Christians did believe this and would easily have been able to distinguish what they experienced from what Crossan thinks of as an apparitional experience.) But we cannot settle on the possibility of miraculous action as the best explanation without further evidence of an extrahistorical nature. Divine agency must be judged at least an intelligible category of causal explanation.

At times both Wright and Crossan tacitly suggest that we should make judgments about such things in light of all that we know. Therefore, in principle, as I see it, if we know that God exists, plus a few other convenient things about God's nature and God's likely intentions in creating the world we inhabit (part of which is the proper object of historical study), then our *historical* data may justify the conviction that Jesus rose bodily from the dead and that he was *raised* from the dead *by God*.

Because the hypothesis of theism does explain the historical data, those data provide some evidence for theism—but again, not enough in isolation from other data. This doesn't worry me at all, since if theism (or Christian theism, at least) is true, we should expect other evidences for this as well; in fact, we should expect enough to justify belief in Christian theism.

Something needs to be said here about so-called methodological naturalism. One typical characterization is that a method of intellectual inquiry is "natural" or "naturalistic" if it proceeds on the assumption that God does not exist or, if God does exist, that God does not intervene in any direct way in the flow of historical events, so that theism should play no role in explaining what is under historical investigation. But that can seem to beg the question in favor of *metaphysical* naturalism, according to which God actually does not exist (that is, metaphysical naturalism entails the denial of theism). In other words, the sort of methodological naturalism just described assumes, provisionally and for the sake of argument, that metaphysical naturalism is true.

But suppose we think of methodology in terms of total abstraction from any general metaphysical framework or worldview—a perspective not easily accomplished, since our historical explanations routinely assume, for example, the operation of laws of nature (regularities of various sorts), which makes sense only against the background of certain metaphysical commitments. But suppose we try for a historical practice that brackets worldview commitments on a more or less grand scale. A radically neutral methodology will leave us high and dry with respect to the data concerning Jesus' resurrection. It may turn up various sources of information and generate relevant data, but it will lack the resources needed to infer any best explanation for what historical investigation turns up.

Let's imagine common ground between Wright and Crossan with respect to the metaphysical neutrality of proper historical research within a shared context of scholarly concern. Let's assume that on that ground they may come to an agreement about pretty much everything that the method deems appropriate for historical knowledge. I leave it to the historians to sort out whether their actual respective, and radically different, conceptions of *bodily resurrection*, framed exclusively in terms of such a shared methodology (shared to the extent that it is metaphysically neutral), are equally "plausible," in a weak sense of plausible. I say a "weak sense of plausible" because neither theory, I maintain, will actually be predicted to any real degree by the data in question following the method in question. Their method is too austere for that. But their theories may both be consistent with the evidence adduced. Again, that's for the historians to sort out.

Of course, it isn't part of Wright's project to do natural theology. Nor do I think that he himself needs to do this sort of thing in detail.

He is a historian, after all. The question is, what does he make of the value of natural theology (both in principle and relative to its positive results), and what are the implications of that for maximally exploiting the historical data concerning Jesus, the resurrection, and the emerging Christian community? I believe that the historical case for a bodily resurrection (to say nothing of the deity of Jesus or the existence of God) needs to be supplemented by the evidence of natural theology. I think Wright disagrees that rational belief in Jesus' bodily resurrection needs to be supplemented in this way. I also suspect that he doubts that a satisfactory case for theism can be made on the basis of evidence (however rich and complex that evidence may be).[11] This is puzzling since his reasons for respecting evidence of a historical nature to draw conclusions about such an admittedly unlikely event as a bodily resurrection from the dead are, it seems to me, basically the same reasons for respecting the evidences of natural theology. Wright's complaint that the post-Enlightenment era exhibits little tolerance for "rationalism" cuts at least as sharply against his evidentialist approach to historical analysis (notwithstanding his qualifying remarks about the value of historical evidence).[12]

So my question for Wright is twofold. First, how can he consistently object to the prospects for a rich program of natural theology on behalf of a revelation-friendly theism while making so much of the method of abduction in historical inquiry, especially when the historical inquiry is thought to justify belief in something that is independently (highly) improbable? Second, what justifies belief in a *bodily* resurrection that doesn't at the same time (*eo ipso*) justify belief that a miracle—a divine act—has occurred?

What about Crossan? Wright's general metaphysical commitments seem obvious enough, even if he strives to prescind from those commitments in his excavation of historical data. In his writings, Wright leaves no doubt that he is a theist in the classical sense. But Crossan's worldview is not so easily identifiable. He speaks of God as if he believes in God. But when pressed about the nature of this belief, he is curiously coy. At times, he seems to regard questions about the specific nature of God, or even questions about the existence of God, as impertinent.[13] This, I think, is part of the ample evidence that Wright is not by any means a classical theist who believes that God is the transcendent creator of the universe, omnipotent, omniscient, and omnibenevolent. The statement "God is the transcendent creator of the universe, omnipotent, omniscient, and omnibenevolent" is one abbreviated way that classical theists describe what the term "God" refers to. If Crossan thinks this statement is unintelligible, then that itself suggests that he does not believe the proposition, whatever it is that he happens to mean when *he* speaks of "God." And he does speak quite liberally about God and God's purposes. For example, in *The Birth of Christianity,* he describes the meaning of the resurrection in terms of God's standing on the side of justice.[14] In the dialogue with Wright earlier in the present book, he speaks of God's purpose to "clean up the world."[15] He depicts Jesus as a Jewish peasant whose attitude was "that of the Jewish God," opposed to violence and so forth.[16] Crossan has unmistakable respect for Jesus, and indeed he refers to himself as a Christian. But does he believe in the God that Jesus himself believed in? And does he believe that God is guaranteed to succeed in cleaning up the world? If so, will Crossan himself be there to enjoy this outcome, and will I be there, if we die in the meantime? Will the Maccabean martyrs partake of this climax in resurrection life? If so, what does that say about what sort of being God is?

I do not yet understand Crossan's conception of the God he speaks of in his writings. I do not understand the point of his using language that (ostensibly) mentions God as if God objectively exists, when it seems that his references to God are themselves metaphorical and not literal. On the other hand, Crossan does not want to be called a "naturalist." In fact, he explains that naturalists are too dismissive when they suggest that the disciples who reported the appearances of Jesus were hallucinating or delusional. He prefers to think of the disciples as normal human beings grieving the loss of someone they cared about, someone who was important to their life orientation. Following the crucifixion, it was a natural human experience for them to have visions of Jesus. In Crossan's view, these were "apparitions" that any normal human being might experience under such conditions.

But even if Crossan is not himself a naturalist, his explanation for the data surrounding the resurrection of Jesus is a naturalistic explanation. It doesn't make reference to anything supernatural or nonnatural. I suspect that one reason he does not believe in a literal bodily resurrection is that this would require a shift in his own world-view commitments. If I'm right, then he has not done his history in a worldview-neutral manner. But precisely what worldview filters his historical judgment?

If Crossan denies *both* philosophical/scientific naturalism *and* classical theism, then the space of possibilities for understanding the historical data concerning the alleged resurrection of Jesus is constricted. He is constrained to formulate his conception of the best explanation for the historical data in terms compatible with denying naturalism on the one hand and forswearing classical theism on the other. It comes as no surprise, then, that for him "bodily resurrection has nothing to do with a resuscitated body coming out of its tomb."[17] If he thinks Jesus could not have been raised bodily from the tomb, it evidently is not because he's a naturalist; more likely it's because he's not a theist. That leaves unclear just what are his positive metaphysical commitments and why those are the commitments he makes.

When asked to accept his selection and interpretation of the *historical* data, I should like to know more about his own metaphysical predilections. I have three basic questions for Crossan. First, what are the general features of his worldview in explicit comparison with what I have called "classical theism"? Second, how, prescinding from whatever worldview he considers most viable, can he rule against the plausibility of Tom Wright's conception of the resurrection in favor of his own, as if *that* were the best explanation? Finally, would Crossan still think his own explanation is the best explanation if he were a classical theist?

As a result of the 2005 Greer-Heard Point-Counterpoint Forum hosted by New Orleans Baptist Theological Seminary in March 2005, we now have on record at least a partial answer to these questions. In his reply to my presentation there, Crossan acknowledged that he is not "presuming theism." He explained his position more fully by suggesting that humans are "hard-wired for religion," and that we are hard-wired to "name the Holy." Everyone does this in one way or another. But every name for the Holy is a "mega-metaphor" that is created by us to name the Holy. Crossan believes there are four basic mega-metaphors for the Holy. First, there is the metaphor of *person*, adopted in Judaism and Christianity. Second, the metaphor of some *state* is used—for example, in Buddhism with its concept of Nirvana, which is not a "being." "Confucianism," Crossan said, "has an *order in the universe*, but no orderer," suggesting a third metaphor. And for a collection of religions that we call, for want of a better name, "native" or "primitive," a fourth metaphor for the Holy is *power*. Crossan stressed that each of these metaphors is valid; none is more intrinsically valid than the other. Nevertheless, there are times when each one breaks down. For Crossan, the metaphor of *person* breaks down when a hurricane rips through town and bypasses his own house while destroying another's.[18]

Although the details of this position are vague, this much seems certain. Crossan is not a classical theist. When he says, "I am not presuming classical theism," he does not mean that in his role as New Testament historian he is prescinding from his own metaphysical commitment to classical theism and drawing whatever conclusions about the resurrection that are permissible in abstraction from that commitment. Rather, he is acknowledging that he is not a classical theist. And while he may use the term *God* when addressing the historical question of Jesus' resurrection, he believes he is merely adopting a metaphor that is useful in that context.

Returning to my three questions, we have a partial answer: Crossan is not a classical theist. His view is pluralistic. (Insofar as it is spelled in his remarks at the conference, it resembles the position of John Hick).[19] The term *God* is a metaphor, just as I suspected, and pretty much the same way *resurrection* is a metaphor when speaking of the "resurrection of Jesus." In other words, it is not literally true that Jesus rose bodily from the dead, and neither is it true that there is a God—omnipotent, omniscient, and omnibenevolent—who might be in a position to will and accomplish the resurrection of Jesus from the dead. No wonder Crossan disagrees with Wright about the nature of the resurrection. No wonder he concludes that Jesus did not literally rise bodily from the dead. For what is denied by his metaphysical commitments precludes the *possibility* of a literal bodily resurrection of Jesus by God. This means that Crossan's verdict on the resurrection is informed by what his metaphysical perspective denies. And so, his verdict as a New Testament historian does not prescind from his worldview commitments at all. It is not metaphysically neutral.

This is by no means a criticism of Crossan's method. In the end, historians must allow their extrahistorical knowledge to inform their historical judgments whenever such knowledge is relevant to understanding the data surrounding the events they investigate. Disagreement will no doubt arise about what counts as extrahistorical knowledge. We cannot expect historians to agree about that when the content and scope of such knowledge are beyond the special purview of historical analysis. But we should require the historian to set forth without equivocation or false modesty his own metaphysical commitments insofar as they inform his historical judgments. He should also be prepared to present whatever evidence persuades him that his metaphysical perspective is more plausible than its alternatives, for the epistemic status of his metaphysical position will haunt his judgments about historical matters. This applies especially to the most metaphysically sensitive matters. A judicious judgment about the occurrence and nature of the resurrection of Jesus depends on a careful assessment of the evidence of natural theology for theism.

N. T. Wright and John Dominic Crossan have written thoughtfully and extensively on the issues of historical evidence and the resurrection of Jesus. While they have not developed full accounts of the issues raised here, their descriptions of their own projects and the conclusions they have advanced touch on matters deserving fuller explication. I should like to see more elaboration of the principles they adopt in assessing the epistemic status of resurrection belief, understood in their respective ways. And I should like to recommend the expansion of their methods and data to include not only the special evidences of history but also anything else that we might know or reasonably believe. I can certainly appreciate the intellectual humility reflected in their reticence to speak of their respective projects in terms of "reasonable belief" and "epistemic justification." We must always take care to recognize, as far as possible, the real limits of our knowledge and understanding. But I submit that epistemological humility should also acknowledge any bona fide source of knowledge as well as the full scope of knowledge. And I suggest that greater attention to evidence available concerning the existence and nature of God will be rewarded with a fuller appreciation of the epistemic status of resurrection belief.[20]

– 6 –

THE GOSPEL OF PETER
Does It Contain a Precanonical
Resurrection Narrative?

Charles L. Quarles

Introduction

The Gospel of Peter (*GP*) is a narrative of the trial, crucifixion, and res-urrection of Jesus.[1] The document is preserved primarily in a Greek fragment consisting of sixty verses that was discovered in an amulet in a tomb in Akhmim in Upper Egypt and dated to the eighth or ninth century. It is also attested in two much smaller Greek fragments con-sisting of two and a half verses from the Oxyrhynchus Papyri written about 200 c.e.[2]

In , the scholar to make the most extensive use of the *GP* is John Dominic Crossan. After a detailed comparison of the *GP* with the intracanonical Gospels, Crossan concluded that the earliest stratum in the *GP* was the hypothetical Cross Gospel.[3] He argued that this early narrative was utilized by the Synoptics and by John and served as the only source of the canonical evangelists for the Passion Narrative.[4]

Although Crossan's theory has not enjoyed wide acceptance in the scholarly community, one recent scholar argued that "one can expect that all future research on *GP* will need to begin with a serious consid-eration of Crossan's work."[5] The remainder of this paper will examine and critique Crossan's arguments for the priority and independence of the Cross Gospel's description of the guards at the tomb (*GP* 8:29-33; 9:35-10:42; 11:45-49\\Matt. 27:62-66; 28:2-4; 28:11-15). In particular, it will question whether the account of the guard at the tomb was a midrashic composition that creatively adapted narrative motifs from Joshua 10 or was an expansion of the Matthean parallel account. It will also examine internal evidence suggesting that the Cross Gospel postdates the canonical Gospels. Finally, it will discuss the implications of Crossan's theory for Christian belief in the resurrection of Jesus.

The Biblical Substratum of the Account of the Guard at the Tomb in the GP

Crossan has argued that almost every element in the trial, abuse, and crucifixion of Jesus was created by Peter based on "Passion prophecy." The Cross Gospel was essentially a midrash on these Old Testament texts that wove Old Testament motifs together into an imaginative narrative.[6] According to Crossan, this extensive dependence on the Old Testament for the details of the Passion Narrative made dependence on the canonical Gospels unnecessary. The traces of dependence also mark the Cross Gospel and, consequently, the canonical Gospels, which depended on it, as "prophecy historicized," that is, narratives created to give the impression of a prophetic fulfillment but which lack any real connection with the actual events of Jesus' Passion.

According to Crossan, the account of the guarded tomb has no connection to "Passion prophecies" but does incorporate narrative motifs from Joshua 10. In that text, Joshua discovered that five defeated Amorite kings were hiding in a cave. He commanded his men to roll stones over the mouth of the cave and left a small detachment of soldiers to guard it while the armies of Israel pursued the kings' men. After slaughtering the Amorites, the soldiers returned to the cave, killed the kings, and hung their corpses on five trees. Crossan observed numerous parallels between the Joshua 10 text and the account of the guarded tomb in the *GP* that suggest a literary dependency. Crossan notes the following parallels in figure 1.

Figure 1

Joshua 10 (NRSV w/LXX)	Cross Gospel (Maurer)
Crucifixion: "Joshua killed them and hung them on five trees" (10:26)	*Crucifixion*: "crucified the Lord in the midst between them" (4:10)
Burial: "threw them into the cave where they had hidden themselves" (10:27b)	*Burial*: "we should bury him" (2:5a)
Guards: "set men by it to guard (φυλάσσειν) it" (10:18b)	*Guards*: "Give us soldiers that we may watch (φυλάξω[μεν]) his sepulcher" (8:30)
Stones: "Roll large stones (κυλίσατε λίθους ἐπί) against the mouth of the cave" (10:18a)	*Stones*: "rolled thither a great stone (κυλίσαντες λίθον μέγαν) and laid it against (ἐπί) the entrance to the sepulcher" (8:32)
Evening: "They hung on the trees until evening. At sunset Joshua commanded, and they took them down from the trees" (10:26b-27a)	*Evening*: "They became anxious and uneasy lest the sun had already set, since he was still alive. For it stands written for them: the sun should not set on one that has been put to death" (5:15)
Opening: "Open (ἀνοίξατε) the mouth of the cave" (10:22)	*Opening*: "That stone which had been laid against the entrance to the sepulcher started of itself to roll and gave way to the side, and the sepulcher was opened (ἠνοίγη)" (9:37)

Several of these parallels are intriguing. However, even if one grants the a priori assumption that connections between the Passion

Narratives and Old Testament motifs betray the presence of prophecy historicized, the evidence for a Petrine dependence on the OT seems slim at best in this case. Even before a close examination of the parallels, several reservations about the supposed connection of the two texts arise. One must wonder whether the author of the *GP* could not have found a more suitable text to supply details for his Passion Narrative. The author of the Gospel clearly reveres Jesus. He consistently refers to him as "the Lord" rather than by his proper name.[7] Would he not have hesitated to describe the death and burial of "the Lord" in a manner that was reminiscent of those of five pagan kings? If any connection between the two texts existed, would one not have expected Jesus to have been cast in the role of his namesake, Joshua, rather than in the role of five Amorites whom the OT law excluded from the congregation of God's people (Deut. 23:1-2)?

Upon closer examination, the initially intriguing parallels between the two texts become much less impressive. One of the most striking parallels, burial before sunset, seems to result from mutual adherence to Mosaic Law (Deut. 21:22-23) rather than from a dependence by Peter on Joshua. Point by point, the two accounts seem more disparate than similar. The suspension of five corpses from a tree differs significantly from execution by crucifixion. The guard at the tomb in Joshua was assigned to prevent the escape of the living kings rather than to prevent followers from stealing their corpses. Numerous stones were used to trap the kings of Joshua 10 in the cave. However, a single large stone sealed the tomb of Jesus.

To demonstrate a literary dependence of one document on another, interpreters must point to (1) a series of verbal parallels between the two documents that cannot be ascribed to coincidence, (2) vocabulary or grammar that varies from the dependent author's normal mode of expression, and (3) vocabulary and grammar that are especially or uniquely characteristic of the alleged exemplar document. Although Crossan has pointed out five examples of vocabulary shared by both texts, the shared vocabulary does not meet these criteria. The vocabulary was a natural choice for the author of the *GP* given the events that he seeks to describe and thus does not betray Petrine dependence on Joshua 10.[8]

Literary Evidence for Matthew's Dependence on the GP

In the pericope of the guard at the tomb, evidence abounds for a close relationship between Matthew and the *GP*. Both accounts refer to the Pharisees gathering before Pilate and expressing concern about a staged resurrection on the third day. Both texts refer to the guarding and sealing of the tomb of Jesus. Both describe the Jews as "the people" (Matt. 27:64 τῷ λαῷ; *GP* 8:28 ὁ λαός).[9] One sustained verbal parallel between Matthew and the *GP* indicates that one document was dependent on the other: μήποτε ἐλθόντες οἱ μαθηταὶ αὐτοῦ κλέψωσιν αὐτὸν (Matt. 27:64; *GP* 8:30). The words do not appear in any OT texts. Thus, the sustained parallelism is best explained by literary dependence by the *GP* on Matthew or vice versa.[10] Crossan agreed with Léon Vaganay that the coincidence of the words and grammar seemed too great to have resulted from mutual dependence by Matthew and Peter on oral tradition.[11] Crossan noted that, although Vaganay argued that *GP* 8:30 was dependent on Matthew 27:64b, he was convinced of an opposite relationship.[12]

An examination of Petrine or Matthean redactional features in the shared words provides the most objective means of determining the direction of the dependency. The vocabulary and grammar strongly suggest Petrine dependence on Matthew. Robert Gundry described the words as a "series of Mattheanisms."[13] Gundry supplied the following statistics for terms and forms in the series. The first number represents the number of Matthean insertions in material paralleled by the other Synoptics. The second number represents the number of occurrences in material unique to Matthew. The third number represents the number of occurrences shared with either Mark or Luke. The numbers in parentheses indicate the total number of occurrences in Matthew, Mark, and Luke, respectively.

μήποτε 2, 4, 2 (8, 2, 7)
ἐλθόντες 10, 10, 8 (28, 16, 12) [nominative circumstantial participial form of ἔρχομαι]
μαθηταί 31, 5, 36–37 (72–73, 46, 37)
κλέψωσιν 2, 2, 1 (5, 1, 1)[14]

In contrast to the frequency with which these terms and forms appear in Matthew's Gospel, "disciple" (μαθητής) never occurs elsewhere in the Cross Gospel. Furthermore, the term appears only one other time in the available fragments of the *GP* (14:59).[15] Similarly, although the verb "steal" appears four other times in Matthew's Gospel, it does not appear elsewhere in the *GP*. Although the conjunction μήποτε occurs seven other times in Matthew, it appears only one additional time in the *GP*, but in a significantly different construction. *GP* 5:15 has "fearing lest the sun set" (μήποτε ὁ ἥλιος ἔδυ) in which the verb with the conjunction is a second aorist indicative verb rather than the expected subjunctive verb as in the text paralleled by Matthew.[16] This telling clue suggests that the author of Peter preferred the indicative with the conjunction and that he used the subjunctive in *GP* 8:30 only because of his dependence on Matthew. Although the participle ἐλθόντες occurs twenty-eight times in Matthew, it never appears elsewhere in the *GP*.[17] John P. Meier seems correct in his conclusion that "when it comes to who is dependent on whom, all the signs point to Matthew's priority. . . . The clause is a tissue of Matthean vocabulary and style, a vocabulary and style almost totally absent from the rest of the *GP*."[18] Since the shared series contains several prominent Mattheanisms, it seems much more likely that the *GP* was dependent on Matthew than that Matthew depended on Peter.[19]

Other Mattheanisms appear in proximity to this one. The words ἴδετε τὸν τόπον ἔνθα ἔκειτο in *GP* 13:56 are very similar to Matthew's ἴδετε τὸν τόπον ὅπου ἔκειτο (Matt. 28:6). The words in Matthew are a redaction of Mark's more rustic Greek, ἴδε ὁ τόπος ὅπου ἔθηκαν αὐτόν.[20] Crossan might object that this is an instance in which Matthew redacted Mark in light of his direct knowledge of the Cross Gospel. However, this would require Mark to have rejected the Cross Gospel's better Greek in favor of a more stilted and primitive expression. The simplest explanation of the above data is that Peter knew and used Matthew's Gospel. Consequently, the argument that the author of the Cross Gospel looked to Passion prophecy and Old Testament narratives, rather than to the canonical Gospels, for the details necessary to flesh out the plot of his Passion Narratives cannot be sustained for this pericope.

Evidence That the *GP* Is a Second-Century Work and Dependent on the Canonical Gospels

Details in the GP's *Account of the Guard at the Tomb That Are Problematic for an Early Date*

LATER CHURCH DOGMA. The question from heaven to the cross—"Did you preach to those who sleep?"—betrays the author's knowledge of the later doctrine of Jesus' descent into Hades between his death and resurrection in order to preach to the dead held there. Recent scholars have questioned whether the doctrine is ever taught in the New Testament.[21] Crossan initially suggested that the doctrine was familiar to first-century Christians since 1 Peter 3:19-20 and 4:6 affirm it.[22] Crossan later reversed his opinion under the influence of Dalton's research[23] and acknowledged that the doctrine "may not even be present in the New Testament."[24]

Although the meaning of these texts remains contested, an emerging consensus in recent Petrine scholarship holds that 1 Peter describes Jesus' declaration of victory over demonic spirits in the lower heavens during his ascent, not descent into Hades to proclaim the gospel to the dead.[25] If the emerging consensus of interpretation regarding 1 Peter is correct, the presence of the reference to preaching to those who sleep in the *GP* suggests that the document was composed no earlier than the first quarter of the second century. However, even if 1 Peter affirms the divine descent, those who reject Petrine authorship of 1 Peter and date the epistle to the early second century must explain how the doctrine emerged in the 40s and why no other Christian documents mention the doctrine for more than sixty years.[26]

THE SEVEN SEALS. Matthew and the *GP* differ slightly in their descriptions of the sealing of Jesus' tomb. Matthew says simply that the tomb was sealed (Matt. 27:66). The *GP* adds that it was sealed with seven seals (*GP* 8:33). However, no evidence suggests that tombs were sealed with seven seals. The reference to seven seals suggests either that seven persons were involved in the sealing of the tomb or that the author of the *GP* embellished Matthew at this point out of apologetic concerns, probably in light of Revelation 5:1.[27]

Daniel 6:18 (see also Bel and the Dragon 14) constitutes the closest biblical parallel to the sealing of the tomb in Matthew and in the *GP*. The text describes the sealing of the stone that covered the mouth of the lion's den. It explains that the king and his lords each sealed the stone. The number of seals was determined by the number of authoritative witnesses present. However, in the *GP*, the number of seals does not seem to relate to the number of witnesses present. *GP* 8:32-33 states that all who were present, including the Jewish leaders and the centurion and his soldiers, rolled the stone and sealed it. Petronius the centurion had at least four soldiers at his disposal since the soldiers guarded "two by two in every watch." In addition, elders and scribes of the Jews assisted in placing the stone over the tomb and sealing it. The plural forms of "elder" and "scribe" show that at least two of each category were present. Thus, one would expect a minimum of nine seals rather than seven.

The text is clearly inconsistent here. Either the text is incorrect in claiming that all present sealed the tomb, or it is inaccurate in mentioning seven seals. The discrepancy between the number of seals and the number of witnesses present becomes even more pronounced when one considers that the assignment of a centurion to the guard probably implies the assignment of his entire century as well.[28] The enumeration of the seals in the *GP* suggests that the author and his readers regarded seven seals as particularly impressive, as offering the ultimate authentication. Apparently, the author adapted his source in order to heighten its apologetic force. Since the involvement of all trusted witnesses in the act of sealing has close parallel elsewhere, the detail of seven seals is, at the very least, an expansion of Matthew driven by apologetic purposes with reference to Roman testamentary law.[29] However, since testamentary law has no obvious connection with the sealing of the tomb, the detail is more likely an allusion to Revelation 5:1. The apparent allusion to later interpretations of 1 Peter 3:19 in *GP* 10:41 strengthens this possibility, as does the description of the first day of the week as the "Lord's day" in *GP* 9:35 and 12:50, since this terminology appears in Revelation alone of the NT documents.

THE LORD'S DAY. The use of the term "Lord's day" may be particularly significant for dating the *GP*.[30] The earliest Christian documents to use the expression are Revelation 1:10 (κυριακὴ ἡμέρα), Didache 14:1 (κατὰ κυριακὴν δὲ κυρίου συναχθέντες), and Ignatius, *Magnesians* 9:1 (μηκέτι σαββατίζοντες ἀλλὰ κατὰ κυριακὴν ζῶντες). The phrase "first day of the week" in the Synoptic Passion Narratives; John 20:1, 19, 26; Acts 20:7; and 1 Corinthians 16:2 is the more primitive form of reference to the day of Jesus' resurrection, which was common in the early church in the middle and later first century. The absence of reference to the "Lord's day" in the early New Testament documents and the presence of the term in Revelation and the Didache suggests that the term became popular in the final decades of the first century. Consequently, the use of "the Lord's day," especially in its abbreviated form, suggests a later date for the Cross Gospel than Crossan allows.[31]

The Compositional Strategies of the Author of the GP

In a recent discussion, Crossan stated that he would acknowledge the *GP*'s dependence on the canonical Gospels only when a rationale is offered to explain how the author of the *GP* produced his work from the canonical Gospels. This section will offer a possible explanation by comparing the compositional strategies of the *GP* to those of second-century apocryphal works.

PROJECTION OF MATERIAL THAT IS ANTECEDENT TO THE PASSION INTO THE PASSION NARRATIVE OF THE *GP*. In the description of the resurrection event in *GP* 9:35-44 and 12:50—13:57, two constructions appear that are oddly reminiscent of the description of Jesus' baptism in the Synoptic Gospels. First, *GP* 9:36 states that the guards at the tomb "saw the heavens opening" (εἶδον ἀνοιχθέντας τοὺς οὐρανοὺς) as two men descended to enter the tomb. The construction sounds like an amalgamation of the Synoptic descriptions of the heavenly phenomenon that occurred at Jesus' baptism. Mark 1:10 states that the baptized Jesus "saw the heavens being split open" (εἶδεν σχιζομένους τοὺς οὐρανοὺς). The *GP* used the plural εἶδον rather than Mark's εἶδεν, but this was required by the new context in which Peter couched the construction. Peter used a form of ἀνοίγω rather than σχίζω, but he appears to have chosen this vocabulary from the descriptions of the heavenly phenomenon in the parallel accounts of

Jesus' baptism in Matthew and Luke, both of whom preferred a form of ἀνοίγω to Mark's σχίζω.[32]

Another clue that Peter drew these descriptions from the Synoptic accounts of the baptism is the awkward shift from the singular "heaven" (μεγάλη φωνὴ ἐγένετο ἐν τῷ οὐρανῷ) to the plural "heavens" (εἶδον ἀνοιχθέντας τοὺς οὐρανοὺς and φωνῆς ἤκουον ἐκ τῶν οὐρανῶν) in his account of the heavenly phenomena that accompanied the resurrection. The Synoptic accounts each refer to heaven(s) twice in the baptismal narratives, first in reference to the opening of the heavens and second in reference to the heavenly voice. Matthew and Mark used the plural form for both references. Luke used the singular form for both references. This consistency in number in the two references within the individual canonical Gospels forms an interesting contrast to the shift in number in the *GP*. Although one might suggest that Peter moved from the singular to the plural form of the noun in order to distinguish the sky from the abode of God (and this best explains the distinction in *GP* 10:40), this is doubtful here since the φωνή that first drew the attention of those surrounding the tomb to the heavens was apparently the sound of the heavens opening. Unlike the later reference to the φωνή from the heavens in 10:41, no divine utterance is recorded here, thus giving the impression that the μεγάλη φωνή was a loud noise caused by the opening of the heavens rather than a "great voice." The shift from the singular "heaven" to the plural "heavens" is best explained as an amalgamation of the Synoptic descriptions of the heavenly φωνή that accompanied Jesus' baptism. The author of the *GP* may have drawn the noun φωνή from any of the Synoptics. The verb ἐγένετο was likely drawn from Mark, and the singular "heaven" was drawn from Luke.[33]

Later, Peter adds that "they heard a voice from heaven saying 'Did you preach to those who are asleep?'" (καὶ φωνῆς ἤκουον ἐκ τῶν οὐρανῶν λεγούσης; *GP* 10:41). The description is very close to Matthew's wording in his baptismal account καὶ ἰδοὺ φωνὴ ἐκ τῶν οὐρανῶν λέγουσα (Matt. 3:17). The placement of the construction in a new context required some grammatical adaptation. The substitution of the verb "hear" in place of the exclamation "behold" required a genitive form of the noun "voice" and the participle "saying." However, the suspicion that Peter has projected the Synoptic descriptions of the heavenly phenomenon accompanying Jesus' baptism into his description of the events surrounding Jesus' resurrection is difficult to escape.

A similar compositional method appears in other Apocryphal literature from the second century. The author of the *Protevangelium of James*, for example, supplied additional details to the canonical birth narratives by retrojecting phrases from Jesus' adult ministry into his account of the nativity.[34] The Passion Narrative in the *GP* appears to share a similar compositional strategy with the birth narrative in the *Protevangelium of James*. However, rather than retrojecting material from later events in Jesus' life into early episodes, he has projected material from earlier episodes into the resurrection event. Such compositional projection and retrojection are absent from the canonical Gospels. This suggests that the authors of the canonical Gospels were constrained to preserve faithfully the traditions about Christ, but that the author of the *GP* felt free to exercise his imagination in creative historiography. The compositional strategy of projection suggests that the *GP* shares a common milieu with second-century pseudepigraphal works and casts doubt on Crossan's claim that the *GP* antedates the canonical Gospels.

MULTIPLICATION OF THE MIRACULOUS IN THE *GP*. The *GP* contains numerous references to miraculous activity that have no parallel in the canonical Gospels. The greatest concentration of these unparalleled supernatural events appears in the pericope related to the guard at the tomb. First, *GP* 9:38 states that when Jesus rose, a great sound/voice came from heaven, the heavens opened, and two men surrounded by a brilliant light descended through the gap in the heavens. Second, as these heavenly figures approached the tomb, the large stone rolled away from the door of the tomb automatically or "by itself" (ἀφ' ἑαυτοῦ).[35] The author prepared his readers to recognize the event as truly miraculous by previously explaining that at least nine men had been required to roll the stone into place (*GP* 8:32). Third, the two heavenly figures entered the tomb but three figures exited it. The first two assisted the third in standing upright. The heads of the first two figures reached to the sky, but the head of the third extended even above the heavens.[36] Obviously, this description of the resurrected

Jesus is fantastic and quite at odds with the descriptions that appear in the canonical Gospels. Fourth, as the three men exited the tomb, a cross, apparently floating through the air, followed them.[37] Fifth, the cross was capable of speech. A heavenly voice asked, "Did you preach to those who are sleeping?" and the cross replied, "Yes."[38]

Second-century apocryphal literature was characterized by several of the features noted above. Not only did these apocryphal texts, such as the *Protevangelium of James* and the *Infancy Gospel of Thomas*, have a greater concentration of supernatural phenomena, but other second-century texts also speak of independently moving crosses and ascribe a supernatural stature to the resurrected Christ.[39] The second-century *Epistula Apostolorum* states that during the second coming Jesus will be carried on the wings of the clouds with his cross going on before him.[40] Similarly, the Ethiopic Apocalypse of Peter describes the returning Christ as coming in a glory seven times as bright as the sun and with his cross going before his face.[41] Beginning in the late first century, Christian texts describe Christ as possessing gigantic stature. Shepherd of Hermas 83:1 described Christ as of such lofty stature that he stood taller than a tower.[42] Similarly, 4 Ezra 2:43 later refers to the unusual height of the Son of God.[43] Again, the common compositional strategy and distinct features shared by the *GP* and the second-century apocryphal works suggest that they belong to the same milieu.

APOLOGETIC EXPANSION IN THE *GP*. The *GP*'s account of the guard at the tomb includes several details without parallel in the canonical Gospels that seek to eliminate any doubt regarding the veracity of the claim that Jesus rose from the dead. First, the *GP* identifies a centurion named Petronius as commander of the detachment of soldiers sent to guard the tomb.[44] The presence of a centurion, which ensured that the guard was properly supervised and that proper procedures, such as a rotating guard, would be used, may hint that approximately eighty stood guard at the tomb, a considerably greater number than Matthew's *custodia* (κουστωδία) would have required. Second, the *GP* has the Roman guard, with the assistance of the scribes and elders, roll the stone over the door of the tomb. This ensured that Jesus' corpse was still in the tomb when the watch began. In Matthew's Gospel, Joseph of Arimathea rolled the stone over the door of the tomb and the Roman guard did not begin its watch until the next day. Thus, someone could have stolen Jesus' body from the tomb during the first few hours after burial without the guard's knowledge. This possibility was eliminated in the *GP* by having the guard close the tomb.[45] Furthermore, all witnesses confirmed that Jesus' body was interred in the tomb with their seal on the stone, so that although Matthew mentions only one seal, Peter mentions seven.

Third, *GP* 9:34 states that early in the morning on the day after Jesus' burial, a crowd from Jerusalem and the surrounding areas went to see the tomb that had been sealed. Thus, even larger numbers of people verified the security of the tomb. Fourth, although the soldiers in Matthew view the angel's descent from heaven and see him roll away the stone, they trembled with fear and fell to the ground like dead men so that they did not personally see Jesus leave the tomb. In the *GP*, two soldiers witnessed Jesus leave the tomb and all the soldiers and Jewish leaders present witnessed the descent of the angel who sat in the tomb to await the disciples' arrival.[46]

The evidence suggests that Peter expanded Matthew's apologetic features rather than that Matthew suppressed Peter's polemical features. Matthew's Gospel clearly has an interest in defending the reality of Jesus' resurrection against Jewish objections that were current at the time he wrote his Gospel (Matt. 28:15). Of the four canonical Gospels, he alone mentioned the guard at the tomb (Matt. 27:62-66; 28:2, 4, 11-15). No sensible explanation for Matthew's elimination of helpful apologetic material available to him from the Cross Gospel exists. This suggests that the author of the *GP* depended on Matthew's Gospel but revised it in order to present a more compelling case for the resurrection.[47]

This apologetic expansion in the *GP* constitutes another close parallel with the compositional strategy of the author of the *Protevangelium of James*.[48] The author inserted several additional scenes into the canonical birth narratives in order to combat the Jewish charge of the illegitimacy of Jesus. First, *Protevangelium of James* 16 has Mary and Joseph tested by bitter water. The test confirms their innocence. Second, *Protevangelium of James* 19-20 has the midwife Salome inspect the hymen of the holy mother with her hand to determine if it had been stretched or torn during the birth. Salome discovered that Mary remained in every sense a virgin, even after the birth. Salome's hand suddenly caught blaze as a punishment for her disbelief. This shared compositional strategy suggests that the *GP*, like the *Protevangelium of James*, belongs to a milieu in which apologetic concerns overrode the church's commitment to preserve faithfully the traditions about Jesus' birth, life, death, and resurrection.

CONCLUSION. Compositional strategies that were popular in the second century can readily explain how the author of the *GP* produced his narrative from the canonical Gospels. Other features of the *GP*, such as the pro-Roman and anti-Jewish tendencies of the book, also have clear parallels in second-century works, such as the Acts of Pilate. These parallels suggest that the *GP* was composed in the same theological and cultural milieu and is a second-century work.

Implications of the Study

The date of the *GP* and its literary relationship to the canonical Gospels are watershed issues that have an enormous impact on one's reconstruction of the events surrounding Jesus' Passion and resurrection. If the Cross Gospel is the earliest narrative of Jesus' Passion and resurrection, and if the canonical Gospels used it as their single source for their Passion Narratives (as Crossan claims), little hope exists for knowing much about Jesus' death, burial, or resurrection. The *GP* is more a product of the author's creative literary imagination than a reflection of eyewitness accounts of actual events. Thus, if the *GP* is the single source for the canonical narratives of the Passion and resurrection, the canonical Gospels are unreliable revisions of an unreliable tradition. None of the Gospels could then be trusted to provide historically reliable testimony about the final events in the life of the historical Jesus. Scholars may only speculate about what happened to Jesus based on their knowledge of the customs of the Jews and Romans; the political situation in Jerusalem in the early 30s; the character of Pilate, Herod Antipas, and the Jewish leaders; and the references to Jesus' death and resurrection in the New Testament epistles. Crossan's theory that Jesus may never have been decently buried at all becomes plausible.[49]

On the other hand, if the canonical Gospels are the earliest record of the Passion and resurrection, as this paper suggests, and if these contain narratives based on eyewitness accounts, as the earliest church testimony affirms and as the internal evidence suggests, the earliest narratives of Jesus' death and resurrection may be viewed as prophecy fulfilled rather than prophecy historicized, and speculation that Jesus was not even buried, much less raised, is groundless.[50]

– 7 –

THE RESURRECTION
Faith or History?

Alan F. Segal

I want to thank the participants and organizers for including my contribution in this collection although I could not be present at the conference. It has been a pleasure and a great help in my scholarship to listen to all the other contributions. I hope that my belated essay can be included in their future discussions.

My own perspective is going to be quite different from most of those offered in the lectures. I hope that it will be considered carefully despite its different perspective. I will begin by saying that, in general, I am in greater sympathy with the scholarly enterprise represented by Dom Crossan, who seeks to understand what the reality of the symbol of resurrection can mean in our society without insisting that it necessarily have a form that is more specific than the NT gives us. On the other hand, I am in general agreement with the historical findings of Tom Wright when he says that the predominant understanding of the New Testament in the first century was that Jesus' resurrection was bodily. But I do think that this is merely the beginning of the question, not its endpoint. Belief in the fleshly resurrection of Jesus is only characteristic of the Gospels, less so of Paul. And it was completely uncharacteristic of the mystics and gnostics who were certainly numerous in the early life of the church.

I have also written extensively on the afterlife in world religions and in Second Temple Judaism, of which Christianity is an important part.[1] As well, I have an abiding interest and fascination with Paul, whose writings I have tried to elucidate in several books.[2] In this paper, I will attempt to show that bodily resurrection in the New Testament means different things to different writers in the New Testament and that the differences in how resurrection is described are both extremely interesting, characteristic of the thinking of the earliest Christian communities, and essential to understanding New Testament faith. The fact that the early Christians did not react in a homogenized, single tradition shows us that the New Testament writers were more interested in a community of opinion than are some more modern interpreters. At the end, I will question whether we can go from New Testament reports to the reality of the transformed fleshly resurrection, as so many of the scholars in this volume claim.

Paul

All of the participants in this volume have affirmed that Paul believes in the literal resurrection of the Christ and that Paul's sermon on the issue, 1 Corinthians 15, stresses both the bodily nature of Christ's resurrection and its spiritual nature. I agree entirely but hasten to point out that Paul explicitly denies that flesh and blood can be resurrected (1 Cor. 15:44, 50, 53-54). We should take this statement completely seriously. There is no reason to suppose that he means anything else than what he says: "Flesh and blood cannot inherit the kingdom of God, nor does the perishable inherit the imperishable" (1 Cor. 15:50). He is not merely denying mortality but suggesting that a transformation (1 Cor. 15:51) must take place before the "spiritual body" is manifest, which will be fully realized at the last trumpet, when death, sin, and the law shall be no more. Whether this spiritual body will be a newly created eschatological body or the same one transformed is moot. But the process itself is described as a transformation of the believer into the body of Christ, which is already transformed by his death and resurrection. The process is progressive and is only realized in the eschaton.

It is, of course, possible that Paul meant that the flesh and blood will be transformed into immortal flesh and blood, as several scholars demand. But Paul is very ambiguous on this issue, and it is certainly not the vocabulary that Paul prefers. This ambiguity is crucial because Paul's writing is the first writing on the subject—or any subject—in Christianity. All future writing either must not know about Paul or must react to it. Very likely, a good deal of the later writing is trying to explicate, even correct, what Paul said on the subject in light of issues that come up in the second and third generations of Christians.

This is certainly true with regard to the Gospels, written at least one and as much as two generations later. Since we know that Luke is very aware of whom Paul is, writing what amounts to a biography of him in the second half of the Acts of the Apostles, I think we should assume that the latter Gospel traditions certainly do know about Paul and that their writing is meant to supplement or correct Paul's. It is crucially important for understanding the distinction between these two bodies of writing—Paul's letters and the Gospels—to note that they do not share a common vocabulary for describing early Christianity or the resurrection body. Paul and the Gospels take very different ways to describe the new revelation of God's plan. That does not assure us that Paul has a different view of the resurrection body than the Gospels do, but it hardly assures us of their unity. Indeed, it can be seriously maintained that Paul had a completely different notion of the relationship between the earthly body and the resurrection body.[3] As I said, I think the issue is frankly ambiguous, so it is hardly settled in the direction of univocality.

The crucial issue is entailed in whether this body is new, created at the resurrection, or merely the old body transformed. The metaphor of the seed that "disappears" before it sprouts suggests a disjunction between the bodies and would seem to argue for the two-body hypothesis, as does the chiastic parallel between Adam and Christ. Critics ask, If there are two bodies, what carries the identity? It is possible that this question bothers us a lot and Paul not at all, since the "person" is in Christ and God is sovereign and can do what he wills. In any event, the issue is moot since the passage creates as many mysteries as it solves. Since many studies assume that Paul talks of the natural body made immortal, I will stress another possibility to show that this is not the only possible, or even the most likely, understanding of Paul's words.

What Paul does say is that the new body will be spiritual and that its spiritual nature does contrast with the earthly body. The earthly body is a *sōma psychikon*, a psychic body or ensouled body, often translated as a "natural body," containing both soul and matter, perhaps even a living soul, as in Genesis. This contrasts with the *sōma pneumatikon*, a spiritual body, which needs to be both shaped like a body and to be spiritual in nature but evidently is not made of flesh and blood. The problem with this vocabulary is that it does not appear to make sense in a Greek context. A spiritual body and a psychic body might easily refer to the same entity in Platonic philosophy. Since Paul is clearly making a distinction between the two bodies, normally one understands the distinction to be between life as we know it and the future, more spiritual life of the spirit, a life that he knows about only from his visionary and religious life.[4]

This is what Paul says about the bodily form of the resurrection:

But someone will ask, "How are the dead raised? With what kind of body do they come?" Fool! What you sow does not come to life unless it dies. And as for what you sow, you do not sow the body that is to be, but a bare seed, perhaps of wheat or of some other grain. But God gives it a body as he has chosen, and to each kind of seed its own body. Not all flesh is alike, but there is one flesh for human beings, another for animals, another for birds, and another for fish. There are both heavenly bodies and earthly bodies, but the glory of the heavenly is one thing, and that of the earthly is another. There is one glory of the sun, and another glory of the moon, and another glory of the stars; indeed, star differs from star in glory.

So it is with the resurrection of the dead. What is sown is perishable, what is raised is imperishable. It is sown in dishonor, it is raised in glory. It is sown in weakness, it is raised in power. It is sown a physical body, it is raised a spiritual body. If there is a physical body, there is also a spiritual body. Thus it is written, "The first man, Adam, became a living being"; the last Adam became a life-giving spirit. But it is not the spiritual which is first but the physical, and then the spiritual. The first man was from the earth, a man of dust; the second man is from heaven. As was the man of dust, so are those who are of the dust; and as is the man of heaven, so are those who are of heaven. Just as we have borne the image of the man of dust, we will also bear the image of the man of heaven. (1 Cor 15:35-49)

This is a very long and notoriously difficult passage, full of ambiguities, but it is possible to make several important points. The body of Christ is equated in kind with the resurrection body of believers. The transformation of the resurrection is analogous with the transformation of Christ and vice versa. This transformation is analogous to the difference between earthly, mortal bodies, and eternal, heavenly bodies. Just as human beings have borne the *image* of the earthly man, Adam, so will we bear the *image* of the heavenly man, Christ, who has joined the immortal company of stars and heavenly bodies. This, arguably, is Paul's understanding of the prophecy of resurrection in Daniel 12:3: "Those who are wise shall shine like the brightness of the sky, and those who lead many to righteousness, like the stars forever and ever." I would suggest that the connection with stars is not fortuitous but is, in fact, a mark that the resurrected body is "angelic," just as the stars themselves are "angelic" in some general sense (Job 38:7; Judg. 5:20). Paul understands all who have been baptized to have been united with Christ's martyr's death, and so all are qualified for the transformation. To me, this represents a democratization of the highest rewards prophesied in Daniel.

Paul's famous description of Christ's experience of humility and obedience in Philippians 2:5-11 also hints that the identification of Jesus with the image of God was reenacted in the church in a liturgical mode:

Let the same mind be in you that was in Christ Jesus,
who, though he was in the form of God,
did not regard equality with God
as something to be exploited,
but emptied himself,
taking the form of a slave,
being born in human likeness.
And being found in human form,
he humbled himself
and became obedient to the point of death—
even death on a cross.

> Therefore God also highly exalted him
>> and gave him the name
>> that is above every name,
> so that at the name of Jesus
>> every knee should bend,
>> in heaven and on earth and under the earth,
> and every tongue should confess
>> that Jesus Christ is Lord,
>> to the glory of God the Father. (Phil. 2:5-11)

This passage has several hymnic features that lead scholars to believe that Paul is quoting a fragment of primitive liturgy or referring to a liturgical setting.[5] Thus, Philippians 2 may easily be the earliest writing in the Pauline corpus as well as the earliest Christology of the New Testament; it is not surprising that it is the most exalted Christology.[6]

In Philippians 2:6, the identification of Jesus with the form of God implies his preexistence. The Christ is depicted as an eternal aspect of divinity that was not proud of its high station but consented to take on the shape of a man and suffer the fate of men, even death on a cross (though many scholars see this phrase as a Pauline addition to the original hymn). This transformation from divinity to earthly human is followed by the converse, the retransformation of the man Jesus back into God. Because of this obedience, God exalted him and bestowed on him the "name that is above every name" (Phil. 2:9).

For a Jew (and Paul remained a Jew his whole life), this phrase can only mean that Jesus received the divine name, the tetragrammaton YHWH, understood as the Greek name *kyrios*, or Lord. Sharing in the divine name is a frequent motif of early Jewish apocalypticism where the principal angelic mediator of God is or carries the name Yahweh, as Exodus 23 describes the angel of Yahweh.

The implication of the Greek term *morphē*, "form," is that Christ has the form of a divine body identical with the *kavod*, the glory, and equivalent also with the *eikōn* (Greek for "image"), for in Greek in Genesis 1:26 man is made after the *eikōn* of God and thus has the divine *morphē* (Greek for "shape" or, in Hebrew, *demuth*). The climax of Paul's confession is that "Jesus Christ is Lord, to the glory of God the Father" (Phil. 2:11), meaning that Jesus, the Messiah, has received the name *Lord* in his glorification, and that this name, not Jesus' private earthly name, is the one that will cause every knee to bend and every tongue to confess.[7]

In paraphrasing this fragment from liturgy, Paul witnesses that the early Christian community directed its prayers to this human figure of divinity along with God (1 Cor. 16:22ff; Rom. 10:9-12; 1 Cor. 12:3). This is all the more striking since the Christians, like the Jews, seemingly refuse to give any other god or hero any worship at all. It turns out, however, that many different Jewish and Christian traditions before the rabbis have tolerated binitarian conceptions of God, especially in view of the passage of Daniel 7:9f, where two divine figures are described.[8] When the rabbis gain control of the Jewish community, they vociferously argue against the worship of any angel and specifically polemicize against the belief that a heavenly figure other than God can forgive sins (*b. Sanhedrin* 38b), quoting Exodus 23:21 prominently among other scriptures to prove their point. The heresy itself they call believing that there are "two powers in heaven." By this phrase the rabbis largely (but not exclusively) referred to Christians who, as Paul says, do exactly what the rabbis warn against—worship the second power.[9]

Concomitant with Paul's worship of the divine Christ is transformation. Paul writes in Philippians 3:10: "I want to know Christ and the power of his resurrection and the sharing of his sufferings by becoming like him in his death" (*symmorphizomenos tōi thanatōi autou*, συμμορφιζόμενος τῷ θανάτῳ αὐτοῦ). The believer shares something of his identity with Christ, in faith and in liturgy, and this reveals the power of resurrection. Later, in Philippians 3:20-21, he writes: "But our citizenship is in heaven, and it is from there that we are expecting a Savior, the Lord Jesus Christ. He will transform [*metaschēmatisei*, μετασχηματίσει] the body of our humiliation so that it may be conformed [*symmorphon*, σύμμορφον] to his glorious body [*tōi sōmati tēs doxēs autou*, τῷ σώματι τῆς δοξῆς αὐτοῦ] by the power that also enables him to make all things subject to himself [κατὰ τὴν ἐνέργειαν τοῦ δύνασθαι αὐτὸν καὶ ὑποτάξαι αὐτῷ τὰ πάντα]."

English does not allow us to build such a vivid image into one word. If we had an English word for it, it would be *symmorphōsis*, like *metamorphōsis* but with a more intimate and transformative meaning. The Greek verb means literally "to be morphed together with," what our word *metamorphose* suggests, except that it states that the reformation will explicitly take place "together with" (*sym-*) his glorious body, suggesting the outcome is a new compound of both. The body of the believer eventually is to be transformed together into the body of Christ. The believer's body is to be changed into the same spiritual body of glory as that of the savior. This is arguably where the identity of the believer is "stored" until the new body is created at the end. But is it the same as his previous mortal body or different? I believe there are no absolute grounds for knowing exactly what Paul meant, a fact that called for commentary in later Christian documents.

We need to coin another new word to understand the next part of this statement, where Paul talks about transformation in a slightly different way. Paul struggles with the expression of his mystic intuition. He also says that the change will *metaschematize* (change the format of) our lowly body so that it will become his glorious body (Phil. 3:10). Again, English does not easily allow us to appreciate this unusual feature of the Greek language. But Paul is suggesting that this transformation from our lowly body to Christ's glorious body creates a new "metascheme," perhaps to be understood as a new immortal body. This vision will, in effect, produce an entirely new understanding of what salvation means because it combines a crucified Messiah with the vision of the end. We know that much of the story is not new. But the identification of the divine figure in heaven with the crucified Messiah on earth, with whose suffering one is to be identified, is entirely new. And it clearly comes not from any preexisting prophecy but from the events of the end of Jesus' earthly life.

Paul exhorts his followers to imitate him as he has imitated Christ: "Brothers and sisters, join in imitating me, and observe those who live according to the example you have in us" (Συμμιμηταί μου γίνεσθε, ἀδελφοί, καὶ σκοπεῖτε τοὺς οὕτω περιπατοῦντας καθὼς ἔχετε τύπον ἡμᾶς). The followers are told to imitate Paul as he himself imitates Jesus. All of this suggests that the body of believers will be literally refashioned into the glorious body of Christ, a process that starts with conversion and faith but ends in the parousia, the shortly expected culmination of history. It will all depend on a notion of body that is a new spiritualized substance, a new body that is not of the flesh and blood, which cannot inherit the kingdom (1 Cor. 15:30).

Paul's depiction of salvation and the transformation of the believer is based on his understanding of Christ's glorification, partaking of early Jewish apocalyptic mysticism for its expression.[10] The basic notion of transformation into an angelic or astral form may even have survived from a pre-Christian setting, because Paul does not mention resurrection here at all. Clearly, glorification is doing the work of resurrection in this passage. Likewise, in Romans 12:2, Paul's listeners are exhorted to "be transformed (*metamorphousthe*, μεταμορφοῦσθε) by renewing of your minds." In Galatians 4:19, Paul expresses another but very similar transformation: "My little children, for whom I am again in the pain of childbirth *until Christ is formed in you!*" (*mechris hou morphōthēi Christos en hymin*, μέχρις οὖ μορφωθῇ Χριστὸς ἐν ὑμῖν).

This transformation, surprisingly, is to be effected by being transformed into Christ *in his death* (*symmorphizomenos tōi thanatōi autou*, συμμορφιζόμενος τῷ θανάτῳ αὐτοῦ; Phil. 3:10). This identification with the death of Jesus is a crucial issue for understanding Paul's religious experience. Paul predicts that the believer will be transformed into the glorious body of Christ through dying and being reborn in Christ. Paul himself sees the phenomenon as being related to baptism. Paul's central proclamation is this: Jesus is Lord and all who have faith have already undergone a death like his and so too will share in his resurrection by being transformed into his form, spirit, and shape. This proclamation perhaps reflects a baptismal liturgy, implying that baptism provides the moment whereby the believer comes to be "in Christ." Christianity may have been a unique Jewish sect in making baptism a central rather than a preparatory ritual, but some of the mystical imagery comes from its Jewish past, probably through the teachings of John the Baptist.[11]

Alternatively, Paul can say, as he does in Galatians 1:16, that "[God] was pleased to reveal his Son *in me* [ἐν ἐμοί]." This is not a simple dative but, rather, refers to his having received in him the Spirit, in his case through his conversion. Being *in Christ* appears to mean being united with or transformed into his heavenly image, which is apparently synonymous with his spiritual body. The same, however, is available to all Christians through baptism. Dying and being resurrected along with Christ in baptism is *the beginning of the process* by which the believer gains the same image of God, his *eikon* (εἰκών), which was made known to humanity when Jesus became the Son of Man— that human figure in heaven who brings judgment in the apocalypse described by Daniel. Likely, it is *eikōn* or one of its synonyms that serves as the marker for identity in the transformation from natural man to spiritual man. It is clear that for Paul the fulfillment of this process is going to come very soon; Paul expected the end of time in his own lifetime.

Paul's conception of the risen body of Christ as the *spiritual body* (1 Cor. 15:43-44) at the end of time and as the body of Glory (Phil. 3:21) thus originates in Jewish apocalypticism and mysticism, modified by the unique events of early Christianity. *Spirit* is a synonym for the "glory" and the "form," which Christ has already received. The meaning of Romans 8:29 can be likewise clarified by Jewish esoteric tradition. There, as we have seen, Paul speaks of God as having "predestined [those whom he foreknew] to be conformed [*symmorphous* again] to the image of his Son" (προώρισεν συμμόρφους τῆς εἰκόνος τοῦ υἱοῦ αὐτοῦ). Paul uses the genitive here rather than the dative as in Philippians 3:21, softening the identification between believer and savior. But when Paul states that believers conform to the image of his Son, he is not speaking of an agreement of mind or ideas between Jesus and the believers. The word behind the English word *conformed* is *symmorphōn* again. Appearing in an oblique case, the word *symmmorphous* itself still suggests a spiritual reformation of the believer's body into the form of the divine image. Paul's language for conversion—*being in Christ*—develops out of mystical Judaism, not Greek philosophy.

This, it seems to me, is the reward that Paul expects believers to gain when they have faith in Christ. They come to be literally *in Christ*. It may be that Paul assumes all who are part of Israel to be saved, as he says in Romans. What he is offering those who believe in Christ is not merely salvation but transformation. This is beyond the rewards offered by the Sadducees certainly and those usually understood by righteous Jews in Pharisaism (see *m. Sanhedrin* 10).[12] He is maintaining that those who believe in Christ—Jew and Gentile alike—will join his heavenly body.

In 1 Corinthians, Paul discusses the issue of the final disposition of the body before he discusses resurrection and transformation themselves. In this passage, he may also be responding to the Greek notion that the body decays while the soul lives on. A. J. M. Wedderburn has astutely observed that the issue in 1 Corinthians 6 is the normal conception of the afterlife in a Greek environment.[13] It is in this context that Paul takes up the issue of the body:

> "All things are lawful for me," but not all things are beneficial. "All things are lawful for me," but I will not be dominated by anything. "Food is meant for the stomach and the stomach for food,"[[14]] and God will destroy both one and the other. The body is meant not for fornication but for the Lord, and the Lord for the body. And God raised the Lord and will also raise us by his power. (1 Cor. 6:12-14)

The Greeks believe that the body is destined for destruction. But Paul does not follow through with a Platonic analysis of the immortality of the soul.[15] Instead, he stays in the apocalyptic-mystical world of Judaism, defending and sharpening that notion in view of the Greek assumptions about the continuity of life after death. Paul immediately suggests that a body will survive death for it belongs to the Lord. God will raise it in glory and perfection by means of the spirit, just as he raised up the body of Jesus, who is even now in his spiritual state. Even so, it is not clear whether the body is to be created from the "*eikōn*" or "form" or "spirit" or "glory" of the Lord or merely to be transformed from natural body.

This kind of talk will demand a clarification in a Greco-Roman context. But, as Paul is still discussing various moral issues within the community, he postpones his discussion until later in the letter, in 1 Corinthians 15, where he sums up his entire religious experience in an apocalyptic vision of the resurrection of believers. Paul begins with a description of his previous preaching and suggests that if his listeners give up belief in the resurrection then they believe in Christ in vain:

Now if Christ is proclaimed as raised from the dead, how can some of you say there is no resurrection of the dead? If there is no resurrection of the dead, then Christ has not been raised; and if Christ has not been raised, then our proclamation has been in vain and your faith has been in vain. We are even found to be misrepresenting God, because we testified of God that he raised Christ—whom he did not raise if it is true that the dead are not raised. For if the dead are not raised, then Christ has not been raised. If Christ has not been raised, your faith is futile and you are still in your sins. Then those also who have died[16] in Christ have perished. If for this life only we have hoped in Christ, we are of all people most to be pitied. (1 Cor. 15:12-19)

Paul claims to have given them, indeed emphasized as of the first importance, the true teaching, as he had himself received it. And that teaching is simply that Christ died for sins in accordance with Scripture, that he was entombed and rose three days later, all in accordance with Scripture. It is quite clear that Paul's knowledge of this process is privileged. It comes from his apocalyptic and visionary life. It is for this reason that he speaks of the spiritual nature of Christ. The Christ's body is spiritual because that is how he has seen it. He expects that it will become actualized in the coming apocalypse, which is soon to arrive, no doubt in Paul's own lifetime. So the actualization of the spiritual nature of Christ is left ambiguous on purpose. I suppose it is because he expects to see exactly how it will happen.

Notice too that Jesus' burial is part of Paul's earliest tradition but that the empty tomb is not. There is no doubt that this is the earliest Christian teaching with regard to the resurrection: it is part of the primitive *kērygma,* or proclamation, of the church. The empty tomb is a Gospel innovation.

The Gospels

If Paul's understanding of the resurrection body is more ambiguous than frequently supposed, the story of the empty tomb is less positive proof than is usually made of it. The Gospels are a much later contribution to the Christian tradition. They are one to two generations later than Paul and, even though their discussion of Jesus' mission has some uniformity, there is almost none in the various Gospels' description of the risen Christ: each Gospel contributes a completely different picture of the resurrected Christ to the tradition, indicating that the resurrection traditions were far less established than the traditions of Jesus' teachings. Furthermore, the years between Paul and the Gospels were difficult ones for early Christianity. Christians had to contend with Jewish criticism of the church's kerygma, as well as the failure of the apocalypse to arrive. Furthermore, the Gospels promote the disciples as church authorities. Faith for the Gospels means faith in those who interpreted the tradition, who were students of students of those who sat as Jesus' original followers—in short, faith in the Gospels means trusting the apostolic tradition. Faith for Pauline Christians meant believing that Paul's personal visions were true. Paul's preaching had little to say about the man Jesus, whom Paul never met. Whereas Paul concentrates on the spiritual nature of his visions, the Gospels concentrate on the stories of Jesus' physical body, and it is his physical body that is valorized in all the postresurrection appearances.

The story of Doubting Thomas in John 20:24-29 is as apt as any, though it is late even for the Gospel traditions. Thomas says, "Unless I see the mark of the nails in his hands, and put my finger in the mark of the nails and my hand in his side, I will not believe" (v. 25). The text does not explicitly say that Jesus was touched. But this is not sufficient grounds to ignore the plain meaning of the story: the risen Christ has appeared and is a revivified corpse, complete with the marks of the crucifixion still upon him. Furthermore, that Jesus appears in a closed room (v. 26) is not demonstration against his flesh-and-blood existence. The point is that Jesus is physically among them as a flesh-and-blood, yet resurrected, being. Thomas wants to put his fingers in the wounds to verify that this is the same man who was crucified, and his skepticism is satisfied by the postresurrection appearance. The moral of the story is inherent in Jesus' answer to Thomas: "Have you believed because you have seen me? Blessed are those who have not seen and yet have come to believe" (v. 29). Paul is one of those who saw Christ, but his generation and the next had gone without the apocalypse. The Gospel sees the faith of its contemporary day as even greater than that which had gone before.

The same point is made by Jesus' eating fish with the disciples in Galilee (John 21:1-15). In short, the difference between Paul and the Gospels is much like the difference between mystical literature and apocalyptic literature: What mystic literature describes as visionary, apocalyptic literature can describe as factual and prophetic. The reasons for this switch must be supposed, but the Gospels certainly want to stress the physicality of Jesus' resurrection over against the spirituality of Paul's description. Were there not so much at stake doctrinally in the modern world in conflating both accounts into one "transformed flesh," this contrast would remain as clear as day. Paul and the Gospels differ in their vocabulary of resurrection. Furthermore, one cannot limit discussion of the Gospels only to the canonical ones. The noncanonical Gospels and the gnostic documents go much further than Paul in spiritualizing the resurrection. It seems to me that there is no ancient consensus about the resurrection body of Christ.

Much has been made at this conference about the empty tomb. But it is not a piece of the ancient kerygma of the church. The empty tomb cannot be traced in Paul's teaching; nor does it bear the kind of test of historicity that contemporary apologists have brought to it. It is, in fact, an argument from silence, which only underlines more strongly that the earliest Christian traditions contain no description of the resurrection itself. In its ancient form, it testifies as much to the church's dismay at Jewish doubt in the resurrection as to anything else. While Paul does certify that Jesus was buried (and we certainly do have evidence that other victims of crucifixion were given burials), there is no pre-Gospel tradition of the empty tomb. When the Gospels were written, it would have been very hard to certify what the tomb had contained. Tombs in that period were not permanent places of burial but only temporary places where the body decayed, leaving the bones. These bones were either pushed to the back of the niche in the tomb (hence the later Gospels' claim that the tomb of Joseph of Arimathea volunteered a new tomb, with no bones), or they were collected in ossuaries. We have no idea what happened to Jesus' body, but there is some ancient evidence in Paul's writing that Paul at least believed it was given a burial.

The Probability of the Physical
Resurrection of Transformed Flesh

I see no reason, therefore, to conclude without further thought that a probability of evidence exists in the early church that Jesus actually was resurrected in a physical, transformed, fleshly way. It is even possible that the early church was barely aware of how important that issue would become. Paul only stresses that the body was buried, which was a victory in itself in the ancient world. The "empty tomb" has become a modern, rationalized apologetic synthesis, constructing scientific certainty from the deep mystery of faith in the ancient world. My conclusion is that modern surety in the empty tomb actually misrepresents the far more ambiguous and ambivalent tradition of the early church.

I believe the whole enterprise of trying to prove that the resurrection is a historical fact is a category mistake. First of all, it does no good to argue that the consensus of NT scholars who have dealt with the problem of the resurrection actually agree that it was a literal resurrection of transformed flesh. I am not sure that such a claim is even valid. No evidence is adduced to this effect, but even supposing its truth, one must take as important the casual comment that Lüdemann would be much happier if he left the field. This only underlines the obvious fact that there exists a group of scholars who are hostile to any other conclusion than that of literal resurrection. Under the circumstances, it is difficult to demonstrate that scholarly disinterestedness has been maintained. The scholars who are mentioned as part of this consensus not only are believers but also have a similar notion of faith, perhaps not entirely unfairly characterized by Dom Crossan as "elegant fundamentalism."

This small scholarly consensus—really a school of scholarship—is beside the point because the vast majority of modern historians looking at the very same story would say that *no evidence at all would ever demonstrate that a unique resurrection took place*. The resurrection is neither probable nor improbable; it is impossible to confirm historically. This is particularly important theoretically: a problem is neither improbable nor probable if it is neither confirmable nor disconfirmable; such a problem is not part of the world of scientific verification.

Historians cannot, in fact, deal with uniquely miraculous appearances. Surely, no one would seriously argue that the early Christians did not believe that Christ had been raised. But just as surely, few if any modern historians would argue that any evidence could move us from this historical fact to the supposition that Jesus was actually and physically raised from the dead and that he appeared in his transformed fleshly body. If so, why not believe not only all the miracles of the Old Testament, including the six-day creation, as well as the miraculous giving of the Quran to Muhammad? If one, then all miracles are possible, since the reports all have credible witnesses. Muslims do believe in the prophecy of Jesus, though not in his physical resurrection. To me, it is absolutely crucial that every one of those who believe in the physical resurrection of Jesus as historical fact is also a believer in Christianity, while those who assert that Jesus was believed by his followers to have been resurrected can come from the spectrum of the whole scholarly and religious community, whether they be New Testament scholars or not. To be part of a rational and historical community of historians, one has to be willing to admit to disconfirmation as well as confirmation. But the consensus comprises all the religious of a particular persuasion. How could they admit to disconfirmation without disconfirming their faith?

This suggests to me that rather than there being a consensus, there is actually a small group of scholars made up entirely of the faithful trying to impose their faith in the form of an academic argument on the general academic community. In other words, one has to be a Christian of a particular theological perspective to believe in the actual, physical resurrection of Jesus, though one may be a Christian even if one does not believe in it in those terms. The community of rational scholarship does not take us to the point that these scholars want us to go. But Dom Crossan's analysis, and many like it, can illuminate any historian's understanding of the events—that is, although the writer is a Christian and believes in the resurrection, the scholar does not make claims that go beyond the canons of rationality today. A historical theory should be available to assent or dissent regardless of one's religious perspective. And that is a truer and more accurate statement of the consensus.

Category Mistakes and the Proper Place of Faith

It seems to me that this only underlines the baroque nature of this recent quest for the historical risen Christ, a Christ that rises directly not into history but "into the kerygma," as Bultmann has said.[17] It is trying to demonstrate something rationally that is rightfully an aspect of faith. So I am not maintaining that believing in the resurrection is wrong, nor am I criticizing it as naive. Rather, I am suggesting that it is not the correct use of faith. I am suggesting that trying to prove the resurrection historically is the same as trying to prove the Trinity historically or trying to prove Adam and Eve scientifically—a category mistake. It was Martin Buber who, for me, best expressed this issue, in his distinction between I-Thou and I-It thinking. I-It thinking—reason in its normal employment, even including historical reason—basically explains any phenomenon by means of proximal causes. I-Thou thinking appreciates the spiritual dimension of reality, starting in the aesthetic realm and ending with statements of human destiny. I-Thou thinking can never be affected—proven or disproved—by I-It thinking. One person looks at a sunset and sees the glowing of pollution in the atmosphere. Another sees the mark of a benign creator. Only I-Thou thinking allows for the latter; that is its greatest and highest usage. But it can never be demonstrated using I-It language. For me, this is the mark of faith; it does not depend on rational argument. If it did, it would be reason, not faith. The same is true with the resurrection. It is one thing to conclude that the early Christians took it as fact; it is another thing to propound that it can be demonstrated historically. Such an endeavor is always bound to fail.

I would not belabor this point were it not so much a part of our contemporary political discussion. So-called scientific creationism was adjudged not scientific by the Supreme Court of the United States, but it was sponsored by people who felt that the six-day creation story of Genesis 1 was as scientifically demonstrable as the theories of evolution. In school boards and local town councils, adherents to this mistake were actually able to put together a consensus of persons who voted for such issues in the science curriculum. But that is not the same thing as achieving the status of a theory, which evolution has slowly done in its almost two centuries of scientific experiment and discussion. Scientific creationism 2.0, now called "intelligent design," has recently been trying to pick up the slack lost when the Supreme Court ruled against scientific creationism 1.0. Indeed, many people in the United States rightfully do believe in some form of "intelligent design," but is it a scientific theory? I think not. It is sure that the new conception will find willing consensus in various places in the United States. In fact, like the Scopes Monkey Trial, it can be shown that these victories often function like scientific proofs in the community that supports it. But is it a scientific proof? Not in any understandable way, despite the fact that our current Republican administration is heavily supporting these enterprises to appease the religious right wing of the party. To me, it shares the same category mistake. It seeks to demonstrate through faulty logic or science or historical reasoning what should be, indeed can only be, affirmed through a faith commitment. In the end, it will do nothing but cheapen the value of faith in our community. So I am arguing that we return faith to its honored position as the arbiter of final meanings in our society. Paul described his faith as a mystery (Rom. 11:25; 16:25; 1 Cor. 2:7; 15:51): "Now to God who is able to strengthen you according to my gospel and the proclamation of Jesus Christ, according to the revelation of the mystery that was kept secret for long ages." I believe that this imposes upon those who follow him the burden of that mystery, which is to live according to faith rather than sure knowledge.

– 8 –

WRIGHT AND CROSSAN ON THE HISTORICITY OF THE RESURRECTION OF JESUS

William Lane Craig

The Resurrection of the Son of God (2003) is N. T. Wright's third volume in his series of books on Christian origins, the sequel to *The New Testament and the People of God* (1992) and *Jesus and the Victory of God* (1996). I find it cause for reflection that, whereas John Meier, that other producer of prodigious tomes on the historical Jesus, refuses even to touch the topic of Jesus' resurrection, Wright has devoted more than eight hundred pages to this subject alone. The result is one of the most impressive studies of the historicity of Jesus' resurrection published to date.

In this chapter, I propose to analyze Wright's argument for the fact of Jesus' resurrection and assess its force in light of John Dominic Crossan's historical critique of the resurrection. In previous exchanges on Wright's book, which I have been privileged to attend, Crossan has declined to engage Wright's argument on the historical level, preferring instead to dialogue about the theology of the resurrection. This lack of engagement should be challenged, since such a modus operandi reflects Crossan's conviction that the historicity of Jesus' resurrection is, after all, not theologically significant, so that even those who deny the historicity of that event can nonetheless be truly said to believe in the resurrection and to be faithful Christians. Unless we insist that

Crossan engage Wright's argument on the historical level, we acquiesce in his pretension that the historical question really does not matter in the end. I hope that at this conference he will take on the specifics of Wright's case and show where it is inadequate or else give up his claim that the resurrection of Jesus is not a historical event.

Wright's Argument Summarized

Wright lays out his argument for the historicity of Jesus' resurrection in part 5 of his book, "Belief, Event and Meaning." Wright's case is very interestingly constructed. Typically, evidences of Jesus' historical resurrection would include (1) the discovery of his empty tomb, (2) his postmortem appearances, and (3) the very origin of the disciples' belief in Jesus' resurrection. In Wright's case, this third element assumes pride of place and actually is used as evidence for the factuality of the other two elements. Having documented the centrality and essentiality of belief in Jesus' resurrection to the early movement named for him, Wright presses the question: "What caused this belief in the resurrection of Jesus?"[1]

Wright presents his answer as the conclusion to a seven-step argument based on necessary and sufficient conditions.[2] His case may be summarized as follows:

1. The striking and consistent Christian alterations of the Jewish belief in resurrection rule out the possibility that the belief in Jesus' resurrection was generated spontaneously from within its Jewish context; rather, the early Christians ascribe the origin of this belief to the facts of Jesus' empty tomb and postmortem appearances.

2. Neither the empty tomb nor the postmortem appearances are individually sufficient to explain the origin of the disciples' belief in Jesus' resurrection.

3. However, the empty tomb and postmortem appearances are jointly sufficient to explain the origin of belief in Jesus' resurrection.

4. The meaning of the term *resurrection* in its Jewish context was such that belief in Jesus' resurrection could not have emerged

unless it were known that his body had disappeared and that he had been discovered to be alive once more.

5. Rival explanations of the origin of the belief in Jesus' resurrection do not possess comparable explanatory power.

6. Therefore, it is historically highly probable that Jesus' tomb was indeed found empty and that the disciples did indeed encounter him alive and well after his death.

7. The empty tomb and postmortem appearances of Jesus are best explained by the hypothesis that Jesus was raised bodily from the dead.

In sum, after showing that primitive Christianity believed that, in the peculiar case of Jesus of Nazareth, a man had risen from the dead in isolation from and in advance of the general resurrection of the dead, Wright argues that the discovery of Jesus' empty tomb conjoined with physical postmortem encounters with Jesus would, in the context of Jesus' own messianic claims, be a sufficient condition for the disciples' coming to believe such a thing about Jesus. On the other hand, Wright insists, in the absence of those two facts there is nothing in the historical antecedents of the Christian movement that would plausibly explain the origin of the disciples' belief that God had raised Jesus from the dead. Wright's argument thus far, then, amounts to the claim that the hypothesis of the facticity of the empty tomb and postmortem appearances has far greater explanatory power with respect to the origin of the belief in Jesus' resurrection than any known rival hypothesis. Notice that this hypothesis is not equivalent to the hypothesis that Jesus rose from the dead and thus far involves only nonmiraculous facts. Only when we come to step 7 does Wright infer Jesus' resurrection as the best explanation of the empty tomb and postmortem appearances.

Wright's Argument Analyzed

Wright's argument is not very tightly formulated. Step 1, for example, is really extraneous to the argument. The inadequacy of the hypothesis that belief in Jesus' resurrection emerged spontaneously as a result of Jewish influences is comprised in step 4 of the argument. The fact that early Christians ascribed the origin of their belief in Jesus' resurrection to the discovery of his empty tomb and his postmortem appearances is ultimately irrelevant, so long as step 4 is true. Crossan would deny that early Christians ascribed the origin of their belief in Jesus' resurrection to the discovery of his empty tomb and his postmortem appearances, but that would not suffice to refute Wright's argument as long as the remaining steps are true. Thus, step 1 does not add anything to the case.

Again, a little reflection shows that step 2 does not contribute to the argument either. What is critical to Wright's argument are the claims that the facts of the empty tomb and postmortem appearances are jointly sufficient (step 3) and individually necessary (step 4) to explain the origin of the disciples' belief in Jesus' resurrection. The fact that the empty tomb and postmortem appearances are individually insufficient to explain the rise of resurrection belief would be freely granted by Crossan without prejudice to his skepticism about the historicity of events of Easter. The skeptic has no problem affirming that the empty tomb and postmortem appearances are individually inadequate to explain the origin of the disciples' belief in Jesus' resurrection.

So the meat of Wright's argument comes with step 3, which implies that the hypothesis of the facticity of the empty tomb and postmortem appearances has the explanatory power to account for the origin of belief in Jesus' resurrection. I think that Wright's claim that the discovery of the empty tomb and the postmortem appearances are jointly sufficient to explain the rise of resurrection belief is relatively uncontroversial, given that we are talking about physical appearances, not mere visions. If Jesus' tomb were found empty and he appeared physically alive after his death, then, given the context of his messianic claims, it seems very probable that the disciples would come to believe that God had raised him from the dead. Even Crossan would, I think, concede the point.

The more controversial claim comes with step 4, that the facticity of the empty tomb and postmortem appearances are individually necessary conditions of the origin of belief in Jesus' resurrection. Wright wants to show that the rise of resurrection belief necessitates the historicity of the empty tomb and postmortem appearances of Jesus. In support of this claim, Wright presents two considerations:

(1) the very meaning of the word *resurrection* rules out most of the rival alternatives, and (2) the principal alternative hypotheses turn out to be insufficient.[3]

The first consideration is not very carefully articulated. What Wright argues is (1) that the vocabulary for resurrection in then-current usage entailed the rising of the dead man to new life, so that an empty grave must be left behind, and (2) that appearances of the dead man are necessary to generate belief in his resurrection, since an empty grave alone is ambiguous. We may grant these points; but it does not follow that "if the body of Jesus of Nazareth had remained in the tomb there would have been no early Christian belief" in Jesus' resurrection.[4] What follows from the the point about the vocabulary of the resurrection is that if the disciples had *thought* Jesus' body remained in the tomb, they would not have come to believe in his resurrection. In other words, the necessary condition of the disciples' belief in Jesus' resurrection, given the meaning of that word, is their *belief* that his body no longer laid in the grave. Kirsopp Lake's wrong tomb hypothesis was consistent with that condition.[5] So is Crossan's hypothesis that Jesus' body was thrown into a common graveyard for criminals and its location forgotten.

Here, Wright's failure to discuss the historicity of the burial narrative in his survey of the Gospels constitutes a shortcoming in his argument. Wright is correct when he characterizes attempts (like Crossan's) to deny Jesus' burial by Joseph of Arimathea as "desperate," but there is a lacuna in his argument here that needs to be filled.[6] Wright could try to fill it by appealing to his arguments earlier in the book that it is highly unlikely that belief in Jesus' resurrection, as attested in Paul's letters, could itself have generated such stories of the empty tomb as we find in the Gospels.[7] But he insisted there that he was arguing not for the historicity of the narratives, but merely their logical and chronological priority to the theology we find in Paul.[8] He needs to show that the *belief* in Jesus' empty tomb could not have arisen unless the tomb of Jesus were in fact empty. His case would be stronger if he were to present independent evidence for the historicity of the burial of Jesus of Nazareth in a tomb whose location was known in Jerusalem. This is easily done. At least nine lines of historical evidence support the historicity of Jesus' burial in a tomb by Joseph of Arimathea.[9] Given the historicity of the burial narrative, it is, indeed, difficult to see how belief in Jesus' resurrection could arise and flourish in Jerusalem in the face of an occupied tomb. The historicity of the burial narrative, which is recognized by the majority of New Testament historians today, is a dagger in the heart of Crossan's skepticism.

What, then, about Wright's second claim: that appearances of the dead man were necessary to generate belief in his resurrection, since an empty grave alone is ambiguous? Clearly, from the meaning of the word *resurrection* one cannot deduce the fact of appearances. Wright's point is, rather, that appearances of Jesus are a necessary condition of the disciples' coming to believe in Jesus' resurrection.[10] His argument here could be stronger, however. He discounts the hypothesis that dreams could have produced belief in Jesus' resurrection because dreams would not lead to belief in a person's resurrection. Quite so, but that only proves that dreams *alone* are not a sufficient condition of the disciples' belief. The question here is whether dreams conjoined with the discovery of Jesus' empty tomb might not have led to belief in his resurrection. Or, more plausibly, visions of Jesus conjoined with his empty tomb? Why are real appearances necessary? On this score, Wright needs to explain more thoroughly the distinction between "resurrection" and "assumption into heaven" in Jewish thinking and then to show how the latter would be an explanation of visionary experiences more consonant with Jewish beliefs than the former. Had the disciples experienced merely visionary appearances of Jesus, such experiences, even when conjoined with the fact of his empty tomb, would at most have led them to believe in and proclaim Jesus' exaltation to heaven, in line with Jewish beliefs, not his resurrection from the dead, in contradiction to Jewish beliefs. This is not to say anything that Wright has not already eloquently explained elsewhere, but he needs to marshal his evidence at this point.

So Wright's first consideration in support of the necessity of the empty tomb and resurrection appearances might be more carefully articulated as the claim that the original disciples would not have proclaimed Jesus' resurrection from the dead had they not experienced appearances of Jesus alive after his death and found his tomb empty. It seems to me that this claim is quite correct and capable of being argued even more forcefully than Wright has done.

Wright's second consideration in support of the necessity of the empty tomb and postmortem appearances, it will be recalled, is the insufficiency of alternative hypotheses to explain the origin of the disciples' belief in Jesus' resurrection. Here he provides an excellent discussion of the hypotheses of cognitive dissonance and a fresh experience of grace.[11] But his critique of the former hypothesis is, again, not as strong as it could be. For the most important point to be made here is that, given the arguments of chapter 13, section 3, "The Surprise of the Resurrection Narratives," the disciples, if they were to have persisted in believing in Jesus due to cognitive dissonance, would not have produced the sort of narratives we find in the Gospels. The lack of scriptural prooftexting and allusion, the absence of any mention of the believers' sharing in the hope of eschatological resurrection, the conspicuous absence of apocalyptic descriptions of the risen Christ in luminous glory, and the prominent role played by women in the narrative all point to these narratives' not being the free creation of persons who imagined the resurrection of Jesus as a means of resolving the cognitive dissonance brought on by his death. These same sorts of consideration weigh heavily against Crossan's view that the resurrection narratives are fictional creations of the early church.

Wright concludes this step of the argument with these words:

> Nobody was expecting this kind of thing; no kind of conversion-experience would have generated such ideas; nobody would have invented it, no matter how guilty (or how forgiven) they felt, no matter how many hours they pored over the scriptures. To suggest otherwise is to stop doing history and to enter into a fantasy world of our own, a new cognitive dissonance in which the relentless modernist, desperately worried that the post-Enlightenment worldview seems in imminent danger of collapse, devises strategies for shoring it up nevertheless.[12]

To my knowledge, nothing that Crossan has written suffices to turn back the force of this conclusion.

On the basis of his argument thus far, Wright judges the historical probability of the dual facts of the empty tomb and postmortem appearances of Jesus to be "so high as to be virtually certain, as the death of Augustus in AD 14 or the fall of Jerusalem in AD 70."[13]

Now comes the final step in the argument: what is the best explanation of the facts of the empty tomb and postmortem appearances? Wright casts his argument here as an inference to the best explanation, but he again focuses on explanatory power, leaving aside such other criteria as explanatory scope, plausibility, degree of ad hoc–ness, and so forth.[14] The resurrection hypothesis explains the empty tomb and appearances; its rivals, he claims, do not.[15]

Wright recognizes that we here come face-to-face with worldview considerations; there is, he says, no neutral ground. It is not entirely clear to me what Wright's answer to Enlightenment naturalism is.[16] He seems to say that the spirit of the Enlightenment is not to close a priori any door to understanding and then to invite the naturalist to shift grounds and see whether the facts do not make better sense within a theistic worldview than they do within a naturalistic view. Of course, such an invitation will appear all the more inviting if a robust natural theology can be given in support of a theistic worldview. Arguments for a creator and designer of the universe, which are analogous to Wright's case for the resurrection, can be provided using historical sciences like cosmology. If one is convinced on the basis of arguments from necessary and sufficient conditions that the origin and fine-tuning of the universe are best explained by the existence of an ultra-mundane creator and designer of that universe, then the argument that Jesus' empty tomb and postmortem appearances are best explained by Jesus' resurrection from the dead will be all the more compelling.

Wright concludes with a summary of reasons for rejecting the principal alternative explanations of the empty tomb and appearances.[17] Unfortunately, here again there is confusion. The four rivals he considers (the immortality of Jesus' soul, Jesus' nonphysical "resurrection," a parallel trajectory of Jesus' exaltation, and retrojection of later Christian beliefs) are in fact denials of the empty tomb and appearances, not explanations of them. These hypotheses should have been considered and rejected in his earlier discussion in step 4 concerning the necessity of the facts of the empty tomb and postmortem appearances in explaining the origin of the disciples' belief in Jesus' resurrection. The rivals that should be considered here are those few hypotheses that concede these two facts and then try to explain them naturally. Wright simply laterals the ball to Gary Habermas at this point, referring the reader to his survey of rival hypotheses. Here I simply register my agreement that attempts to explain the empty tomb and postmortem appearances apart from the resurrection of Jesus are hopeless. That is precisely why skeptics like Crossan have to row against the current of scholarship in denying facts like the burial and empty tomb. Once these are admitted, no plausible naturalistic explanation of the facts can be given.

Wright's Argument Recast

The foregoing analysis suggests that Wright's argument might be more perspicuously recast along the following lines.

1. Early Christians believed in Jesus' (physical, bodily) resurrection.
2. The best explanation of that belief is the hypothesis of the disciples' discovery of Jesus' empty tomb and their experience of postmortem appearances of Jesus.
   - 2.1 The hypothesis of the disciples' discovery of Jesus' empty tomb and their experience of postmortem appearances of Jesus has the explanatory power to account for that belief.
   - 2.2 Rival hypotheses lack the explanatory power to account for that belief.
     - 2.21 Hypothesis of spontaneous generation within a Jewish context
     - 2.22 Hypothesis of dreams about Jesus
     - 2.23 Hypothesis of cognitive dissonance following Jesus' death
     - 2.24 Hypothesis of a fresh experience of grace following Jesus' death
     - 2.25 And so forth
3. The best explanation for the facts of Jesus' empty tomb and postmortem appearances is the hypothesis that Jesus rose from the dead.
   - 3.1 The resurrection hypothesis has the explanatory power to account for the empty tomb and postmortem appearances of Jesus.

3.2 Rival hypotheses lack the explanatory power to account
for the empty tomb and postmortem appearances of
Jesus.
3.21 Conspiracy hypothesis
3.22 Apparent death hypothesis
3.23 Hallucination hypothesis
3.24 And so forth

In short, I think that Wright's book is best seen as the most
extensively developed version of the argument for the resurrection
of Jesus from the fact of the origin of the disciples' belief in Jesus'
resurrection, an argument that may be supplemented by comparably
strong, or even stronger, independent arguments for the historicity of
the empty tomb and postmortem appearances of Jesus and, then, for
his resurrection. Wright's book is an invaluable reference work and a
benchmark of resurrection scholarship.

– 9 –

THE FUTURE OF THE RESURRECTION

Ted Peters

The historian looks for the resurrection in the past. The theologian looks for resurrection in the future. When it comes to resurrection as Christians explicate it, the future resurrection of all of us depends on the past resurrection of Jesus. Or is it vice versa? Could it be that what we see as a past event, Jesus' original Easter resurrection, is contingent on the eschatological new creation still promised by God?

To render a judgment as to whether Jesus' Easter resurrection really happened is, like all historical judgments, a matter of probability. N. T. Wright concludes that it is quite probable; John Dominic Crossan concludes that it is improbable. Both recognize to greater or lesser degrees that the Scripture we have inherited links what happened to Jesus on the first Easter with what God promises to us for our future. Jesus' resurrection is the first fruits of "those who have died" (1 Cor. 15:20). The link between the historical Jesus and the advent of the new creation is a theological link; it is a link between a probable historical judgment and an eschatological hope.

Theologians explicate Scripture. To do so, they employ a double hermeneutic. On the one hand, theologians watch the historians go backward, following a historical hermeneutic to reconstruct the likely historical background of what eventually became the text of the Bible.

On the other hand, theologians explicate the Christian faith as it travels from century to century, from culture to culture, and becomes understood within the horizon of a modern, post-Enlightenment, global context. Both hermeneutical directions begin from the same point of departure, Scripture.

The accounts of Jesus' exit from the tomb and post-Easter appearances as we find them in Scripture come shrink-wrapped in an eschatological package complete with understandings of Jesus as the Son of God and Savior of the world. For the historical hermeneutic to go backward and imagine a preconfessional Jesus without divinity and without soteriology is a matter of speculation. Such history is speculative reconstruction. The most concrete Jesus we have is the Jesus of Scripture, and this is a Jesus already confessed to be our Lord. A Jesus who is not claimed to be our Lord would be an imagined Jesus.

The truth of the biblical claim has to do with the eschatological Jesus, the one whose Easter resurrection is inextricably tied to the general resurrection, the advent of the new creation. What will confirm or disconfirm the Bible's claim will be the future. In principle, if the future does not include a divine eschatological act of consummation, then Jesus did not rise on Easter, at least not as the Bible describes it.

Let me clarify. Without the eschatological complement, the historian is still free to speculate about the possibility of an empty tomb or apparitions to disciples. But the event of Jesus' Easter resurrection as an eschatological event is contingent upon what lies in our future. This is the theologian's problem, not that of the historian. The historian is responsible for understanding the biblical claims regarding Jesus' resurrection as eschatological claims.

Even if it turns out that the past is contingent on the future, we find ourselves today in a situation where Christian claims about the Easter Jesus are subject to considerable doubt. A parish pastor writes in a recent issue of the *Christian Century* that, in mainline churches, "we no longer speak of heaven as an actual destination, a hope to be realized. Now, heaven is a figure of speech, a consoling metaphor to pull out for funeral services. I am not saying that we have stopped believing in heaven. Rather, I am suggesting that like Timbuktu, heaven is treated as if it were a term for something foreign and far away."[1]

Such a hopeless faith is unnecessary, in my judgment. The passion and energy of Christian living come from reliance on the biblical promise. Yet, it is a promise; it is not sure knowledge. This has always been the case. Why demure? Carl Braaten reminds us: "It would be foolishness to hold that an explanation is needed to gain access to the life it [resurrection] promises. That would be like refusing to watch television until one could explain electricity, or refusing to admit one had fallen in love before explaining how it happened."[2] This is not to strain credulity. Rather, the point is that Christian belief is dependent upon an as-yet-unfulfilled future expectation of resurrection.

In the meantime, we historians and theologians need to be busy about our work. In what follows, I would like to offer brief expositions of the work of John Dominic Crossan and N. T. Wright followed by briefer expositions of Wolfhart Pannenberg and John Polkinghorne. The central historical question is this: did it really happen? In order to get at this question, the move from Scripture to history will begin with a slightly different question: what must have happened to explain the rise of the early church and the writing of the Bible as we have it? When we turn from these historical questions to the theological question, we ask: did it really happen *as an eschatological event*, as a prolepsis of what is yet to come? And, because of the emphasis we find especially in the work of N. T. Wright on the *bodily* character of the resurrection, we will conclude by asking a scientific question: how can we speculatively preconstruct what new laws of nature the eschatological resurrection would require?

John Dominic Crossan

John Dominic Crossan understands his work to be that of a historian stepping up to meet the need to "give an accurate but impartial account of the historical Jesus as distinct from the confessional Christ."[3] He calls his method *historical study*, which "means an analysis whose theories and methods, evidence and arguments, results and conclusions are open, in principle and practice, to any human observer, any disciplined investigator, any self-conscious and self-critical student."[4]

Beginning with canonical and extracanonical texts, Crossan reconstructs the historical Jesus.

Crossan's historical study locates the historical Jesus where three independent vectors cross: cross-cultural anthropology, Greco-Roman and especially Jewish history, and literary or textual criticism.[5] The third vector, textual criticism, reveals that the primary biblical texts are structured according to three successive levels: first, retention of *original* or historical Jesus materials; second, the *transmission* or development of those materials; and third, *redaction* that includes creation of wholly new or fictional materials.[6] The composition of the canonical text of the Bible, which includes all three levels, says Crossan, is a result of deliberate theological or confessional interpretations of Jesus. Crossan's task, then, is to penetrate the levels beneath the theological or confessional interpretations to locate the original Jesus materials.

Crossan concludes that "the historical Jesus was a *peasant Jewish Cynic*. . . . His strategy, implicitly for himself and explicitly for his followers, was the combination of *free healing and common eating*, a religious and economic egalitarianism that negated alike and at once the hierarchical and patronal normalcies of Jewish religion and Roman power."[7] A key component in this conclusion for Crossan is that Jesus proffered open commensality—that is, dining at table in an egalitarian and antihierarchical fashion. Jesus advocates "an open commensality, an eating together without using table as a miniature map of society's vertical discriminations and lateral separations."[8] This was politically disruptive. Crossan writes: "Open commensality is the symbol and embodiment of radical egalitarianism, of an absolute equality of people that denies the validity of any discrimination between them and negates the necessity of any hierarchy among them."[9]

Crossan finds a similar social or political significance in the miracles. An exorcism, for example, is a social phenomenon, not a physical or spiritual one. This must be the case because, as Crossan assumes, no such things as demons exist: "I myself . . . do not believe that there are personal supernatural spirits who invade our bodies."[10] As long as such an assumption obtains, then a historical explanation other than the supernaturalistic one must also obtain—hence, the social explanation.

Even though miracles are important, Crossan does not assume that Jesus could actually cure diseases. This opens room for "healing the illness without curing the disease" and the social interpretation of healing miracles. He writes: "Miracles are not changes in the physical world so much as changes in the social world, and it is society that dictates, in any case, how we see, use, and explain that physical world." Jesus helps make "the social world humanly habitable."[11]

Jesus and his missionary disciples "share a miracle and a Kingdom, and they receive in return a table and a house. Here, I think, is the heart of the original Jesus movement, a shared egalitarianism of spiritual and material resources."[12] After removing the transmissional and redactional levels of biblical text, Crossan finds a rural Jewish Cynic with a message of social equality that upsets the existing hierarchical worldview.

When it comes to the big miracle, the Easter resurrection, Crossan announces emphatically what he assumes: "I do not think anyone, anywhere, at any time brings dead people back to life."[13] If resurrection, then, is a reported miracle that could not have happened as it is reported, what might its theological or confessional purpose be? Crossan answers: the conferral of leadership authority. At the redactional level, the biblical writers were countering the historical Jesus' original egalitarianism by establishing a hierarchy. To show this, Crossan places together for shared analysis a number of miracles he dubs "nature miracles": Jesus' Easter resurrection, walking on water, the surplus of fish, and the meal miracles, such as the feeding of the five thousand or Luke's postresurrection breakfast on the beach. These all belong together, he avers. According to Crossan, the "nature miracles of Jesus are actually creedal statements about ecclesiastical authority, although they all have as their background Jesus' resurrectional victory over death, which is, of course, the supreme nature miracle."[14]

These nature miracles appear not at the original or historical level but only at the transmissional or redactional levels. As later redactions, they confer authority on apostolic leadership. The "very early traditions about a resurrectional and ritualized meal of bread and fish involving Jesus and the believing *community* as a whole" suggest that "the Eucharistic presence of the Risen Lord" were "without any discriminating emphasis on leadership in general or on any one leader in particular."[15] The problem with the apparition accounts of the resurrected Jesus is that they conferred individual authority on individual persons and thereby justified for the developing church its clerical hierarchy. From Scripture onward, a male priest presides at the eucharistic table and the women serve. Jesus' original egalitarianism has disappeared. That is the net impact of the nature miracles, including the appearances of the risen Lord.

No resurrection occurred at level one, the original or historical level. Is the report of a resurrection a lie? Crossan wrestles with the idea of the Bible as a lie. He elects to avoid using that term. Rather, he says, the "*words and deeds* of Jesus were updated to speak to new situations and problems, new communities and crises. They were adopted, they were adapted, they were invented, they were created."[16] What eventually develops over time from the adoption and adaptation process is a resurrection community of believers who intend to continue beyond Jesus' death what he embodied while still alive. Crossan places Jesus' postresurrection appearance story in Luke 24:13-33 in the representative role: "Resurrected life and risen vision appear as offered shelter and shared meal. Resurrection is not enough. You will need scripture and eucharist, tradition and table, community and justice; otherwise, divine presence remains unrecognized and human eyes remain unopened."[17]

N. T. Wright

Like Crossan, N. T. Wright understands his work to be that of historical study. Wright, too, penetrates behind the layers of textual tradition to find the original or historical accounts of Jesus in their preconfessional or pretheological state. By asking a focal question—just what must have happened for the early Christian church to come into existence?—he looks for an answer that a historian can embrace.

Why did the early Christian church come into existence? Wright answers: "The *only* possible reason why early Christianity began and took the shape it did is that the tomb really was empty and that people really did meet Jesus, alive again. . . . The best historical explanation for all these phenomena is that Jesus was indeed bodily raised from the dead."[18] Wright's conclusion is his thesis: "The combination of empty tomb and appearances of the living Jesus forms a set of circumstances which is itself *both necessary and sufficient* for the rise of early Christian belief. Without these phenomena, we cannot explain why this belief came into existence, and took the shape it did. With them, we can explain it exactly and precisely."[19]

Wright is unhappy with what he calls the "dominant paradigm" that reigns among biblical historians of the present era. It is a paradigm that he himself utterly rejects. Referring to the paradigm he plans to shift, Wright describes it this way: (1) in the ancient Jewish context, "resurrection" had no one stable meaning and did not necessarily imply a real body leaving a real tomb; (2) the earliest Christian account of the resurrection, Paul's, did not affirm a "bodily" resurrection but proposed a "more spiritual" view; (3) the earliest Christians believed that Jesus had been exalted or glorified, and at first they used the language of "resurrection" to denote that belief; (4) the resurrection accounts in the Gospels are later inventions designed to bolster this confessional belief; (5) appearances of Jesus are best understood in terms of Paul's conversion experience, which itself is to be explained as a subjective "religious" experience; and (6) whatever became of Jesus' body (which may not have even been buried), it was certainly not "resuscitated" nor was it "raised from the dead" in the literal way that the Gospel stories seem to imply. In summary, the "dominant paradigm" assumes that Paul, with his "spiritual" view of the resurrection, is our earliest and most reliable witness, and that the Gospels, with their stories of an empty tomb and appearances by a visible, tangible Jesus, are late and unreliable.[20]

Wright's own counterproposal is as follows: (1) from the very earliest days, Christians shared stories of both the empty tomb and of appearances of the resurrected Jesus, and those early oral stories were very similar to the ones we now have in written form in our Gospels; (2) Paul, far from offering a different, more spiritual view of Jesus' resurrection, is actually summarizing those early stories in the opening verses of 1 Corinthians 15 and elsewhere, and his great contribution was to provide, not a different story, but a theological way of thinking about those traditional stories, already well known in his day: "The gospel stories are not dependent on Paul. . . . Irrespective of when the gospels reached their final form, the strong probability is that the Easter stories they contain go back to genuinely early oral tradition."[21]

Here is the contrast in a nutshell. Whereas the dominant paradigm contends that the early church created first the stories of the appearances and then those of the empty tomb, Wright contends that the empty tomb combined with the appearances created the church.

On the particular question regarding the historicity of the empty tomb and Gospel appearance narratives as raised by the dominant paradigm, Wright and Crossan would disagree. Whereas Crossan sees the synoptic and Johannine resurrection accounts as late, at the third level, Wright sees them as early, at the first level. Whereas Crossan declares them fictional creations, Wright grants them historical status. Wright states: "Crossan traces the origins of resurrection stories themselves to an educated, middle-class scribal movement which developed away from the pure, early peasant roots of Jesus himself. . . . The resurrection narratives are thus declared worthless as history: they are projected politics, and the politics (what is more) of the wrong sort of people, the wicked educated scribes instead of the noble virtuous peasants. . . . It looks as though Crossan is saying it can't be done when he means that it shouldn't be."[22] Such argumentation is unsatisfactory to Wright.

Crossan, as we saw earlier, does not believe anybody has risen or will rise from the dead. Wright concedes that this was also the assumption made by New Testament Christians: "*The fact that dead people do not ordinarily rise is itself part of early Christian belief*, not an objection to it. The early Christians insisted that what had happened to Jesus was precisely something new; was, indeed, the start of a whole new mode of existence, a new creation."[23] The methodological issue at stake is whether the kind of assumption Crossan makes becomes a nonnegotiable when evaluating the historical evidence. Crossan appears to be applying Ernst Troeltsch's principle of analogy—that is, because he has himself not observed a dead person rising, he argues by analogy that it is not plausible to argue that Jesus or anybody else could have risen in the past. Wright will allow the historical evidence to override this use of analogy: "It is precisely the uniqueness of the rise of the early church that forces us to say: never mind analogies, what happened?"[24]

The concept of resurrection with which the early Christian community worked did not derive from the surrounding pagan cultures, for no precedents for what became Christian belief can be found in those contexts. Rather, Wright describes the distinctively Christian belief in resurrection as a mutation, or set of mutations, in the evolving Jewish view. The mutations are identifiable: (1) resurrection moves to the center of Christian belief, whereas it had been more marginal in previous Jewish thought; (2) the Christians sharpened a previously vague notion by emphasizing physical immortality; (3) virtually all early Christians held the same understanding, demonstrating a sense of clarity regarding the idea; (4) the resurrection event becomes split into two stages—stage one, which began with Jesus at Easter, and stage two, which will include the promised general resurrection; (5) use of the term *resurrection* in both literal and metaphorical ways; and (6) attachment of the idea of death and resurrection to the concept of the Messiah, leading to a hermeneutical retrieval of Old Testament textual anticipations of death and resurrection. Wright surmises that only a startling event such as the Easter resurrection of Jesus could have produced this set of beliefs.

Wright, like Crossan, is aware of the political significance of Jesus. They both agree that humanly constructed hierarchies and systems of domination are antithetical to the kingdom of God associated with Jesus. The two scholars differ, however, on where they locate that significance. Crossan locates it in commensality, in the affirmation of peasant egalitarianism during Jesus' own lifetime that was continued by his disciples following his death. Wright, in contrast, locates the political significance in the Easter resurrection. The reality of resurrection of the body means that rulers cannot use the threat of death to enforce their dominion. The resurrection is testimony that God will overthrow the bullies and dictators of human oppression. Curiously, Wright places the earthly rulers in league with scholars of the dominant paradigm and rejects both: "No wonder the Herods, the Caesars and the Sadducees of this world, ancient and modern, were and are eager to rule out all possibility of actual resurrection. They are, after all, staking a counter-claim on the real world. It is the real world that the tyrants and bullies (including intellectual and cultural tyrants and bullies) try to rule by force, only to discover that in order to do so they have to quash all rumours of resurrection, rumours that would imply that their greatest weapons, death and deconstruction, are not after all omnipotent."[25]

Prolepsis

What does resurrection look like? A metaphor for the political ascendancy of Israel? Plato's disembodied soul? The rise of faith in the enduring community? Wright, offering an exposition of what the early church believed, says it is a *bodily* resurrection, first for Jesus and then for the rest of us: "Early Christianity was a 'resurrection' movement through and through, and . . . indeed, it stated much more precisely what exactly 'resurrection' involved (it meant going through death and out into a new kind of bodily existence beyond, and it was happening in two stages, with Jesus first and everyone else later); second, . . . though the literal 'resurrection' of which the early Christians spoke remained firmly in the future, it coloured and gave shape to present Christian living as well."[26]

The anticipation of new creation that affects present living as well brings up the issue of prolepsis. This is not a term Wright exploits, yet as a theological concept it moves us from the basic historical experience with Jesus to the eschatological significance or meaning of Jesus: "The heart and centre of it all, then, is the defeat of death in the future, based on the proleptic defeat inflicted in the resurrection of Jesus himself; or, to put it another way, it is the final completion of the 'age to come', which was inaugurated, in the midst of the 'present evil age', through the Messiah's death and resurrection."[27] With prolepsis, we are understanding the Easter resurrection of Jesus as a prefiguration of the advent of the eschatological new creation. This is a theological judgment, already present in the New Testament. It is built right into the meaning of the history of Jesus.

Robert H. Smith fears that Wright, along with Crossan and the Jesus Seminar, truncates his exegesis by limiting his questions to whether certain things happened or not. Wright does not read the evangelists as theologians. He does not ask about Matthew's theology of the resurrection nor that of Mark, Luke, or John. He does not ask how the particular resurrection narrative we find in each Gospel functions within that Gospel. In the Gospel narratives, Smith writes, "the evangelists explore multiple layers of meanings of the resurrection. . . . Resurrection faith is something more than 'believing that the tomb is empty and he has appeared alive.'"[28]

Regardless of this criticism, what Wright is after is the earliest stratum or level. He prefers to date the bare sources employed by the Gospels as early, as pre-Pauline. At this first level, these accounts are not quite ready to make the connection between Jesus' Easter resurrection and our future resurrection, at least to the degree we would find in Paul's interpretation, where Jesus at Easter is the first fruits of those of us having fallen asleep (1 Cor. 15:20). If not yet with a fully developed Pauline eschatology, then the historical Jesus was immediately understood with at least a proto-eschatology. Though not absent at the historical beginning, it takes a somewhat more developed form by the time we get to the theologies of Matthew, Mark, Luke, and John.

Wright recognizes the need to move beyond the strictly historical judgment regarding what the early church believed and why they believed it. What comes next is the question, what does this mean? What is its theological meaning? To move from history to theology, Wright recaptures the hermeneutical distinction between referent and meaning. By "referent," he refers to the historical judgment that Jesus rose bodily from the dead. By "meaning," he draws out its significance, namely, Jesus is the Son of God: "The resurrection, in other words, declares that Jesus really is God's Son: not only in the sense that he is the Messiah, though Paul certainly intends that here, not only in the sense that he is the world's true lord, though Paul intends that too, but also in the sense that he is the one in whom the living God, Israel's God, has become personally present in the world, has become one of the human creatures that were made from the beginning in the image of this same God."[29]

Might we have a small hermeneutical problem here worth pointing out? Is Wright working with the assumption that the historian can begin with the referent (historical fact) and then add the meaning (theological interpretation)? Almost, though not quite. To tease the issue out further, we might ask: do we have access to the referent independently of the meaning? Do we have the luxury of pouring theological meaning on top of a historical event, like hot fudge over ice cream? No, we do not, because our only access to the referent is through a text already laden with meaning. Or, to put it another way, the only Easter resurrection of Jesus we know is the eschatological event.

Hence, if we ask, "Did it happen?" we still need to ask, "What is the 'it' that happened?" The "it" in the case of the Easter resurrection is the proleptic or anticipatory instantiation of the eschatological kingdom of God.

The Birth of the Church

If we ask both scholars the same question—how do you explain the rise or the birth of the Christian church?—they give quite different answers. John Dominic Crossan answers: "The birth of Christianity is the interaction between the historical Jesus and his first companions and the continuation of that relationship despite his execution."[30] N. T. Wright answers: "The proposal that Jesus was bodily raised from the dead possesses unrivaled power to explain the historical data at the heart of early Christianity."[31] For Crossan, Jesus was executed and remained dead, while his followers provided continuity between the pre-executed Jesus and the birth of the early church. For Wright, the executed Jesus rose bodily from the dead, and this historical fact accounts for the rise of faith in the early church.

Crossan, curiously, also uses the image of embodiment to stress the extradoctrinal life of the early Christian community. In what appears to be the Crossan credo, he writes: "Justice is always about bodies and lives, not just about words and ideas. Resurrection does not mean, simply, that the spirit or soul of Jesus lives on in the world. And neither does it mean, simply, that the companions or followers of Jesus live on in the world. *It must be the embodied life that remains powerfully efficacious in this world.* I recognize those claims as an historian, and I believe them as a Christian."[32] Does Crossan mean by "embodiment" what Wright would mean? Not quite. Wright is concerned about the literal body of the person of Jesus emerging from the tomb and appearing to his followers, whereas Crossan is concerned about the metaphorical body of Christian believers.

Did the first Christians introduce something new? Or did everybody in the ancient world believe in resurrection? Crossan asserts that the early Christian claim—namely, that Jesus rose from the dead—was commonplace in the context of the Jewish and Roman world within which the Christian mission took place. What happened to Jesus was not unique but ordinary: "Visions of risen corpses or apparitions of resurrected bodies are not uniquely special. . . . I draw this hypothesis: the birth of Christianity is the interaction between the historical Jesus and his first companions and the continuation of that relationship despite his execution."[33] The logic seems to be this: if resurrections were an everyday news item in the ancient Roman Empire, and if nothing unique is attached to the report of what happened to Jesus, then reports of his resurrection are insufficient to explain the birth of Christianity. What can explain this, then, must be the commitments of Jesus' companions prior to his execution.

Crossan's historical judgment is disputable on three counts and amendable on another count. First, other historians do not picture the early missionary context as one in which widespread reports of resurrections similar to that of Jesus were common. Quite to the contrary, the early Christian missionaries confronted misunderstanding and even conflict. In her history of Christian theology, Margaret Miles identifies a conflict regarding the role of the body in claims of immortality: "Belief in the resurrection of body seemed at best misguided, at worst an ignorant superstition, a confusion of two very different beliefs, immortality of the soul and resurrection of body. . . . Against the Platonic teaching that the soul is naturally immortal, Christians insisted that immortality of the soul was a gift from God, and that it was insufficient without the resurrection of the body."[34] In sum, what the early Christians were saying about Jesus and about our future did not fit with widespread beliefs about what happens after we die.

The second count is that Crossan's reconstructed historical Jesus is divorced from the message of salvation, especially the power of salvation exercised in the Easter resurrection. This seems arbitrary and unnecessary. The Jesus of the Bible is inextricably tied to the message of salvation, so the burden of proof lies with one who wishes to cut the tie. In Arland Hultgren's account of the birth of the early church, the historical resurrection and its salvific significance come in a single package: "For the earliest faith community, which included disciples of the earthly Jesus, Jesus' death and resurrection would have been not only the most memorable event of his fate, but also the event that marked the turn of the ages, beginning a new era in which sin and death had been surpassed, and righteousness and life were gifts of God through the Spirit."[35] This means that the historical Jesus Crossan constructs is an abstraction, a figure abstracted from his embeddedness in a community claiming to have experienced Christ's saving power.

Third, Crossan seems to reverse causal logic. He argues that the confessional bias of the written biblical tradition superimposed a theology of resurrection on a history without a resurrection. One might ask: from whence did these writers get their confessional bias? What precipitated it? Could it have been reports of Jesus' Easter resurrection? Günther Bornkam recognizes, as does Crossan, that the Gospel accounts differ from one another and are "stamped" with each author's faith commitments. Yet, this observation does not compromise the causal logic: "The appearances of the risen Christ and the word of his witnesses have in the first place given rise to this faith."[36] Luke Timothy Johnson asks Crossan rhetorically: "If the resurrection appearance accounts are mere legitimations for the authority of leaders within the movement, how do we account for the rise of the movement in the first place?"[37]

In addition to these three criticisms, we might amend what Crossan says on another count—that is, the need to apprehend more fully the biblical meaning of Jesus' Easter resurrection in light of its original eschatological horizon, a horizon within which we today still need to explicate the commitments of the Christian faith.[38] At which level do we find the eschatological meaning, the first or the third? Crossan says the third or redactional level, whereas Wright places it at the first level of the original experience with Jesus. Wright observes: "The prediction of 'Jesus' apocalyptic return' occurs in the first stratum, and is multiply attested, but is regarded [by Crossan] as 'from the later Jesus tradition' rather than from Jesus himself, because Crossan has decided that such 'apocalyptic' material is uncharacteristic of Jesus."[39]

What the systematic theologian needs is a two-directional hermeneutic. The first direction is backward, back from the biblical text toward speculation about the history that must have given rise to the text as we read it. The second direction is forward toward our contemporary context, toward an explication of the Christian faith within the modern, post-Enlightenment horizon of meaning. Both directions start from the same location, from what Scripture says. Both history and explication are interpretations of Scripture. The horizon of the future plays a significant role in both.

Wolfhart Pannenberg

The message of Jesus, which included the announcement of the coming kingdom of God, was anticipatory. It anticipated the prophesied messianic rule of God and the advent of the new creation.[40] Jesus' commensality, to use Crossan's apt term, combined with Jesus' healing miracles anticipated eschatological commensality and healing. The embodiment of the promised future in advance is what is meant by the term *prolepsis*. Munich systematic theologian Wolfhart Pannenberg emphasizes the pre-realization of the eschatological promise: "The ministry of Jesus shared with prophecy the character of an anticipation, but not only as in prophecy and apocalyptic in the sense of mere pre-*cognition*, but, so to say, as a pre-*realization* of the future, as its proleptic dawning."[41]

Built into the original meaning of Jesus' Easter resurrection is the dawning of the general or universal resurrection previously anticipated in apocalyptic prophecies. Whether Jesus' Jewish listeners believed or disbelieved in the apocalyptic vision of resurrection, they understood it; and they could understand why what happened to Jesus on Easter would be interpreted within this horizon. Jesus' resurrection is the "first fruits" of "those who have died" (1 Cor. 15:20). What was expected for all of us has already happened individually to the person of Jesus: "Jesus' expectation of the speedy realization of the eschatological reality did not simply fail. It was fulfilled, and thus confirmed, though only in his own person. . . . The general human destiny has occurred in Jesus—if he *really was* resurrected from the dead."[42]

Note how Pannenberg makes his theological assertion contingent on a historical one: "If he *really* was resurrected from the dead." Theological commitment is dependent on the historicity of the founding event, Jesus' personal resurrection. Faith is dependent on history. Faith, even though it is a subjective appropriation of Christian belief, is not reducible to its subjective character; it requires grounding in the objective realm of fact. This means, among other things, that a historical judgment against the authenticity of the biblical claim regarding Jesus' resurrection would undermine Christian belief.

For Pannenberg, this means theology requires a reintegration of fact and meaning, what Wright calls "referent" and "meaning." Pannenberg writes: "Such splitting up of historical consciousness into a detection of facts and an evaluation of them . . . is intolerable to Christian faith, not only because the message of the resurrection of Jesus and of God's revelation in him necessarily becomes merely subjective interpretation, but also because it is the reflection of an outmoded and questionable historical method. It is based on the futile aim of the positivist historians to ascertain bare facts without meaning in history. . . . Against this we must reinstate today the original unity of facts and their meaning."[43]

A systematic theologian who thinks like this would find it impossible to proceed to explicate the Christian faith if Crossan is right in denying the historicity of biblical claims about the Easter Jesus; the theologian might also find it difficult, though manageable, to proceed if Wright is correct in separating historical fact from its meaning. While waiting for the jury to come in with a verdict, the theologian could take a risk and proceed on the assumption of historicity. This is what Pannenberg is willing to do: "Now let us assume that the historical question concerning the resurrection of Jesus has been decided positively, then the meaning of this event as God's final revelation is not something that must be added to it; rather, this is the original meaning inherent in that event within its own context of history and tradition."[44]

Is this a safe assumption? Gary Habermas would say so: "My position is that Jesus' resurrection is best considered a historical event of the past. . . . Most critical scholars, whether conservative or liberal, agree that the resurrection of Jesus is the key to the Christian faith."[45] If I understand Habermas correctly, he is saying that the theological meaning still requires independent historical judgment to support it, and that it is safe for the theologian to assume history will be supportive.

Even if it is a relatively safe assumption, it still incorporates a historical judgment. Historical judgments are at best probable judgments, not apodictic. This indicates that theological explications based on historical judgments are hypothetical. This should not be surprising. In principle, all faith commitments are hypothetical, contingent on their confirmation by God. As Pannenberg writes: "Anticipation therefore always involves hypothesis."[46] So, it is necessary for the systematic theologian to proceed with the explication of the meaning of Jesus' resurrection while incorporating the probable status of its historical foundation.

What is the meaning of Jesus' Easter resurrection? This is the theological significance of the Easter resurrection of Jesus according to Pannenberg: if Jesus has been raised, then (1) the end of the world has begun; (2) God himself has confirmed the pre-Easter activity of Jesus; (3) Jesus is the expected Son of man; (4) God is ultimately revealed in Jesus; (5) the universality of Israel's God motivates the gentile mission; and (6) Jesus' words and appearances should be interpreted as having the same content.[47] The methodological point is that both for the early oral and written tradition and for people of Christian faith today, the historical report of Jesus' Easter resurrection comes prepackaged, so to speak, with the eschatological promise of new creation and the advent of God's everlasting kingdom. Both this referent and the meaning of this historical event are contingent on their eschatological confirmation or disconfirmation.

Panennberg explicates this systematically by arguing that the proleptic events surrounding the historical Jesus and the eschatological event of new creation are a single reality, a single act by an eternal God within a temporal world:

> The coming again of Christ will be the completion of the work of the Spirit that began in the incarnation and with the resurrection of Jesus. From the standpoint of eternity we have here one and the same event because the incarnation is already the inbreaking of the future of God, the entry of eternity into time. For us, however, confession of the incarnation has its basis in Jesus' resurrection, and only at his return will debate concerning the reality of the Easter event be at an end and will that reality definitively and publicly come into force, for the resurrection of Jesus is a proleptic manifestation of the reality of the new, eschatological life of salvation in Jesus himself.[48]

Only in the future will we know the past for certain.

A New Law of Nature?

Crossan admits that he does not believe that dead people rise from the dead, and this must apply to the historical Jesus as well. Wright observes that this was the general belief in the ancient world of the New Testament: dead people do not rise from the dead, at least not in the way Jesus is described to have risen. What we have learned about the laws of nature during the era of modern biology only confirms our expectation that dead people stay dead. If our universe is in fact a closed causal nexus governed by the inexorable natural laws we have come to learn, then no exceptions to this rule can be rationally allowed. Troeltsch's principle of analogy must obtain: because people who die remain dead, it follows that Jesus must have remained dead as well. So will all human beings in the future.

Yet, if the God of Israel described by the Bible exists, then the laws of nature as we have come to know them are not the final word. They are not ultimate. The laws of nature belong to the creation, placed here by the Creator. In the event that the divine creator decides to change them, we can expect surprises.

Theologians working with a Humean definition of miracle would look on the Easter resurrection of Jesus as a moment when God abrogated the existing laws of nature. But this misses the eschatological import. It misses the intrinsic connection between what happened historically on Easter and what the Scriptures promise will happen in the eschatological future, namely, the advent of the new creation. The biblically envisioned new creation cannot operate exhaustively with the laws of nature as we currently know them. The creator will need to do some re-creating.

My colleague in Berkeley, Robert John Russell, founder and director of the Center for Theology and the Natural Sciences at the Graduate Theological Union, has been inspired by Pannenberg. He views the Easter resurrection of Jesus as "the first instantiation of a new law of nature," or FINLON for short. Because Christian theology posits an eschatology complete with a promised new creation yet to come, theologians can conceive of a world guided by laws of nature different from the ones we currently have.[49]

In order to open us up to perceive and acknowledge the possibility of FINLON, Russell critically suspends two philosophical assumptions made by scientists and by most historians, namely, analogy and nomological universality. According to the principle of analogy, the past and future should look like the present. This means that, based on analogy from observations about the natural world we make now, we can make judgments about past events and can project that future people will die and remain dead. This needs critique. If in the near or distant future God acts to transform and redeem this world so that dead people rise, it would be unpredictable according to the principle of analogy.

Underlying analogy is nomological universality. According to the principle of nomological universality, the same laws that govern the past and present will govern the future as well. This too needs critique. Again, should God the creator re-create the world so that different laws obtain—such as wolves living with lambs and the elimination of death—then existing laws would no longer apply. The law that dead people stay dead would no longer apply. We are now ready to ask about the truth status of the Pauline stratum of the New Testament where Jesus is described as the "first fruits of those having fallen asleep" (1 Cor. 15:20). On Easter, God inaugurated a new law of nature, one that we will see become universal at some point in the future.

Cambridge physicist and theologian John Polkinghorne would agree: "The new creation represents the transformation of that universe when it enters freely into a new and closer relationship with its Creator, so that it becomes a totally sacramental world, suffused with the divine presence." This suffusion of divine presence translates into healing. Polkinghorne writes: "Its process can be free from suffering, for it is conceivable that the divinely ordained laws of nature appropriate to a world making itself through its own evolving history should give way to a differently constituted form of 'matter', appropriate to a universe 'freely returned' from independence to an existence of integration with its Creator."[50]

Conclusion

The central point of this essay has been that an understanding of Jesus' Easter resurrection entails an understanding of its inextricable tie to the eschatological new creation that has been promised by God. The empty tomb reports and appearance reports come to us in Scripture already interpreting Jesus' historical resurrection as the dawning of the new reality of God's kingdom. The resurrection is not the resurrection without the eschatological component.

Even so, asking historical questions is our responsibility. Did Jesus really rise from the tomb? Is it necessary for Jesus to have been raised from the tomb and to appear to his disciples in order to explain the rise of the early church and the transcription of the Bible? Crossan answers "no" to each of these; Wright answers "yes."

It is my judgment that if Crossan should prove to be correct, then the faith built on an explication of Scripture would be in vain. If Wright is correct, the trust people of faith place in Scripture would be provided with supplemental, though not apodictic, support. The theological task would be wounded by Crossan, healed by Wright.

Scholars seem to agree that what is meant by resurrection in reference to Easter is not the simple return of a corpse to ordinary life; nor is it the escape of Jesus' soul from the body as it was for Socrates. Built into the very definition of resurrection is the prophetic expectation of Israel's Messiah, the coming of the kingdom of God, and the rising of the dead into the new creation. This expected transformation included the expectation of divine action, of a decisive transformation that only God could bring about. Easter could not help but mean that this man, Jesus, was raised by God as part of this eschatological transformation. Or, better, Easter is a prolepsis of the eschatological event yet to come. This is what is meant by the historical event of the resurrection told with its significance.

Now, this claim may be true or false. If Crossan could demonstrate (rather than assume) that the empty tomb stories and the appearance stories are false, then we would have something that disconfirms the Christian faith. Or, should history roll on interminably without any eschatological divine action, then this would disconfirm the Christian faith. In the latter case, it would matter little or nothing at all even if

Jesus himself were to rise from the dead if this event is not connected to the eschatological resurrection of all of us. What is at stake is the comprehensive Christian claim, not merely the details surrounding the historical person of Jesus.

Looking backward at a historical reconstruction of Jesus is a form of speculation. Looking forward and preconstructing a hypothetical picture of resurrection is a form of speculation. This is what Robert John Russell provides. Like Crossan and Wright, Russell interprets Scripture and draws a speculative landscape of the world to come. The systematic theologian needs both history and eschatology, two forms of constructive interpretation of the one Bible.

– Appendix –

BODILY-RESURRECTION FAITH

John Dominic Crossan

"To speak of someone 'going up to heaven' by no means implied that the person concerned had (a) become a primitive space-traveller and (b) arrived, by that means, at a different location within the present space-time universe. We should not allow the vivid, indeed lurid, language of the Middle Ages, or of many hymns and prayers which use the word 'heaven' to denote, it seems, a far-off location within the cosmos we presently inhabit, to make us imagine that first-century Jews thought literalistically in that way too. Some indeed may have done so; there is no telling what things people will believe; but we should not imagine that the early Christian writers thought like that."
N. T. Wright, *The Resurrection of the Son of God*

Mode and Meaning in the Emmaus Story

In the epigraph, Tom emphasizes, first, that "early Christian writers" knew quite well the distinction between literal and metaphorical language, second, that they took such phases as "going up to heaven" or "heaven" itself metaphorically rather than literally, and third, that it was only later misinterpretation that took such phrases literally rather than metaphorically.

For this dialogue, I use the term *mode* to distinguish between one type of language that is literal, factual, actual, or historical (Jesus is the peasant from Nazareth) and another type of language that is metaphorical, fictional, symbolic, or parabolic (Jesus is the Lamb of God). Problems arise, of course, not so much in abstract theory as in practical application. In which mode is this given statement or that cited story to be placed? And, if it be in metaphorical mode, what is the metaphor's referent and what does it mean to assert? I insist, by the way, that a metaphorical statement or a parabolic story may have a very, very concrete referent in, say, a person's character, a group's identity, a movement's program, or an empire's destiny. I exemplify with the Emmaus story in Luke 24:13-32.

A couple, presumably male and female and possibly husband and wife, since with standard Mediterranean chauvinistic politeness only the male is identified, encounter Jesus as they leave Jerusalem on what we call Easter Sunday. Unlike all other such risen apparitions, Jesus is disguised as a normal stranger. Their hearts, as they said, burned within them as he opened the Scriptures to reveal therein his destiny (24:32) but it was only in the breaking of bread that "their eyes were opened, and they recognized him; and he vanished from their sight" (24:31). That climactic revelation only happened because of these preceding verses: "As they came near the village to which they were going, he walked ahead as if he were going on. But they urged him strongly, saying, 'Stay with us, because it is almost evening and the day is now nearly over.' So he went in to stay with them" (24:28-29). Only when the stranger was invited to share their meal in what was presumably their home was he revealed as the Risen Lord. Jesus opened his Scriptures for them and they opened their table for him.

Think now of two routes for commentary on that story. First, we could argue whether it was intended and/or should be interpreted as fact or fiction, history or parable. And we could stop at that discussion of *mode*, never get beyond it, and neither side might change its initial position. Or, second, we could finish that debate or even bracket it entirely and move on to discuss *meaning*. If you take it historically, what does it mean for you? If you take it as absolutely literal, why did the Risen Lord decide to act that way and not some other way with those people on that day? In fact, the more literally you take it and the more fully you believe that Jesus could do anything he wanted, the more you must ponder why he did this rather than that, appeared in this rather than some other way. If you take it metaphorically, what does it mean for you? If you consider it a parable, what is its intention, purpose, effect, teaching? Could it, would it, should it be that in either mode the meaning is the same?

APPENDIX: BODILY-RESURRECTION FAITH

Even a perfectly valid discussion about *mode* cannot negate an equally or even more valid discussion about *meaning*. But, first, an argument over mode often unconsciously precludes or consciously avoids the challenge of meaning. And, second, focusing exclusively or even primarily on mode often ends by hardening actual disagreement on that issue rather than exploring beyond it into potential agreement on meaning. We may certainly debate on whether that Emmaus story was intended and/or should be interpreted as historical or parabolic, but on either option and in either case, it challenges us beyond mode to meaning: Do we or do we not believe that the Risen Lord is present to us, initially, when we search and find him in the Scriptures and, ultimately, when we invite him in the stranger to share our world as one that belongs not to us but to God?

Go back, for a second, from parables about Jesus to parables by Jesus.[1] Having heard the Good Samaritan story from Jesus, we could argue forever on whether it was factual history or fictional parable. And that concentration on *mode* allows us to avoid the challenge of *meaning*. Which is: Would you or would you not save your cultural alien found dying in a ditch? Or, better: Would you or would you not accept that your cultural alien might save you found dying in a ditch?

Over a decade ago, I said, "Emmaus never happened. Emmaus always happens."[2] That was simply a terse summary of my view that the story was a parable intended as permanent challenge. But the first half of that aphorism was about *mode*, the latter half about *meaning*. And, in the following treatment of the resurrection of Jesus, I will always try, first, to distinguish mode from meaning, and, second, where there is terminal disagreement on mode, to at least insist on raising the question of meaning. Might it be possible for what this forum terms evangelical and non-evangelical scholars to bracket the irreconcilable debate on mode and meet instead on the field of meaning? Maybe we can no longer afford the luxury of perpetual controversy on mode and perpetual postponement of meaning among Christians even as God's world is more and more taken over by injustice and violence.

The Origin and Claim of Bodily-Resurrection Faith

I consider the origin of faith in the general bodily resurrection, first, within Jewish tradition and, second, within that pre-existing tradition, the origin of faith in Jesus' resurrection for Christian Judaism. In that former section I think I am in substantial agreement with Tom's position.[3] In the latter section I add some major qualifications which, in my impertinent opinion, are *amicus curiae* briefs that he could accept within his own principles and should accept to strengthen his own views. It is only after we clarify the situation on historical origin that we can move to the more profound questions of linguistic mode and theological meaning.[4]

In Jewish Tradition

COSMIC TRANSFORMATION. If your faith tells you that this world belongs to and is ruled by a just divinity and your experience tells you that the world belongs to and is ruled by an unjust humanity, utopia or *eschatology* becomes almost inevitable as the reconciliation of that global discord. God, you sing, will overcome, someday. God will act, indeed must act, to make new and holy a world grown old in evil. Eschatology is not, positively not, about the end of this time-space cosmos but rather an end of cosmic time-space evil and impurity, injustice, violence, and oppression. It is not about the evacuation of earth for God's heaven but about the divine transfiguration of God's earth. It is not about the destruction but about the transformation of God's world here below.

As one ever-more-powerful empire after another took over cosmic control, the imminence of God's *justification* as global *making-just* here below, the proximity of God's Great Cosmic Clean-Up, became more and more fervently proclaimed and expected. An *apocalypse* is a revelation about that eschatological event, and while, strictly speaking, it could apply to any aspect or element of it, *apocalyptic eschatology* usually refers to the imminence of God's transformation of this world here below from one of violent justice to one of nonviolent justice. It never refers, *in our sense*, to the imminent end of the world as such. We, of course, can easily imagine that scenario because *we* can do it already in about five different ways: atomic, biological, chemical, demographic, ecological—and we are only up to *e*!

That apocalyptic eschatology is the absolutely inescapable background and presupposition for Jewish faith in the general bodily resurrection. It was to be the climax or grand finale of the process whereby the Creator made just and holy a world become unholy and unjust. But why was it important to include that element?

BODILY RESURRECTION. There was both a general and specific reason. The former had to do with the transfiguration of nature, the latter with the vindication of martyrdom.

The *general* reason was because the renewal of an all-good creation here below upon this earth demanded it. How could you have a renewed creation without renewed bodies? Any full-service apocalyptic eschatology has three levels of transformation: the *physical* world must become a place of unlabored fertility and unworked prosperity; the *animal* world must become a place of vegan serenity and feral harmony; and the *social* world must become a place of nonviolent justice and global peace. In that or any other such utopian context, therefore, I do not find Tom's chosen word for the risen body of Jesus, namely, "transformed physicality" or "transphysicality"[5] any more surprising than the necessary transphysicality of any eschatological consummation. For example, those lambs lying down with wolves in Isaiah 11:6 or those technicolored rams in Virgil's *Fourth Eclogue* 42–45 would surely be transphysical ones.

The *specific* reason was the problem of martyrdom during the Seleucid persecution in the 160s B.C.E. The question was not about their survival but about God's justice faced specifically with the battered, tortured, and executed *bodies* of martyrs. I agree with Tom that, in the context of the Syrian religious persecution of the 160s B.C.E., Daniel 12:2-3 refers "to concrete, bodily resurrection . . . not, of itself, an 'otherworldly' idea, but a very much 'this-worldly' one" since in a "renewed bodily life, God will give everlasting life to some and everlasting contempt to others," will give life to "the righteous who have suffered martyrdom on the one hand" and contempt to "their torturers and murderers on the other.[6] I also agree with Tom that, in response to those same martyrs, 2 Maccabees (in contrast to 4 Maccabees!)

"provides far and away the clearest picture of the promise of resurrection anywhere in this period."[7] Since martyrdom is about *tortured bodies*, the justice of God requires *transfigured bodies* in the future for those *disfigured bodies* in the past.

In Christian Tradition

THIRD MUTATION. Faith in imminent eschatology was a first great mutation within Jewish covenantal faith, and bodily resurrection was a second great mutation within that first one. I agree, therefore, with Tom's standard description of Christian Judaism's faith in Jesus' resurrection as a "mutation" of general Jewish and specific Pharisaic faith.[8] That transformation was, as it were, a third and final mutation. This *Christian mutation proclaimed that the general bodily resurrection was not just imminent but had already begun with that of Jesus.* God's Great Clean-Up of cosmic violence and injustice had begun with Jesus' bodily resurrection. There was, in other words, no way that the term *resurrection* could have meant some privilege however transcendental for Jesus alone. *Resurrection* meant the general bodily resurrection and to apply that term to Jesus could only mean that the eschatological transformation of the world was not just imminent but had already started. That, of course, is why Paul can argue in either direction: no Jesus resurrection means no general resurrection, and no general resurrection means no Jesus resurrection (1 Cor. 15:12-13). It is hard to over-emphasize the breathtaking creativity and stunning originality of that claim, and I agree with Tom that its advent requires precise historical explanation.

TWOFOLD CAUSALITY. Throughout his book, Tom argues clearly that the only sufficient and necessary *historical* explanation for Christian Judaism's stunning mutation of Pharisaic Judaism's resurrection is twofold: the *historical* discovery of Jesus' empty tomb accompanied by the *historical* experience of Jesus' bodily presence.[9] In dissenting from that explanation, I do not for here and now debate the historicity of either Jesus' burial or the empty tomb's discovery. Instead, for here and now (*dato non concesso*, to be sure) *I take the Gospel stories of the empty tomb's discovery and of all those risen apparitions as historically factual in their entirety.*

APPENDIX: BODILY-RESURRECTION FAITH

Put negatively, however, I cannot see how Tom's twin conditions, even granting them their fullest historicity, can explain anything beyond believers concluding to an *absolutely unique assumption* or *extraordinary heavenly exaltation* of Jesus as Christ, Lord, and Son of God. They could certainly bring them to, say, Psalm 2, Psalm 110, or even Phil. 2:9-11, but I do not think (speaking historically) it would get them beyond exaltation to resurrection. At this point the two major theses of Tom's book contest one another. The more he correctly emphasizes the extraordinarily powerful swerve of Christian Judaism (the general resurrection is here!) from within to beyond Pharisaic Judaism (the general resurrection is near!) the more his twofold causality of empty tomb and risen apparition becomes inadequate as a historical explanation.

Put positively, one *more* condition was absolutely necessary and this is what is crucial for me. This missing condition is the historical Jesus' own proclamation that the kingdom of God was not just imminently future but already present, a proclamation that was not only individual vision but corporate program as his companions entered that kingdom by living as he did and thereby experiencing for themselves the power of its presence. My own answer to Tom's question about sufficient and necessary causality is that two conditions were indeed simultaneously necessary, but those two were (1) the historical Jesus' individual living and communal communicating of the kingdom as already present even if not yet fully consummated, and (2) appearances of that same Jesus after his death—the experiences summarized in 1 Corinthians 15 and presumed but totally reformulated in the Gospels' Easter stories. For the record and also for present discussion, I consider both those elements to be historical events.

For the record but not for present discussion, I consider that, first, the story of the empty-tomb discovery was created by Mark precisely to avoid any apparitions to the (by him) discredited outer Twelve or inner Three or, especially, Peter himself. And, second, the apparition stories now present in our gospels are about authority rather than apparition or, better, about authority by apparition. But, of course, both those conclusions point to original risen apparitions as taken absolutely for granted and I fully accept them as historical events even though details are now lost to us forever.

I do not focus our dialogue on eliminating the empty tomb from Tom's twosome (that's a minor matter for me) but rather on adding the communal experience of Jesus' already-present kingdom of God (that's the major matter for me). In basic summary, then, these are the two options:

1. Resurrection Faith =   Empty Tomb   + Risen Apparitions
2. Resurrection Faith =   Historical Jesus (±Empty Tomb) + Risen Apparitions

Tom's twosome, I repeat, could get you to an exaltation-surprise but not to a resurrection-mutation. In other words, Jesus' kingdom of God is isomorphic with Paul's Resurrection of Christ in that both proclaim in different theological language that God's Great Clean-Up has already begun.

COLLABORATIVE ESCHATON. A second stunningly original mutation follows immediately and almost inevitably from that first one. As long as eschatological transformation, general resurrection, and cosmic judgment were imagined as, say, a blinding moment of divine light, human cooperation could hardly be discussed except, of course, through preparatory prayer and persistent piety. But now, said Christian Judaism, all of that has been mutated from an instant of divine time to a period of human time. Eschaton and resurrection had already started and would proceed to their eventual consummation (soon, they thought, but they were off on that by two thousand years and counting). Similarly and consequently, an exclusively divine initiative had now mutated into an inclusively divine-human collaboration as believers were called to live the radical ethics of a new creation or a transformed life and thereby to co-create with God a nonviolent world of justice and peace. In one sense, Christian Judaism's eschaton-as-collaboration was even more stunningly original than its eschaton-as-process but it was probably also an inevitable corollary from it. That is why Jesus could tell his companions to go out and do exactly what he was doing: heal the sick, eat with those they healed, and announce that the kingdom of God had already started in that mutual sharing of spiritual (healing) and physical (eating) power. The coming of the kingdom meant, as the Lord's Prayer said, the doing of God's will on earth—and it had already begun. So also with Paul. It was not ecstasy but accuracy which made him declare in 1 Cor. 3:18 that "all of us, with unveiled faces, seeing the glory of the Lord as though reflected in a mirror, are being transformed into the same image from one degree of glory to another; for this comes from the Lord, the Spirit." That presumes, of course, that believers are *living* the resurrected life that incarnates the nonviolent God of justice and peace who was revealed in Christ. We are not waiting for God to act. God has already acted and is waiting for us to react, to collaborate, to cooperate, to get with the divine program.

I think that understanding of a collaborative eschaton, of a new creation, of a radical cosmic mutation from violence and injustice to nonviolence and justice, is a better way of describing the breathtaking challenge of Christian Judaism than either of the two ways in which Tom's book articulates it.

First, Tom's standard way of describing this mutation is to say that resurrection was *split into two parts*,[10] namely the past of the Jesus resurrection and the future of the general resurrection. Is that the best way to describe Christianity's intra-Pharisaic modification, innovation, or mutation? I would prefer to describe exactly that same phenomenon as *instant become process* or *moment becomes event* or any other way that holds *beginning, middle, and end*, or *initiation, continuation, and completion* together as one persistent process here below upon an earth in the process of divine justification (that is, finally making it just).

Second, following from that *split-into-two* interpretation of resurrection, Tom takes the twin poles of starting with the Jesus resurrection and ending with the general resurrection *literally* but in between resurrection is to be taken *metaphorically*. Throughout his book, Tom speaks repeatedly of "the metaphorical uses of 'resurrection', in relation to present Christian living."[11] But that Christian understanding of resurrection as literal → metaphorical → literal does not seem to me an appropriate model. I think the resurrection as redeeming human time rather than just ending it challenges us to take the entire process *as all literal or all metaphorical, and in either case the concrete referent is God's present justification of the world.* That is the ultimate claim made by the resurrection announcement of Christian Judaism. It proclaims, to put it clearly, accurately, and bluntly, that, at Easter, God's Cosmic Clean-Up has already begun. To repeat: *whether resurrection is taken all-literally or all-metaphorically,* it claims that something has literally started and is therefore literally present. If it only spoke of a future event, it would be, like all such future announcements, beyond proof or disproof. But, once you announce that something has begun (in this case, God's transfiguration of all creation), you must be able to show something. And Jesus or Paul would have accepted that challenge by saying: Come and see how our communities live. Come and see how God-in-us and we-in-God are transforming the world. Come and see how surprised we are at the way God is actually doing it!

The Mode and Meaning
of Bodily-Resurrection Faith

Ancients knew just as well as moderns the distinction between, say, myth and history, fable and parable, or literal and metaphorical language. In the abstract, all was clear, then and now. In fact, if you raise that issue with classicists, their answers tend to be dismissively truculent. Of course, they tend to say that the ancients knew that distinction just as well as we do. But my question is not an abstract and general one but a specific and particular one. My question is this: With regard to this or that given phenomenon, into which category was it placed? And the given phenomenon that interests me here is the dialectic between Christian resurrection theology and Roman imperial theology.

Resurrection—Mode and the Harrowing of Hell

If you read an earlier eschatological vision in, for example, Isaiah 11:1-9, it involves what I would call a *prospective* paradise on earth. That utopian consummation will be magnificent for some *future* world when it finally arrives, but it says nothing about the *past* at that moment (something actually true of most similar visions?). But, especially because of the Maccabean martyrs, the antecedents of what would become "Pharisaic" theology insisted on *retrospective* as well as *prospective* eschatology. Since this was not primarily about the survival of us but about the justice of God, that backlog of injustice could not be ignored.

This means for me that the harrowing (or robbing) of hell, the proclamation of liberation (not the preaching of a sermon!) to the righteous dead, must be taken much more seriously than Tom does. If a mutated "Pharisaic" theology started the general bodily resurrection with that of Jesus, it could not have announced an exclusively individual rather than an inclusively communal event. What about the bodies of the martyrs? Jesus, of course, did not rise as simply one among many but as the cause and liberator of "them that sleep." Nowhere, for example, is that proclaimed more beautifully than in the *Odes of Solomon* 42:21 where Jesus liberates the just from Sheol, proclaiming that "they are free and they are mine."

In a text of 738 pages, which only reaches the New Testament Gospels on page 584 and studies Tertullian, Irenaeus, Hippolytus, and Origen on pages 510–27 before Matthew, Mark, Luke, and John on pages 586–682, I would want more space given to that Christ-led but communal resurrection as the corporate first-fruits of God's Great Cosmic Clean-Up. Whether in hymn, narrative, image, or weird residual fragment (as in Matt. 27:52-53), that theology emphasizes most forcefully that Jesus' resurrection begins God's justification of an unjust world by transforming first the past and only then the future. It also makes impossible any interpretation of what happened to Jesus as supreme individual exaltation rather than initial corporate resurrection.

Somewhere between the Apostles' Creed and the Nicene Creed we lost the harrowing or robbing of hell. And, for me at least, it was one of the most serious losses from earliest Christian theology because it clearly emphasized that Jesus' resurrection was about God's justification of the world and not just about the exaltation of Jesus. No divine justice for the future would be credible without initial divine justice for the past, for the backlog of injustice already there, for all those in Sheol who had died for justice or from injustice. But it was, indeed, almost impossible to retain that communal resurrection of the just *and* Jesus's pre-ascension (but only pre-ascension, of course) apparitions to the apostles. Matthew 27:52-53 is one attempt to retain both elements and, however Matthew understood it, the magnificent harrowing of hell is already lost in that fragment's present redaction. Also,

Matthew 27:52-53 shows what happens when ecstatic ode or liturgical poem is transformed into gospel story. (I think, actually, that the *Gospel of Peter* does a better job of that impossible task.)

I make the following suggestion gently and delicately but also firmly and strongly. The cover of Tom's book and the advertising poster for our present dialogue display a buffed Jesus who looks more like an athlete leaving the gym than a savior leaving the tomb. I suggest it might have been better to use one of those Christ-led but communal deliverance scenes from the harrowing of hell tradition—for example, that *Anastasis* fresco in the conch of the parekklesion's apse from what was once the Chora Monastery and is now the Kariye Museum in Istanbul.

One final point of admission on mode. It is possible that I underline the harrowing of hell because that Christ-led communal resurrection is what persuades me most strongly to prefer an intended metaphorical to a literal understanding of resurrection. I have difficulty imaging the harrowing of hell intended literally, and indeed, if it were, there would be not just one but very many empty tombs for inspection around Jerusalem that first Easter Sunday morning. In any case, emphasizing or not emphasizing the harrowing of hell may correlate with a metaphorical (for me) and literal (for Tom) understanding of earliest Christian resurrection faith.

Resurrection—Meaning and the Empire of Rome

Before Jesus was born, Caesar Augustus was proclaimed as Divine, Son of God, God, and God from God, as Lord, Redeemer, Liberator, and Savior of the World. Those claims of Roman imperial theology were found everywhere through texts, images, inscriptions, and structures.[12] They were as ubiquitous and immediate[13] as advertising is all around us everywhere today. Question: What percentage of the empire's population took them *literally* and what percentage took them *metaphorically*?

LITERAL OR METAPHORICAL? I think the honest answer is: we do not have the faintest idea, and we do not even know how to figure it out. But we have a relatively clear idea what percentage took them *programmatically*, that is, took them as operational announcements of heavenly mandate and functional proclamations of manifest destiny. Or again, when an Augustan coin depicted the meteor of Julius Caesar's apotheosis, how many took it as a *literal* message, how many took it as a *metaphorical* message, and how many never made that distinction but took it as a transcendental *programmatic* imperative to accept and promote their newly-peaceful (because Roman-controlled) Mediterranean world? In all those cases, the challenge to faith was quite clear: to believe meant to accept, support, and internalize Roman imperial theology and to enter the world it was creating as the only first-century reality. Maybe they, like us, were quite capable of hearing and seeing, accepting and following a *commercial* message without ever pondering too closely that distinction between the literal and the metaphorical?

Maybe even to ask that question about literal or metaphorical message and acceptance is to force a post-Enlightenment distinction on a pre-Enlightenment world? In a pre-Enlightenment world where all wonders were collectively possible in theory, even if individually deniable in practice, the criterion that counted was not presence claimed but relevance demonstrated. What has your wonder or miracle, your god(dess)'s divinity or your hero(ine)'s divinization done for the world?

In that context, on the one hand, how are we sure what percentage of believers took Christian resurrection faith *literally* and what percentage took it *metaphorically*? On the other hand, we are much more sure what percentage took it *programmatically*—were, for example, willing to die for it. I insist, of course, that literal and metaphorical are not the same as real and unreal. I never, ever, confuse or equate the literal and the real. The real can be proclaimed literally and/or metaphorically but the deeper that reality, the more metaphorical its proclamation. Also, was it possible, then and now, to take it literally and get it wrong? And, was it possible, then and now, to take it metaphorically and get it right? Also, vice versa?

Imagine, for a moment, a spectrum of ancient (and/or modern) understanding about Roman imperial theology from 100 percent literal to 100 percent metaphorical. Now imagine Christian resurrection theology along that same spectrum of ancient (and/or modern) interpretation. No matter where on that spectrum you locate either theology, they are in absolute confrontation with one another. Put another way, *majestas* or high treason may be expressed equally in either literal or metaphorical mode. Each mode claimed that, at the least, a criminal executed by Rome has been resurrected by God and that put Rome on a collision course with God. Either mode claimed that, at the most, God's Great Clean-Up of the world had begun and that, once again and on the deepest level, that put Rome, as the contemporary normalcy of civilization, on a collision course with God.

CAESAR OR CHRIST? Tom and I agree on one absolutely vital implication of resurrection faith, and it flows from what has already been discussed. Once it is clear that early Christian resurrection faith (and I add: whether taken literally or metaphorically) proclaims that God's transfiguration of this world here below has already started, it is equally clear that we are dealing with a religio-political vision and/or program that is nonviolent but also revolutionary. Tom is quite emphatic on that point, and I agree completely with him on it.[14]

I would ask, however, what exactly is involved in Christ *versus* Caesar when both are entitled Lord, Redeemer, Liberator, Savior of the world, and also Divine, Son of God, God, and God from God? And I do not ask for an answer that simply repeats those titles in other terms that must then be addressed with the same question. What is the basic structural and fundamental systemic difference between them?

My suggestion is that, first, Christ incarnates the Jewish sequence of *first justice then peace* or *peace through justice* in this world by nonviolence while Caesar incarnates the Roman sequence of *first victory then peace* or *peace through victory* in this world by violence (the first word of Virgil's *Aeneid* is *arma*—weapons; the terse summary in Augustus' *Res Gestae* is *parta victoriis pax*—peace through victories). Put more fully, the program of Jesus and Paul is the sequence of *covenant, nonviolence, justice, and peace*, but the program of Rome is *piety, war, victory, and peace*. But my suggestion is also, second, that Rome was not the evil empire of the first century, the axis of evil in the Mediterranean world. It was no more and no less than the normalcy of civilization or even the cutting-edge (pun intended) of history because civilization has always been imperial, that is, violent and unjust. It is only a question of who has lost it, who has got it, who wants it, and who is next.

It is necessary, therefore, to take literally and not metaphorically the statement of Jesus that his kingdom is not *of* this world because it is not a violent one and so his companions will not attack Pilate to release him (John 18:36). It is equally necessary to take quite literally Paul's claim that a just and nonviolent world demands a "new creation," demands a world we have never experienced and can only gropingly imagine (Gal. 6:15; 2 Cor. 5:17). That, by the way, probably means that our everyday distinctions of mode are radically inadequate in the situation of a "new creation," which both staggers our imagination and challenges the normalcy of civilization and language.

We now have two routes to follow in discussions of Christian resurrection faith. First, we may continue to debate whether it was and is to be taken literally or metaphorically. It is not my position that such a debate is invalid. It is simply that it is not the more important question and may well be used, consciously or unconsciously, to avoid that harder one. It is also that it is probably unanswerable, that it has already been argued to impasse, and that it seems to change few minds not already inclined one way or another before it began.

If taken literally, polemical arguments for its *impossibility* by unbelievers or apologetic arguments for its *uniqueness* by believers are equally invalid in dealing with a pre-Enlightenment world where it was culturally accepted that great wonders could and did happen. In that original world, with impossibility and uniqueness equally ruled out, one was confronted less with disbelief than with unconcern. *How wonderful! How nice for Jesus! So what? So why should I care?* It is precisely in such a world that claims for a God who has thereby begun to redeem and save a broken world in Christ are at least relevant especially as an alternative to the same claims of salvation and redemption made for Caesar. In that world, one had to get beyond transcendental "wow!" to speak of divine counter-program and, interactive with it, of community counter-life. And also, of course, if one takes it literally today, one still has to do the same. Taken literally, resurrection faith may be about Jesus coming bodily from his tomb, but one still has to get beyond exaltation to resurrection, to proclaim and to promote God's Great Clean-Up of the earth.

If taken metaphorically, it cannot mean just anything one wants. It does not *only* mean that there is always hope although it *also* means that. It does not *only* mean that Jesus will always be with believers although it *also* means that. It does not *only* mean that God has reversed Rome's verdict on Jesus although it *also* means that. It means that God's Great Clean-Up of a world grown old in evil and impurity, injustice and violence has already begun and that it involves a period of human time from start to finish rather than an all-encompassing instant of divine time. It means this above all else: God's Great Clean-Up has begun (a first miracle!) and we are called to participate in it (a second miracle!).

The second route is to concede historically, theologically, and especially pastorally that, while Christians must believe in the resurrection of Jesus, they may do so *either* literally *or* metaphorically but that, in either case, the meaning is constrained by what it meant inaugurally for those who first proclaimed it. In either option, we must say clearly what we believe. We are not proscribed from argument and debate on the subject, but I also invite us (indeed, implore us) to move beyond mode to meaning and to take back God's world from the thugs. Finally, to the extent that we Christians do not display an eschatological life of justice-as-the-body-of-love and love-as-the-soul-of-justice, we lose the right to speak of Christ's earthly resurrection and have at best a right to speak of his heavenly exaltation.

~ Notes ~

Preface

1. N. T. Wright, *The Resurrection of the Son of God*, Christian Origins and the Question of God, vol. 3 (Minneapolis: Fortress Press; London: SPCK, 2003).

2. Craig Blomberg, review of *The Resurrection of the Son of God, by N. T. Wright, Denver Journal: An Online Review of Current Biblical and Theological Studies* 6 (2003), http://www.denverseminary.edu/dj/articles2003/0200/0208. php; accessed June 27, 2005.

3. John Dominic Crossan, *The Historical Jesus: The Life of a Mediterranean Jewish Peasant* (San Francisco: HarperSanFrancisco, 1991).

4. N. T. Wright, *Jesus and the Victory of God*, Christian Origins and the Question of God, vol. 2 (Minneapolis: Fortress Press; London: SPCK, 1996), 65.

Introduction

1. John Dominic Crossan, *Jesus, A Revolutionary Biography* (San Francisco: HarperSanFrancisco, 1994), 123–26.

2. Ibid., 125–27.

3. John Dominic Crossan, *The Historical Jesus: The Life of a Mediterranean Jewish Peasant* (San Francisco: HarperSanFrancisco, 1991), 394.

4. Crossan, *The Historical Jesus*, 393. Cf. Crossan, *Jesus, A Revolutionary Biography*, 156–58.

5. John Dominic Crossan and Richard G. Watts, *Who Is Jesus?: Answers to Your Questions about the Historical Jesus* (Louisville: Westminster John Knox, 1996), 121.

6. N. T. Wright, *Jesus and the Victory of God*, Christian Origins and the Question of God, vol. 2 (Minneapolis: Fortress Press; London: SPCK, 1996), 658–59; N. T. Wright, *The New Testament and the People of God*, Christian Origins and the Question of God, vol. 1 (Minneapolis: Fortress Press; London: SPCK, 1992), 399–401, 460.

7. N. T. Wright, "How Jesus Saw Himself," *Bible Review* 12 (June 1996): 29.

8. N. T. Wright, *The Resurrection of the Son of God*, Christian Origins and the Question of God, vol. 3 (Minneapolis: Fortress Press; London: SPCK, 2003).

9. Ibid., 686–93.

10. Albert Schweitzer, *The Quest of the Historical Jesus: A Critical Study of Its Progress from Reimarus to Wrede*, trans. W. Montgomery (New York: MacMillan, 1968; repr. Baltimore: The Johns Hopkins University Press, 1998), 15; Hermann

Samuel Reimarus, "Concerning the Intention of Jesus and His Teaching," in *Reimarus: Fragments*, ed. Charles H. Talbert, trans. Ralph S. Fraser, 59–269, Lives of Jesus Series, ed. Leander Keck (Philadelphia: Fortress Press, 1970).

11. See also Schweitzer, *The Quest of the Historical Jesus*, 13–15. Schweitzer does mention briefly a life of Jesus that predated Reimarus that was written in Persian by the Jesuit Hieronymus Xavier, a missionary to India for a Moghul emperor. Schweitzer concludes that it was a "skilful falsification of the life of Jesus in which the omissions, and the additions taken from the Apocrypha, are inspired by the sole purpose of presenting to the open-minded ruler a glorious Jesus, in whom there should be nothing to offend him." Schweitzer, *The Quest of the Historical Jesus*, 13–14.

12. See Reimarus, *Reimarus: Fragments*. At the time of publication, Lessing was librarian to the Duke of Brunswick at the ducal library in Wolfenbüttel, hence the name of the series.

13. Colin Brown, "Reimarus, Hermann Samuel," in *Major Biblical Interpreters*, ed. Donald K. McKim (Downers Grove, Ill.: InterVarsity, 1998), 346.

14. Reimarus, *Reimarus: Fragments*, 64–65.

15. Ibid., 61.

16. Ibid., 61–150.

17. Ibid., 243–50.

18. Peter Gay, *Deism: An Anthology* (Princeton: Princeton University Press, 1968), 10.

19. David Friedrich Strauss, *The Life of Jesus Critically Examined*, ed. Peter C. Hodgson, trans. George Eliot, Lives of Jesus Series, ed. Leander E. Keck (Philadelphia: Fortress Press, 1972), lii.

20. Ibid., 39–92.

21. Ibid., 49.

22. Ibid., 39–44.

23. Ibid., 53.

24. David Friedrich Strauss, *Das Leben Jesu: fur das deutsche Volk. Bearb. von David Friedrich Strauss* (Leipzig: F. A. Brockhaus, 1874).

25. Robert Morgan, "Strauss, David Friedrich," in *Major Biblical Interpreters*, ed. Donald K. McKim (Downers Grove, Ill.: InterVarsity, 1998), 367.

26. Stephen Neill and Tom Wright, *The Interpretation of the New Testament 1861–1986* (Oxford: Oxford University Press, 1988), 116–17.

27. Karl Lachmann, "*De Ordine Narrationum* in *Evangeliis Synopticis*," *Theologische Studien und Kritiken* 8 (1835): 570.

28. Christian Hermann Weisse, *Die evangelische Geschichte kritische und philosophisch bearbeitet Leipzig*, 2 vols. (Leipzig: Breitkopf and Hartel, 1838); Christian Hermann Weisse, *Die Evangelienfrage in ihrem gegenwärtigen Stadium* (Leipzig: Breitkopf und Härtel, 1856).

29. Heinrich Julius Holtzmann, *Die Synoptischen Evangelien: Ihr Ursprung und geschichtlicher Charakter* (Leipzig: Wilhelm Engelmann, 1863), 64–67.

30. Ibid., 470.

31. Ibid., 1–9.

32. Albrecht Ritschl, *The Christian Doctrine of Justification and Reconciliation: The Positive Development of the Doctrine*, ed. H. R. Mackintosh and A. B. Macaulay (Clifton, N.J.: Reference Book Publishers, 1966), 1.

33. Ibid., 385–484.

34. Adolf von Harnack, *What Is Christianity?* trans. Thomas Bailey Saunders (New York: Harper & Row, 1957), 19–78.

35. Ben F. Meyer, *The Aims of Jesus* (London: SCM, 1979), 40.

36. Theodor Keim, *The History of Jesus of Nazara*, 2 vols., trans. Arthur Ransom (London: Williams & Norgate, 1876); Karl Hase, *Geschichte Jesu Nach Akademischen Vorlesungen* (Leipzig: n.p., 1876); Karl Heinrich Weizsäcker, *Untersuchungen uber die evangelische Geschichte, ihre Quellen und den Gang ihrer Entwicklung* (Leipzig: n.p., 1863); Bernard Weiss, *Das Leben Jesu*, 2 vols. (Berlin: Wilhelm Hertz, 1882).

37. The first truly significant biography of Jesus was Renan's. Ernst Renan, *La Vie de Jesus* (Paris: Michel Lévy Frères, 1863).

38. William Wrede, *The Messianic Secret*, trans. J. C. G. Greig (Cambridge: James Clarke, 1971), 6.

39. Ibid., 216–19.

40. Ibid., 219–30.

41. While Wrede insists that Mark is not alone responsible for the content of his Gospel in that it reflects the theology of the early church, he does nevertheless see Mark as providing a distinctive touch (ibid.). From this, one can see how both form and redaction criticism are well in line with Wrede's skepticism.

42. Albert Schweitzer, *The Mystery of the Kingdom of God: The Secret of Jesus' Messiahship and Passion*, trans. Walter Lowrie (New York: Macmillan, 1950).

43. Schweitzer wrote of his philosophy of reverence for life as a superior version of Nietzsche's concern for life lived to the fullest degree. Albert Schweitzer, *The Philosophy of Civilization*, trans. C. T. Campion (London: A. & C. Black, 1946), 174–76.

44. Schweitzer was not the first to advocate an eschatological Jesus. Johannes Weiss, Ritschl's son-in-law, had previously written that Jesus' proclamation of the kingdom of God was eschatological in nature. Johannes Weiss, *Jesus' Proclamation of the Kingdom of God*, trans. and ed. Richard H. Hiers and D. Larrimore Holland, Lives of Jesus Series, ed. Leander E. Keck (Philadelphia: Fortress Press, 1971). The primary difference between Weiss and Schweitzer is that while Weiss understood eschatology as the central motif of Jesus' teaching, Schweitzer saw it as the key to Jesus' personality and ministry.

45. Schweitzer, *The Mystery of the Kingdom of God,* 173. Following Schweitzer's summary of the life of Jesus, there is a one-page postscript recognizing that the nature of Jesus is bound forever to be a mystery to modern man and that modern culture can be revived only by grasping the nature of his conscious sacrifice for

others. It fittingly concludes with a sentence reminiscent of Nietzsche: "Only then can the heroic in our Christianity and in our *Weltanschauung* be again revived." Schweitzer, *The Mystery of the Kingdom of God,* 174.

46. For a thorough treatment of the response to Schweitzer's work, see Walter P. Weaver, *The Historical Jesus in the Twentieth Century, 1900–1950* (Harrisburg, Pa.: Trinity Press International, 1999), 31–38.

47. Schweitzer, *The Quest of the Historical Jesus.*

48. Ibid., 403. Those familiar with Schweitzer's life and philosophy will immediately see that this was for Schweitzer not simply a pithy phrase but a credo for life.

49. Martin Kähler, *The So-called Historical Jesus and the Historic Biblical Christ,* ed. and trans. Carl Braaten (Philadelphia: Fortress Press, 1964), 46.

50. Ibid., 111.

51. Ibid., 63.

52. Ernst Troeltsch, *Die Bedeutung der Geschichtlichkeit Jesus für den Glauben* (Tübingen: J. C. B. Mohr, 1929), 34. For an insightful discussion of Troeltsch's significance for biblical interpretation, see Anthony C. Thiselton, *The Two Horizons: New Testament Interpretation and Philosophical Description* (Grand Rapids, Mich.: Eerdmans, 1980), 69–74.

53. Ernst Troeltsch, *Gesammelte Schriften* (Tübingen: J. C. B. Mohr, 1912–25), 2:734. Troeltsch is particularly critical of Christian theologians who attempt to use part of the historical-critical method but reject the presuppositions of it. Ibid., 2:730.

54. Wilhelm Bousset, *Kyrios Christos: A History of Belief in Christ from the Beginnings of Christianity to Irenaeus,* trans. John E. Steely (Nashville, Tenn.: Abingdon, 1970).

55. Colin Brown, "Historical Jesus, Quest of," in *Dictionary of Jesus and the Gospels* (Downers Grove, Ill.: InterVarsity, 1992), 334.

56. Rudolf Bultmann, *The History of the Synoptic Tradition,* trans. John Marsh (Oxford: Blackwell, 1963), 3–4.

57. Rudolf Bultmann, *Jesus and the Word,* trans. Louise Pettibone Smith and Erminie Huntress Lantero (New York: Scribner, 1958), 8.

58. Rudolf Bultmann, "The Study of the Synoptic Gospels," in *Form Criticism: Two Essays on New Testament Research,* ed. R. Bultmann and Karl Kundsin, trans. Frederick C. Grant (1934; reprint, New York: Harper Torchbook, 1962), 17.

59. Other influences on Bultmann include Luther, Collingwood, and the history-of-religions school, as well as the liberal theology of his teacher Harnack. For a general discussion of influences on Bultmann, see Thiselton, *The Two Horizons,* 205–51.

60. Bultmann, *Jesus and the Word,* 9–12.

61. Bultmann, "New Testament and Mythology," in *Kerygma and Myth,* ed. Hans Werner Bartsch, trans. Reginald Fuller (London: SPCK, 1953), 11–12.

62. Ernst Käsemann, "The Problem of the Historical Jesus," in *Essays on New Testament Themes,* trans. W. J. Montague (London: SCM, 1964), 15–47.

63. Ibid., 20.

64. Ibid., 46.

65. Ibid., 37.

66. James M. Robinson, *A New Quest of the Historical Jesus and Other Essays* (1959; reprint, Philadelphia: Fortress Press, 1983).

67. Ibid., 22–25.

68. Günther Bornkamm, Gerhard Barth, and Heinz Joachim Held, *Tradition and Interpretation in Matthew*, trans. Percy Scott (Philadelphia: Westminster, 1963); Hans Conzelmann, *The Theology of St. Luke*, trans. G. Buswell (New York: Harper & Row, 1960).

69. Grant R. Osborne, "Redaction Criticism," in *New Testament Criticism and Interpretation*, ed. David Alan Black and David S. Dockery (Grand Rapids, Mich.: Zondervan, 1991), 199–224.

70. Schweitzer, *The Quest of the Historical Jesus*, 398.

71. Wright, *Jesus and the Victory of God*, 28–124. Wright coined the term "Third Quest." Neill and Wright, *The Interpretation of the New Testament*, 363.

72. For example, see John H. Elliot, *What Is Social-Scientific Criticism?* Guides to Biblical Scholarship, New Testament Series, ed. Dan O. Via Jr. (Minneapolis: Fortress Press, 1993); Gerd Theissen, *The First Followers of Jesus: A Sociological Analysis of the Earliest Christianity*, trans. John Bowden (London: SCM, 1978); Gerd Theissen, *Sociology of Early Palestinian Christianity: Essays on Corinth*, ed. and trans. John H. Schutz (Philadelphia: Fortress Press, 1982); Bruce J. Malina, *The New Testament World: Insights from Cultural Anthropology* (Louisville, Ky.: Westminster John Knox), 1993; Bruce J. Malina, *Christian Origins and Cultural Anthropology: Practical Models for Biblical Interpretation* (Louisville, Ky.: Westminster John Knox), 1986.

73. Audio recordings of the entire conference can be obtained at http://www.greer-heard.com.

1. The Resurrection: A Dialogue

1. N. T. Wright, *The Resurrection of the Son of God*, Christian Origins and the Question of God, vol. 3 (Minneapolis: Fortress Press; London: SPCK, 2003), 655.

2. Wright, *The Resurrection of the Son of God*, 558–59.

3. Stephen J. Patterson, *Beyond the Passion: Rethinking the Death and Life of Jesus* (Minneapolis: Fortress Press, 2004). See also Stephen J. Patterson, *The God of Jesus: The Historical Jesus and the Search for Meaning* (Harrisburg, Pa.: Trinity Press International, 1998).

2. The Dominical and Thomistic Traditions

1. John Dominic Crossan, "Empty Tomb and Absent Lord (Mark 16:1–8)," in *The Passion in Mark*, ed. W. Kelber (Philadelphia: Fortress Press, 1976), 135–52; C. A. Evans, "Mark's Use of the Empty Tomb Tradition," *Studia Biblica et Theologica* 8, no. 2 (1978): 50–55.

2. John Dominic Crossan, *The Historical Jesus: The Life of a Mediterranean Jewish Peasant* (San Francisco: HarperSanFrancisco, 1991). I review the book in *Trinity Journal* 13 (1992): 230–39.

3. John Dominic Crossan, *Who Killed Jesus? Exposing the Roots of Anti-Semitism in the Gospel Story of the Death of Jesus* (San Francisco: HarperCollins, 1995). I review the book in "The Passion of Jesus: History Remembered or Prophecy Historicized?" *Bulletin for Biblical Research* 6 (1996): 159–65.

4. John Dominic Crossan, *Who Killed Jesus?* 189–210. The major themes of this book are anticipated in Crossan's *Jesus: A Revolutionary Biography* (San Francisco: HarperCollins, 1994), 123–58 (on death and burial), 159–92 (on resurrection).

5. John Dominic Crossan, *The Birth of Christianity: Discovering What Happened in the Years Immediately after the Execution of Jesus* (San Francisco: HarperCollins, 1998), xiii–xxxi, 527–73; John Dominic Crossan, "Historical Jesus as Risen Lord," in J. D. Crossan, L. T. Johnson, and W. H. Kelber, *The Jesus Controversy: Perspectives in Conflict* (Harrisburg, Pa.: Trinity Press International, 1999), 1–47; John Dominic Crossan, "The Resurrection of Jesus in Its Jewish Context," *Neotestamentica* 37 (2003): 29–57.

6. N. T. Wright, *The New Testament and the People of God*, Christian Origins and the Question of God, vol. 1 (Minneapolis: Fortress Press; London: SPCK, 1992); N. T. Wright, *Jesus and the Victory of God*, Christian Origins and the Question of God, vol. 2 (London: SPCK; Minneapolis: Fortress Press, 1996).

7. N. T. Wright, *The Resurrection of the Son of God*, Christian Origins and the Question of God, vol. 3 (Minneapolis: Fortress Press; London: SPCK, 2003).

8. See the mostly appreciative review by L. M. McDonald in *Bulletin for Biblical Research* 14 (2004): 313–18.

9. And for this reason Wright assigns the work of the Jesus Seminar to the 1950s–1960s New Quest of the historical Jesus, rather than to the current Third Quest.

10. R. Bultmann, *Jesus* (Berlin: Deutsche Bibliothek, 1926); English translation: *Jesus and the Word* (New York: Scribner, 1934).

11. Bultmann, *Jesus and the Word*, 16–22.

12. Ibid., 16.

13. R. Bultmann, *Theology of the New Testament*, 2 vols. (New York: Scribner, 1951–55), 1:11.

14. R. Bultmann, *The History of the Synoptic Tradition* (Oxford: Blackwell, 1972), 374.

15. John Dominic Crossan, *Four Other Gospels: Shadows on the Contours of Canon* (1985; reprint, Sonoma, Calif.: Polebridge, 1992).

16. John Dominic Crossan, *The Cross That Spoke: The Origins of the Passion Narrative* (San Francisco: Harper & Row, 1988).

17. In *First Apology* 15.10–12, Justin Martyr blends portions of dominical tradition from the respective Matthean and Lukan forms of the Sermon on the

Mount (or Plain) and introduces this pastiche as a single utterance of Jesus. In 16.9–13, we find Synoptic materials blended together with elements from the Gospel of John, all of which is presented as a single utterance, introduced as a "word" of Jesus.

18. See C. A. Evans, R. L. Webb, and R. A. Wiebe, eds., *Nag Hammadi Texts and the Bible: A Synopsis and Index*, NTTS 18 (Leiden: Brill, 1993), 88–144; and N. Perrin, *Thomas and Tatian: The Relationship between the Gospel of Thomas and the Diatessaron*, Academia Biblica 5 (Atlanta: Society of Biblical Literature, 2002).

19. See the chapter by Charles L. Quarles in the present volume. There is no better assessment of the secondary nature of the *Gospel of Peter*.

20. Smith published two books on Secret Mark, one learned and one popular, respectively: *Clement of Alexandria and a Secret Gospel of Mark* (Cambridge, Mass.: Harvard University Press, 1973); and *The Secret Gospel: The Discovery and Interpretation of the Secret Gospel according to Mark* (New York: Harper & Row, 1973).

Voss (1618–1689) presents the text in parallel columns in Latin and Greek (*Epistolae genuinae S. Ignatii martyris; quae nunc primum lucem vident ex bibliotheca Florentina. Adduntur S. Ignatii epistolae, quales vulgo circumferuntur. Adhaec S. Barnabae Epistola. Accessit universis translatio vetus* [The genuine letters of Saint Ignatius the martyr; now seeing the first light out of the library of Florence. To which are added the letters of Saint Ignatius that are commonly circulating. To which is added the letter of Saint Barnabas in its entirety in old translation], ed. and with notes by Isaac Voss [Amsterdam: Ioannem Blaeu, 1646]). His notes are in Latin. As the title indicates, the volume contains the "genuine" letters of Ignatius and the Letter of Barnabas. The handwritten Clementine letter containing references to Secret Mark appears at the end of the volume, right after Barnabas.

21. J. H. Hunter, *The Mystery of Mar Saba* (New York: Evangelical Publishers, 1940). The book was reprinted annually until 1946. A few scholars have noticed the remarkable parallel. See P. Jenkins, *Hidden Gospels: How the Search for Jesus Lost Its Way* (New York: Oxford University Press, 2001), 102; and R. M. Price, "Second Thoughts on the Secret Gospel," *Bulletin for Biblical Research* 14 (2004): 127–32.

22. Smith's signature is not clear in the photos published in Smith's 1973 books, but it is clear in C. W. Hedrick and N. Olympiou, "Secret Mark: New Photographs, New Witnesses," *The Fourth R* 13, no. 5 (September–October 2000): 10. With regard to Smith's signature, Price ("Second Thoughts," 130) asks rhetorically, "Was he signing his own work?"

Several scholars have defended the authenticity of the letter and have, at the same time, defended Morton Smith. For example, S. J. Patterson ("The Secret Gospel of Mark," in R. J. Miller, ed., *The Complete Gospels* [Sonoma, Calif.: Polebridge, 1992], 402) complains: "Early discussion of [the letter] was marred by accusations of forgery and fraud, no doubt owing in part to its controversial contents. Today, however, there is almost unanimous agreement among Clementine scholars that the letter is authentic." B. Ehrman (*Lost Christianities: The Battles for Scripture and the Faiths We Never Knew* [Oxford: Oxford University Press, 2003], 79) affirms that "it would be well nigh impossible to imagine someone other than Clement being able to write it." Some, however, have no problem imagining that the letter is indeed a forgery and that Smith is the forger. Besides Jenkins and Price mentioned in the preceding note, see also D. H. Akenson, *Saint Saul: A Skeleton Key to the Historical Jesus* (Oxford: Oxford University Press, 2000), 88–89; as well as the suspicions expressed at the outset by Q. Quesnell, "The Mar Saba Clementine: A Question of Evidence," *CBQ* 37 (1975): 48–67. In my view, Quesnell's penetrating and judicious assessment has not been accorded the attention by Smith's defenders that it deserves.

The debate over the authenticity of the Clementine letter and Secret Mark, including the possibility, even probability, that Morton Smith forged the writing, not only continues but seems to be intensifying. A major new defense of the letter has been offered in S. G. Brown, *Mark's Other Gospel: Rethinking Morton Smith's Controversial Discovery* (Waterloo, Ont.: Wilfrid Laurier University Press, 2005). In support of this book, J. S. Kloppenborg states that Brown "lifts the discussion of 'Longer Mark' from the mire of innuendo and pseudo-scholarly opinion and sets it on the footing of serious and balanced discussion, showing that there are good reasons both to suppose that the Clementine letter is genuine and to conclude that the gospel fragments are Markan" (promotional blurb). However, a new assault on the letter has been offered by S. C. Carlson, *Uncovered: Morton Smith's Secret and the Anatomy of an Academic Hoax* (Waco, Tex.: Baylor University Press, 2005). Carlson has tested samples of Morton Smith's handwriting. He concludes that Morton Smith most certainly is the author of the controversial Clementine letter!

23. E. P. Sanders, *Paul and Palestinian Judaism: A Comparison of Patterns of Religion* (London: SCM Press; Philadelphia: Fortress Press, 1977), 33–428; Crossan, *The Historical Jesus*, 1–224.

24. Crossan, *The Historical Jesus*, 421.

25. Archaeological investigations at Sepphoris subsequent to the publication of Crossan's *Historical Jesus* (1991) have found, among other things, a first-century dump. Archaeologists have discovered no pig bones among the faunal remains dating to the pre-70 C.E. period, in contrast to 30 percent pig bones in the post-70 period. The absence of a significant presence of Gentiles, or at least persons who did not keep *kashruth*, weakens Crossan's hypothesis of a Cynic presence in Sepphoris. The finds of the 1990s have identified fragments of several stone vessels and *miqvaoth* (ritual immersion pools). These finds, along with the absence of pagan artifacts and architecture, strongly suggest that Sepphoris was a Torah-observant, Jewish city in the time of Jesus. For more on this, see M. A.

Chancey, *The Myth of a Gentile Galilee* (SNTSMS 118; Cambridge: Cambridge University Press, 2002); and, in popular form, M. Chancey and E. M. Meyers, "How Jewish Was Sepphoris in Jesus' Time?" *Biblical Archeologist Reader* 26, no. 4 (2000): 18–33, 61.

26. M. Casey, "Where Wright Is Wrong: A Critical Review of N. T. Wright's *Jesus and the Victory of God*," *Journal for the Study of the New Testament* 69 (1998): 95–103. Another review essay appears in the same issue: C. Marsh, "Theological History? N. T. Wright's *Jesus and the Victory of God*," 77–94. Wright responds to these essays in "Theology, History and Jesus: A Response to Maurice Casey and Clive Marsh," 105–12.

27. I discuss the issue, including Casey's objections, in "Jesus and the Continuing Exile of Israel," in *Jesus and the Restoration of Israel: A Critical Assessment of N. T. Wright's Jesus and the Victory of God*, ed. Carey C. Newman (Downers Grove, Ill.: InterVarsity, 1999), 77–100, 304–8. Wright responds to all of the essays in this book in "In Grateful Dialogue: A Response," 244–77.

28. I am referring to the opening section in chapter 1 of *Who Killed Jesus?* 1–13, which Crossan calls "History Remembered and Prophecy Historicized."

29. An illustrative case in point is the scriptural citations linked to Judas Iscariot's betrayal of Jesus. Did passages from Zechariah 11 and Jeremiah 19 give rise to the story of the thirty pieces of silver flung into the temple and the purchase of the potter's field (Matt. 27:3–10), or did the sorry story of Judas prompt a search of the prophetic scriptures, or was it a little of both?

30. I do not think the tradition in Matthew 27:51b–53, which describes at the time of Jesus' death the resurrection of several saintly persons, has any claim to authenticity. This legendary embellishment, which may actually be a late-first- or early-second-century scribal gloss, is an attempt to justify the Easter appearances of Jesus as resurrection, in the sense that Jesus and several other saints were the "first fruits" of the general resurrection. This is, of course, exactly how Paul explains the anomaly (see 1 Cor. 15:23).

31. This point has been driven home very persuasively by D. C. Allison Jr., *Resurrecting Jesus: The Earliest Christian Tradition and Its Interpreters* (London: T. & T. Clark, 2005).

3. The Hermeneutics of Resurrection

1. For a much fuller treatment of these issues, as well as several others related to hermeneutics and Jesus research, see my forthcoming *The Quest of the Hermeneutical Jesus: The Impact of Hermeneutics on the Jesus Research of John Dominic Crossan and N. T. Wright* (Lanham, Md.: University Press of America, forthcoming).

2. N. T. Wright, *The New Testament and the People of God*, Christian Origins and the Question of God, vol. 1 (Minneapolis: Fortress Press; London: SPCK, 1992), 65.

3. Ibid.

4. Wright, *The New Testament and the People of God*, 122–24; N. T. Wright, *Jesus and the Victory of God*, Christian Origins and the Question of God, vol. 2 (Minneapolis: Fortress Press; London: SPCK, 1996), 137–38.

5. Wright, *The New Testament and the People of God*, 122.

6. Ibid., 77–80.

7. Ibid., 95–96.

8. N. T. Wright, *The Resurrection of the Son of God*, Christian Origins and the Question of God, vol. 3 (Minneapolis: Fortress Press; London: SPCK, 2003), 719–20.

9. Wentzel Van Huyssteen, *Essays in Postfoundationalist Theology* (Grand Rapids, Mich.: Eerdmans), 43.

10. Wright, *The New Testament and the People of God*, 35.

11. Ibid., 48.

12. John Dominic Crossan, *In Parables: The Challenge of the Historical Jesus* (New York: Harper & Row, 1973), xv.

13. John Dominic Crossan, *In Fragments: The Aphorisms of Jesus* (San Francisco: Harper & Row, 1983), vii.

14. Crossan, *In Parables*, 13.

15. James M. Robinson, "Hermeneutic since Barth," in *The New Hermeneutic*, vol. 2, *New Frontiers in Theology: Discussion among Continental and American Theologians*, ed. James M. Robinson and John B. Cobb Jr. (New York: Harper & Row, 1964), 60–61.

16. John Dominic Crossan, *The Dark Interval: Towards a Theology of Story* (Sonoma, Calif.: Eagle, 1988).

17. Ibid., 100.

18. John Dominic Crossan, *Finding Is the First Act: Trove Folktales and Jesus' Treasure Parable*, Semeia Supplements (Philadelphia: Fortress Press, 1979), 120.

19. Stanley Cavell, "Ending the Waiting Game," in *Must We Mean What We Say? A Book of Essays* (New York: Scribner, 1969), 149. See also John Dominic Crossan, *Raid on the Articulate: Comic Eschatology in Jesus and Borges* (New York: Harper & Row, 1976), 32–33.

20. John Dominic Crossan, *Cliffs of Fall: Paradox and Polyvalency in the Parables of Jesus* (New York: Seabury, 1980), 5–13.

21. Crossan, *Cliffs of Fall*, 9–10.

22. See Crossan, *The Dark Interval*, 42.

23. John Dominic Crossan, "The Parables of Jesus," *Interpretation* 56, no. 3 (July 2002): 249.

24. Ibid., 253.

25. Ibid., 254.

26. Ibid., 258.

27. Wright, *The New Testament and the People of God*, 69–70.

28. Ibid., 70.

29. Ibid., 82.

30. Ibid., 109–12.

31. Ben F. Meyer, *The Aims of Jesus* (London: SCM, 1979), 19–21, 174–220.

32. For more on basic beliefs, aims, consequent beliefs, and intentions, see Wright *The New Testament and the People of God*, 110–11, 125–26.

33. Ibid., 66.

34. Ibid., 127.

35. Ibid., 130.

36. Ibid., 133–36.

37. Ibid., 121.

38. Ibid., 126–30.

39. Ibid., 126.

40. Crossan, *Raid on the Articulate*, 128.

41. Ibid., 129.

42. Crossan, "Responses and Reflections," in *Jesus and Faith: A Conversation on the Work of John Dominic Crossan*, ed. Jeffrey Carlson and Robert A. Ludwig (Maryknoll, N.Y.: Orbis, 1994), 144.

43. Crossan, *Raid on the Articulate*, 123–24.

44. Crossan, *Cliffs of Fall*, 101.

45. Crossan, *Finding Is the First Act*, 1–2; see also Crossan, *In Parables*, 4.

46. Crossan, *Finding Is the First Act*, 2.

47. Crossan, "The Parables of Jesus," 259.

48. John Dominic Crossan, "Divine Immediacy and Human Immediacy: Towards a New First Principle in Historical Jesus Research," *Semeia* 44 (1988): 125.

49. Wright, *The New Testament and the People of God*, 81–82, 88.

50. Ibid., 81–82.

51. Ibid., 82.

52. Ibid., 109–10.

53. N. T. Wright, "In Grateful Dialogue: A Response," in *Jesus and the Restoration of Israel: A Critical Assessment of N. T. Wright's Jesus and the Victory of God*, ed. Carey C. Newman (Downers Grove, Ill.: InterVarsity, 1999), 246–48.

54. Wright, "In Grateful Dialogue," 249.

55. Wright, *The New Testament and the People of God*, 99–100.

56. Ibid., 100.

57. Ibid., 101–4.

58. See C. S. Peirce, *Philosophical Writings of Peirce*, ed. Justus Buchler (New York: Dover, 1955), esp. vol. 5, 150–56, 190–217.

59. Crossan, "The Historical Jesus in Earliest Christianity," 3–4.

60. John Dominic Crossan, *The Historical Jesus: The Life of a Mediterranean Jewish Peasant* (San Francisco: HarperSanFrancisco, 1991), 423.

61. Ibid., 423.

62. Crossan, *The Birth of Christianity: Discovering What Happened in the Years Immediately after the Execution of Jesus* (San Francisco: HarperSanFrancisco, 1998), 42–45.

63. Ibid., 45–46.

64. Ibid., 20.

65. Ibid., 45.

66. John Dominic Crossan, *Four Other Gospels: Shadows on the Contour of the Canon* (Minneapolis: Winston, 1985), 7–11.

67. Crossan, *The Historical Jesus*, xxxiv.

68. Crossan, *The Birth of Christianity*, 44.

69. Marcus J. Borg and N. T. Wright, *The Meaning of Jesus: Two Visions* (San Francisco: HarperSanFrancisco, 1998), 118.

70. Wright, *The Resurrection of the Son of God*, 9, 28.

71. Ibid., 28.

72. N. T. Wright, "How Jesus Saw Himself," *Bible Review* 12 (June 1996): 29.

73. Wright, *Jesus and the Victory of God*, 111.

74. Who Jesus was and what he said and did factored into this radical mutation. Wright, *The New Testament and the People of God*, 399–400; Wright, *Jesus and the Victory of God*, 487–89.

75. Wright, *The Resurrection of the Son of God*, 6.

76. Ibid., 9.

77. Ibid., 448.

78. Ibid., 680.

79. Ibid., 686–93. Wright grants that it is more difficult to establish the empty tomb and resurrection appearances as *necessary* conditions.

80. Wright uses "highly probable" in a "common-sense historian's way," that is, "as a way of indicating that the historical evidence, while comparatively rarely permitting a conclusion of 'certain', can acknowledge a scale from, say, 'extremely unlikely', through 'possible', plausible' and 'probable', to 'highly probable.'" Wright, *The Resurrection of the Son of God*, 687, n. 3. For a philosophical analysis of Wright's argument, see the essay by William Lane Craig in the current volume.

81. Ibid., 719–20.

82. Ibid., 727.

83. Ibid., 729.

84. Ibid., 731.

85. Ibid., 737.

86. Crossan, "The Historical Jesus in Earliest Christianity," 16. See also John Dominic Crossan, *Jesus: A Revolutionary Biography* (San Francisco: HarperSanFrancisco, 1994), 145.

87. Martin Hengel, *Crucifixion in the Ancient World and the Folly of the Message of the Cross*, trans. John Bowden (Philadelphia: Fortress Press, 1977).

88. Crossan, *Jesus*, 123–26.

89. Ibid., 125–27.
90. Crossan, *The Historical Jesus*, 393. See also Crossan, *Jesus*, 156–58.
91. Crossan, *The Historical Jesus*, 372.
92. Crossan, *The Birth of Christianity*, xxx.
93. Ibid., xxxi.
94. John Dominic Crossan and Richard G. Watts, *Who Is Jesus?: Answers to Your Questions about the Historical Jesus* (Louisville, Ky.: Westminster John Knox, 1996), 121.
95. Crossan, "The Parables of Jesus," 254.
96. Ibid., 254.
97. John Dominic Crossan, "The Resurrection of Jesus in Its Jewish Context," *Neotestamentica* 37, no. 1 (2003): 29–30.
98. Ibid., 29–30.
99. Ibid., 30.
100. Ibid., 31–35.
101. Ibid., 34–37.
102. Ibid., 38–43.
103. Ibid., 42–43.
104. Ibid., 48–51.
105. Ibid., 55.
106. Ibid., 55–56.
107. Wright, *The Resurrection of the Son of God*, 697–706.

4. The Trend toward Bodily Resurrection Appearances

1. For a more detailed look at this material, particularly the broader range of current attempts to popularize naturalistic theories, see Gary R. Habermas, "The Late Twentieth-Century Resurgence of Naturalistic Responses to Jesus' Resurrection," *Trinity Journal*, New Series, 22 (2001): 179–96.
2. For details on each of these points, including critical attestation and agreement, see Gary R. Habermas, *The Risen Jesus and Future Hope* (Lanham, Md.: Rowman & Littlefield, 2003), ch. 1.
3. The most popular choices are drawn from Acts 1:21-22; 2:22-36; 3:13-16; 4:8-10; 5:29-32; 10:39-43; 13:28-31; 17:1-3; 17:30-31.
4. For more details here, see Habermas, *The Risen Jesus*, esp. 21–25; see also Gary R. Habermas, "Experiences of the Risen Jesus: The Foundational Historical Issue in the Early Proclamation of the Resurrection," forthcoming.
5. Reginald H. Fuller, *The Foundations of New Testament Christology* (New York: Scribner, 1965), 142.
6. Reginald H. Fuller, *The Formation of the Resurrection Narratives* (Minneapolis: Fortress Press, 1980), 169 (emphasis added).
7. James D. G. Dunn, *The Evidence for Jesus* (Louisville, Ky.: Westminster, 1985), 75 (emphasis in original).

8. Norman Perrin, *The Resurrection according to Matthew, Mark, and Luke* (Philadelphia: Fortress Press, 1977), 80.

9. Helmut Koester, *Introduction to the New Testament*, vol. 2, *History and Literature of Early Christianity* (Philadelphia: Fortress Press, 1982), 84. Koester does not explain the sense in which he thinks that Jesus appeared.

10. Peter Carnley, *The Structure of Resurrection Belief* (Oxford: Clarendon, 1987), 246 (emphasis added).

11. Bart D. Ehrman, *Jesus: Apocalyptic Prophet of the New Millennium* (Oxford: Oxford University Press, 1999), 231.

12. We will not discuss in any depth the agnostic position.

13. It should be noted carefully that both of these views postulate that Jesus did not rise from the dead. Therefore, neither "internal" nor "external" has any reference to supernatural workings. These terms simply describe the direction of the disciples' sensory stimulation.

14. It also should be noted carefully that both of these views postulate that Jesus actually rose from the dead. Thus, "internal" is not to be taken in the sense that the resurrection appearances were only subjective in nature. Rather, it is usually contended that even when the risen Jesus manifested himself to groups of persons, he did so in a nonbodily manner, perhaps communicating telepathically with each witness, without thereby casting doubt on the reality of the resurrection appearances. While "external" is a reference to Jesus' bodily appearances, it does not specify further differences between commentators.

15. Habermas, "Twentieth-Century Resurgence," esp. 184–86.

16. Harold I. Kaplan, Benjamin J. Sadock, and Jack A. Grebb, *Synopsis of Psychiatry*, 7th ed. (Baltimore: Williams & Wilkins, 1994), 306–7.

17. Gerd Lüdemann, *The Resurrection of Jesus: History, Experience, Theology*, trans. John Bowden (Minneapolis: Fortress Press, 1994), 106–7, 174–75, 180. A popular version is Gerd Lüdemann with Alf Ozen, *What Really Happened to Jesus: A Historical Approach to the Resurrection*, trans. John Bowden (Louisville, Ky.: Westminster John Knox, 1995).

18. See Hansjürgen Verweyen, ed., *Osterglaube ohne Auferstehung? Diskussion mit Gerd Lüdemann* (Freiburg: Herder, 1995). Another example of such a critique is the lengthy book review by Andreas Lindemann in *Wege zum Menschen* 46 (November-December 1994): 503–13.

19. Willi Marxsen, *The Resurrection of Jesus of Nazareth*, trans. Margaret Kohl (Philadelphia: Fortress Press, 1970), esp. 88–97. The prototype was an earlier essay by Marxsen, "The Resurrection of Jesus as a Historical and Theological Problem," in C. F. D. Moule, ed., *The Significance of the Message of the Resurrection for Faith in Jesus Christ* (London: SCM, 1968), 5–50.

20. Willi Marxsen, *Jesus and Easter: Did God Raise the Historical Jesus from the Dead?* trans. Victor Paul Furnish (Nashville, Tenn.: Abingdon, 1990), 70–74.

21. Rudolf Pesch, "Zur Entstehung des Glaubens an die Auferstehung Jesu," *Theologische Quartalschrift* 153 (1973): 219-26; Rudolf Pesch, "Materialien und

Bemerkungen zu Entstehung und Sinn des Osterglaubens," in Anton Vogtle and Rudolf Pesch, *Wie kam es zum Osterglauben?* (Dusseldorf: Patmos, 1975), 157–68.

22. Rudolf Pesch, "Zur Entstehung des Glaubens an die Auferstehung Jesu: Ein neuer Versuch," *Freiburger Zeitschrift für Philosophie und Theologie* 30 (1983), esp. 87; see also John Galvin, "The Origin of Faith in the Resurrection of Jesus: Two Recent Perspectives," *Theological Studies* 49 (1988): 27–35, for an excellent summary of the shift in Pesch's thinking.

23. Margaret Lloyd Davies and Trevor A. Lloyd Davies, "Resurrection or Resuscitation?" *Journal of the Royal College of Physicians of London* 25 (April 1991): 167–70.

24. "Letters to the Editor," *Journal of the Royal College of Physicians of London* 25 (July 1991): 268–72.

25. David Strauss, *The Life of Jesus Critically Examined*, trans. George Eliot, 4th German ed. (1835; reprint, n.p.: Sigler, 1994), esp. 678–79; see also 734, 737–39. See also Albert Schweitzer, *The Quest of the Historical Jesus: A Critical Study of Its Progress from Reimarus to Wrede*, trans. W. Montgomery (1906; reprint, New York: Macmillan, 1968). Schweitzer describes Strauss's attack (56–57) and does not list any nineteenth-century proponents of the swoon theory after 1838. Actually, Strauss's later critique, published in 1864, was even more influential in denouncing the apparent death thesis. See his *A New Life of Jesus* (Edinburgh: Williams & Norgate, 1879), 1:408–12.

26. See Eduard Riggenbach, *The Resurrection of Jesus* (New York: Eaton & Mains, 1907), 48–49; James Orr, *The Resurrection of Jesus* (1908; Grand Rapids, Mich.: Zondervan, 1965), 92; George Park Fisher, *The Grounds of Theistic and Christian Belief*, rev. ed. (New York: Scribner, 1909), 193.

27. John Dominic Crossan, *Jesus: A Revolutionary Biography* (San Francisco: Harper Collins, 1994), 152–58; John Dominic Crossan, *The Historical Jesus: The Life of a Mediterranean Peasant* (San Francisco: HarperSanFrancisco, 1991), 392–94.

28. For examples, Michael Martin, *The Case against Christianity* (Philadelphia: Temple University Press, 1991), 95; A. N. Wilson, *Jesus* (London: Sinclair-Stevenson, 1992), 242.

29. Wells develops this thesis in volumes like *Did Jesus Exist?* 2nd ed. (London: Pemberton, 1986), esp. chs. 2 and 3; *The Historical Evidence for Jesus* (Buffalo, N.Y.: Prometheus, 1988), esp. chs. 1 and 4; *A Resurrection Debate: The New Testament Evidence in Evangelical and Critical Perspective* (London: Rationalist Press, 1988), esp. chs. 5, 7, and 8.

30. Evan Fales, "Successful Defense? A Review of *In Defense of Miracles,*" *Philosophia Christi*, Second Series, 3 (2001): 29–34.

31. Kaplan, Sadock, and Grebb, *Synopsis of Psychiatry*, 307. See also Jerrold Maxmen and Nicholas Ward, *Essential Psychopathology and Its Treatment* (New York: Norton, 1995), 483–85.

32. Martin, *Case against Christianity*, 92–95.

33. Wells, *A Resurrection Debate*, 39–40.

34. Michael Goulder, "The Baseless Fabric of a Vision," in *Resurrection Reconsidered*, ed. Gavin D'Costa (Oxford: Oneworld Publications, 1996), 52–55.

35. For several examples, see Habermas, "Twentieth-Century Resurgence," esp. 180–84.

36. Raymond Brown, *An Introduction to New Testament Christology* (New York: Paulist, 1997), 163–66.

37. N. T. Wright, "Christian Origins and the Resurrection of Jesus: The Resurrection of Jesus as a Historical Problem," *Sewanee Theological Review* 41 (1998): 118–22.

38. Dunn, *The Evidence for Jesus*, 76.

39. Stephen T. Davis, "Is Belief in the Resurrection Rational?" *Philo* 2 (1999): 57–58.

40. Richard Swinburne, "Evidence for the Resurrection," in *The Resurrection: An Interdisciplinary Symposium on the Resurrection of Jesus,* ed. Stephen T. Davis, Daniel Kendall, and Gerald O'Collins (Oxford: Oxford University Press, 1997), 201.

41. Some examples include Paul Tillich, *Systematic Theology* (Chicago: University of Chicago Press, 1957), vol. 2, esp. 155–56; Karl Barth, *Church Dogmatics*, ed. G. W. Bromiley and T. F. Torrance (Edinburgh: T. & T. Clark, 1956), 4:340; Michael C. Perry, *The Easter Enigma* (London: Faber & Faber, 1959), 120-33; Günther Bornkamm, *Jesus of Nazareth*, trans. Irene and Fraser McLuskey with James M. Robinson (New York: Harper & Row, 1960), 181–85; A. M. Ramsey, *The Resurrection of Christ*, rev. ed. (London: Collins, 1961), 48–53; A. M. Hunter, *Bible and Gospel* (Philadelphia: Westminster, 1969), 111–12; Helmut Thielicke, "The Resurrection Kerygma," in *The Easter Message Today*, trans. Salvator Attanasio and Darrell Likens Guder (London: Thomas Nelson, 1964), 87–91, 103–4; Jürgen Moltmann, *Theology of Hope: On the Ground and the Implications of a Christian Eschatology*, trans. James W. Leitch (New York: Harper & Row, 1967), 186, 198–200; Neville Clark, *Interpreting the Resurrection* (Philadelphia: Westminster, 1967), 99–105; Joachim Jeremias, "Easter: The Earliest Tradition and the Earliest Interpretation," in *New Testament Theology: The Proclamation of Jesus*, trans. John Bowden (New York: Scribner, 1971), 302; John A. T. Robinson, *Can We Trust the New Testament?* (Grand Rapids, Mich.: Eerdmans, 1977), 123–25; Ulrich Wilckens, *Resurrection: Biblical Testimony to the Resurrection: An Historical Examination and Explanation,* trans. A. M. Stewart (Edinburgh: Saint Andrew, 1977), 117–19; Wolfhart Pannenberg, *Jesus—God and Man,* 2nd ed., trans. Lewis L. Wilkins and Duane A. Priebe (Philadelphia: Westminster, 1977), 88–97; Pinchas Lapide, *The Resurrection of Jesus: A Jewish Perspective* (Minneapolis: Augsburg, 1983), 120–26; Hugo Staudinger, "The Resurrection of Jesus Christ as Saving Event and as 'Object' of Historical Research," *Scottish Journal of Theology* 36 (1983): 326; Murray J. Harris, *Raised Immortal: Resurrection and Immortality in the New Testament* (Grand Rapids, Mich.: Eerdmans, 1983), 57–71; John Drane, *Introducing the New Testament* (San Francisco: Harper &

Row, 1986), 106; David Samuel, "Making Room in History for the Miraculous," *Churchman* 100 (1986): 111; John Macquarrie, "The Keystone of Christian Faith," in *'If Christ Be Not Risen . . .': Essays in Resurrection and Survival,* ed. John Greenhalgh and Elizabeth Russell (San Francisco: Collins, 1986), 18–22; C. E. B. Cranfield, "The Resurrection of Jesus Christ," *Expository Times* 101 (1990): 171; Luke Timothy Johnson, *The Writings of the New Testament: An Interpretation* (Philadelphia: Fortress Press, 1986), 99–107; Paul Barnett, Peter Jenson, and David Peterson, *Resurrection: Truth and Reality* (Sydney, Australia: Aquila, 1994), 27; Paul Maier, *In the Fulness of Time: A Historian Looks at Christmas, Easter, and the Early Church* (San Francisco: Harper Collins, 1991), 193–96; Anthony Baxter, "Historical Judgement, Transcendent Perspective and 'Resurrection Appearances,'" *Heythrop Journal* 40 (1999): 22–23, 28, 37. See also the recent scholars listed in notes 36–40 above.

42. Published in Berlin in three volumes between 1867 and 1872, this critique is made in vol. 3 (1872), esp. 594–600. The English version is translated by E. M. Geldart and A. Ransom (London: Williams & Norgate, 1883); see esp. 361–65.

43. Keim, 600–605.

44. Hans Grass, *Ostergeschehen und Osterberichte,* 2nd ed. (Göttingen: Vandenhoeck and Ruprecht, 1962), 93, 118–19, 242, 279.

45. Fuller, *Resurrection Narratives,* esp. 48–49, 179–82.

46. One concern to both Fuller and Grass is the term *objective* (for example, see Fuller, *Resurrection Narratives,* 202n48). Although Fuller apparently notes approvingly that the word refers to God's activity, he wants the eschatological implications to be made clear as well (33).

47. Besides Grass and Fuller, just a few examples of these scholars include Pannenberg, *Jesus—God and Man,* esp. 92; Moltmann, *Theology of Hope,* esp. 198; Jeremias, *New Testament Theology,* esp. 308, 310; Werner Georg Kümmel, *The Theology of the New Testament: According to Its Major Witnesses, Jesus—Paul—John* (Nashville, Tenn.: Abingdon, 1973), 103–4; Gerald O'Collins, *What Are They Saying about the Resurrection?* (New York: Paulist, 1978), 54–55; and Wilckens, *Resurrection,* 112, 119.

48. N. T. Wright, *The Resurrection of the Son of God,* Christian Origins and the Question of God, vol. 3 (Minneapolis: Fortress Press; London: SPCK, 2003).

49. For just a few of these scholars, see Thomas F. Torrance, *Space, Time, and Resurrection* (Grand Rapids, Mich.: Eerdmans, 1976), esp. ix–xi (following Karl Barth), 25–26, 87, 164, 171; Joseph A. Fitzmeyer, "The Ascension of Christ and Pentecost," *Theological Studies* 45 (1984): 423; Robert H. Gundry, *Soma in Biblical Theology with Emphasis on Pauline Anthropology* (Cambridge: Cambridge University Press, 1976), chs. 12 and 13; Stephen T. Davis, "'Seeing' the Risen Jesus," (126–47); and William P. Alston, "Biblical Criticism and the Resurrection" (148–83) in Davis, Kendall, and O'Collins, *The Resurrection*; William Lane Craig, *Assessing the New Testament Evidence for the Historicity of the Resurrection of* Jesus (Lewiston, N.Y.: Edwin Mellen, 1989), 325–47; with some qualifications,

see also Raymond E. Brown, *The Virginal Conception and Bodily Resurrection of Jesus* (New York: Paulist, 1973), 127–29, for instance.

50. Lüdemann with Özen, *What Really Happened to Jesus*, 103.

51. John Dominic Crossan and Jonathan L. Reed, *In Search of Paul: How Jesus's Apostle Opposed Rome's Empire with God's Kingdom* (San Francisco: HarperSanFrancisco, 2004), 6–10 (emphasis in original).

52. Ted Peters, Robert John Russell, and Michael Welker, eds., *Resurrection: Theological and Scientific Assessments* (Grand Rapids, Mich.: Eerdmans, 2002).

53. For examples, see the conclusions in the essays by Robert John Russell (25), Michael Welker (38), John Polkinghorne (49), Jeffrey P. Schloss (68–71), Peter Lampe (105–10), and Hans-Joachim Eckstein (116–23). At least the latter two authors also raise a few questions for the reconstitutionalist view (Lampe, 110–14; Eckstein, 120–21).

54. Wright, *The Resurrection of the Son of God*, xvii–xix, 31, 71, 82–83, 200–206.

55. Wright, *The Resurrection of the Son of God*, (on Paul) chs. 5–8, esp. 273, 314, 350–74; (on the other New Testament authors) chs. 9 and 10, esp. 424, 476-79.

56. As noted in Crossan's main lecture, "Bodily-Resurrection Faith," included in this volume as the appendix; see pp. 174, 176f., and 216n3 below.

57. Crossan, "Bodily-Resurrection Faith," 216n3, and as noted in his opening statement, pp. 24–26 above. Compare also John Dominic Crossan, "The Resurrection of Jesus in Its Jewish Context," *Neotestamentica* 37/1 (2003): 29–57, esp. 37–40, 46–49, 55.

58. For these ideas, see Crossan and Reed, *In Search of Paul*, 133–35, 173–74, 296, 341–45.

59. I am implying not that Lüdemann, Crossan, and Reed hold this supernatural external view themselves but that they are among those who acknowledge that both Paul and the Gospel authors taught that Jesus was raised from the dead and appeared bodily.

60. This could be for more than one reason. Maybe this is why some scholars do not state their own positions, though this sounds suspiciously like an argument from silence. However, it appears more likely that while agnosticism may not be the first option, it becomes a default setting when some scholars are pushed to provide an answer.

61. Of course, I am not claiming to have done an exhaustive study of the scholars who answer this question. Still, my survey was quite extensive.

5. The Epistemology of Resurrection Belief

1. See John Dominic Crossan, *The Birth of Christianity: Discovering What Happened to Jesus in the Years Immediately after the Resurrection of Jesus* (San Francisco: HarperSanFrancisco, 1998), xxxi.

2. Crossan, *The Birth of Christianity*, xvii, xviii.

3. N. T. Wright, *The Resurrection of the Son of God*, Christian Origins and the Question of God, vol. 3 (Minneapolis: Fortress Press; London: SPCK, 2003), 717.

4. Crossan, *The Birth of Christianity*, xviii.

5. Wright, *The Resurrection of the Son of God*, 686–87. His method is also concisely stated in Marcus J. Borg and N. T. Wright, *The Meaning of Jesus: Two Visions* (San Francisco: HarperSanFrancisco, 1998), ch. 2.

6. Wright, *The Resurrection of the Son of God*, 717.

7. R. Douglas Geivett, "Why I Believe in the Possibility of Miracles," in *Why I Am a Christian: Leading Thinkers Explain Why They Believe*, ed. Norman L. Geisler and Paul K. Hoffman (Grand Rapids, Mich.: Baker, 2001), 97–110.

8. Wright, *The Resurrection of the Son of God*, 718.

9. Ibid.

10. Wright, *The Resurrection of the Son of God*, 736. It is unclear exactly what he means by "first principles" here.

11. Wright, *The Resurrection of the Son of God*, 714, 717–18, 733, 736, and elsewhere.

12. Wright, *The Resurrection of the Son of God*, 714–18.

13. See, for example, his remarks in Paul Copan, ed., *Will the Real Jesus Please Stand Up?: A Debate between William Lane Craig and John Dominic Crossan* (Grand Rapids, Mich.: Baker Academic, 1998).

14. See Crossan, *The Birth of Christianity*, xxx, 182–208.

15. See pp. 24–25 above.

16. Crossan, *The Birth of Christianity*, xxx.

17. Ibid., xxxi.

18. R. Douglas Geivett, "The Epistemology of Resurrection Belief," 2005 Greer-Heard Forum audio compact disc. Available at http://www.greer-heard.com.

19. Geivett, "The Epistemology of Resurrection Belief." See John Hick, *An Interpretation of Religion: Human Responses to the Transcendent*, 2nd ed. (New Haven, Conn.: Yale University Press, 2005).

20. I have argued elsewhere that the evidence of natural theology is strong enough to justify belief in God; that this and other evidence indicates that God is powerfully motivated to participate in a direct way in the flow of human history, especially for the purposes of ameliorating the human condition; and that the historical evidence for the bodily resurrection of Jesus against this backdrop makes belief for us today in the bodily resurrection of Jesus a genuinely reasonable hope. For a recent development of this perspective, see my chapter "David Hume and a Cumulative Case Argument," in *In Defense of Natural Theology*, ed. James F. Sennett and Douglas Groothuis (Downers Grove, Ill.: InterVarsity, 2005).

6. The Gospel of Peter

1. Present knowledge of the content of the *GP* is limited since complete texts are no longer extant. The most extensive fragment of the *GP* begins at the end

of Jesus' trial and breaks off at the beginning of a description of a postresurrection appearance of Christ to the Twelve. The original *GP* may have included an account of Jesus' birth, childhood, youth, adult ministry, and so forth. This supposition is supported by Origen's claim (*In Matt.* 10.17) that the *GP* claimed that Joseph, Mary's husband, had children from a previous marriage.

2. See Helmut Koester, *Ancient Christian Gospels: Their History and Development* (London: SCM, 1990), 216–17. The complete Greek text of the Akhmim fragment appears in H. B. Swete, *The Apocryphal Gospel of Peter: The Greek Text of the Newly Discovered Fragment* (London: n.p., 1893); Erich Klostermann, *Apocrypha I: Reste des Petrusevangeliums, der Petrusapokalypse und des Kerygma Petri* (Berlin: De Gruyter, 1933); and M. G. Mara, *Évangile de Pierre: Introduction, texte critique, traduction, commentaire et index* (Paris: Gabalda, 1973). For an extensive, though now somewhat dated, bibliography on the *GP*, see James H. Charlesworth, *The New Testament Apocrypha and Pseudepigrapha: A Guide to Publications, with Excurses on Apocalypses* (Metuchen, N.J.: Scarecrow, 1987), 321–27. David Wright has suggested the possibility that Papyrus Egerton 2 is an early version of the *GP* ("Papyrus Egerton 2 [the *Unknown Gospel*]—Part of the *GP*?" *Second Century* 5 (1985–86): 129–50.

3. John Dominic Crossan, *Four Other Gospels: Shadows on the Contours of Canon* (Chicago: Winston, 1985), 132–34; Crossan, *The Cross That Spoke: The Origins of the Passion Narrative* (San Francisco: Harper & Row, 1988), 16–30; Crossan, *Historical Jesus: The Life of a Mediterranean Jewish Peasant* (New York: HarperCollins), 429.

4. Crossan acknowledged Koester's theory that Mark, John, and the *GP* may have independently relied on an earlier source. However, he insisted: "Composed by the fifties C.E., and possibly at Sepphoris in Galilee, it [Cross Gospel] is the single source of the intracanonical passion narratives" (Crossan, *Historical Jesus*, 429).

5. *Anchor Bible Dictionary*, s.v. "Peter, Gospel of."

6. See Crossan, *Four Other Gospels*, 138–48, esp. 138; Crossan, *Cross That Spoke*, 276. For a thorough introduction and critique of Midrash criticism, see Charles L. Quarles, *Midrash Criticism: Introduction and Appraisal* (Lanham, Md.: University Press of America, 1998).

7. See *GP* 1:2; 2:3 (2x); 3:6, 8; 4:10; 5:19; 6:21, 24; 9:35; 12:50 (3x); 14:59, 50.

8. Furthermore, the only precise verbal parallel between the two texts is the preposition ἐπί.

9. The Greek text of the *GP* utilized in this paper is E. Klostermann's text, which appears in full in various portions of Kurt Aland, *Synopsis Quattuor Evangeliorum: Locis parallelis evangeliorum apocryphorum et partum adhibitis edidit* (Stuttgart: Deutsche Bibelgesellschaft, 1986). Klostermann's text differs from that of Maria G. Mara, the most recent critical edition, in only a few conjectures. For a comparison of these two editions, see F. Neirynck, "Apocryphal Gospels and Mark," in *The New Testament in Early Christianity: La reception des écrits*

néotestamentaires dans le christianisme primitive, ed. Jean-Marie Sevrin (Leuven, Belgium: Leuven University, 1989), 140–41.

10. Inferences drawn from the precise wording of the *GP* must be tentative since the text of the Gospel that is presently available is most likely significantly different from the original text. See the research of Jay C. Treat, "The Two Manuscript Witnesses to the *GP*," in *Society of Biblical Literature Seminar Papers* (Atlanta: Scholars, 1990), 398–99.

11. Léon Vaganay, *L'Évangile de Pierre*, 2nd ed. (Paris: Gabalda, 1930).

12. Crossan, *Cross That Spoke*, 271.

13. Robert Gundry, *Matthew: A Commentary on His Handbook for a Mixed Church under Persecution* (Grand Rapids, Mich.: Eerdmans, 1994), 584.

14. Gundry, *Matthew*, 674–82.

15. See also *GP* 12:50, which uses the related term *female disciple* (μαθή-τρια).

16. Friedrich Blass, Albert Debrunner, and Robert Funk, *A Greek Grammar of the New Testament and Other Early Christian Literature* (Chicago: University of Chicago, 1961), 188, shows that μήποτε with the aorist indicative was used in classical Greek in an expression of apprehension. Both of the usages of the conjunction in the *GP* involve expressions of apprehension though, and Blass, Debrunner, and Funk note that these expressions of apprehension may depend on any verb, so one still must explain the grammatical inconsistency in the *GP*. In the New Testament, the conjunction never occurs with the aorist indicative.

17. The force of these arguments from redactional tendencies is somewhat diminished by the brevity of the fragments of the *GP* in comparison with Matthew. However, even if one draws the vocabulary and grammatical statistics from the Matthean Passion narrative alone, a couple of the terms and constructions are far more frequent in Matthew than in *GP*. The word μήποτε occurs five times (Matt. 27:64; 28:7,8,13,16) and the participle ἐλθόντες occurs four times (Matt. 27:33, 64; 28:11, 13) in chapters 27 and 28 of Matthew.

18. John P. Meier, *The Roots of the Problem and the Person*, vol. 1 of *A Marginal Jew: Rethinking the Historical Jesus* (New York: Doubleday, 1991), 117.

19. This evidence for dependency was probably the result of Peter's memory of Matthew's account. See Raymond Brown, *The Death of the Messiah: From Gethsemane to the Grave: A Commentary on the Passion Narratives in the Four Gospels* (New York: Doubleday, 1994), 2:1334–36.

20. Matthew changed the exclamation "Behold!" into a truly imperatival form. If Mark's ἴδε were imperatival rather than exclamatory, he would have used the accusative τὸν τόπον rather than the nominative form. Mark's expression results in an incomplete sentence that seems abrupt and harsh compared to Matthew's smoother Greek. Matthew uses the verb κεῖμαι only three times (Matt. 3:10; 5:14; 28:6). The uses in both Matthew 5:14 and 28:6 are redactional. However, the use in Matthew 3:10 is part of the double tradition. The verb appears six times in Luke's Gospel but never in Mark.

21. John Elliot, *1 Peter* (New York: Doubleday, 2000), 706–10; Bo Reicke, *The Disobedient Spirits and Christian Baptism: A Study of 1 Peter III.19 and Its Context* (Copenhagen: Munksgaard, 1946), 115–18; E. G. Selwyn, "Unsolved New Testament Problems: The Problem of the Authorship of I Peter," *Expository Times* 59 (1947): 340.

22. Crossan, *Four Other Gospels*, 166. In his later work after reading Dalton's work, Crossan acknowledged that "it may not even be present in the New Testament." He argued that the doctrine was supported by the statement of the Apostle's Creed, "He descended into hell" (Crossan, *Historical Jesus*, 388). However, Philip Schaff has demonstrated that the earliest version of the Apostle's Creed did not contain the reference to Christ's descent into Hades. The reference first appeared in the creed of Aquilcia in 390 C.E. See Philip Schaff, *The Greek and Latin Creeds*, vol. 2 of *The Creeds of Christendom* (Grand Rapids, Mich.: Baker, 1996), 46, 54.

23. W. J. Dalton, *Christ's Proclamation to the Spirits: A Study of 1 Peter 3:18–4:6* (Rome: Pontifical Biblical Institute, 1989).

24. Crossan, *Historical Jesus*, 388.

25. See esp. W. J. Dalton, *Christ's Proclamation to the Spirits*, 26. See also *Luther's Works* 30:113; J. P. Jenson, *Laeren om Kristi Nedfahrt til de Döde* (Copenhagen: n.p., 1903), 181; K. Gschwind, *Die Niederfahrt Christi in die Unterwelt. Ein Beitrag zur Exegese des Neuen Testaments und zur Geschichte des Taufsymbols*, NTabh 2 (Münster: Aschendorff, 1911), 88–89, 97–114; J. N. D. Kelly, *The Epistles of Peter and of Jude*, HNTC (New York: Harper and Row, 1969), 175–76; Elliot, *1 Peter*, 647–62; J. Ramsey Michaels, *1 Peter*, WBC 49 (Waco, Tex.: Word, 1988), 205–11; and Peter H. Davids, *The First Epistle of Peter*, NICNT (Grand Rapids, Mich.: Eerdmans, 1990), 140–41.

26. Crossan (*Historical Jesus*, 432) stated that 1st Peter was "written from Rome and pseudepigraphically attributed to Peter . . . around 110 C.E."

27. Mara, *Évangile de Pierre*, suggests that this reference to the apocalyptic imagery of Revelation is part of a string of such allusions. The glorious Christ's ability to break the seven seals closely matches Revelation 5:1 (170). The loud voice from heaven on the Lord's Day parallels John's experience in Revelation 1:10. Revelation 11:11-12, like the *GP*, describes a loud voice, a resurrection, and an ascent to heaven (177–78). Revelation 10:1-3 describes a heavenly figure of enormous size (183–84). See also Brown, *Death of the Messiah*, 2:1296.

28. Although the name "century" implies a group of one hundred soldiers, Roman centuries typically consisted of eighty soldiers. See *Anchor Bible Dictionary*, s.v. "Roman Army."

29. Roman law stated that a testament was to be sealed by the testator and by six witnesses. See *Theological Dictionary of the New Testament*, s.v. "σφραγίς." The number of seals related to the number of people authenticating the document.

30. Several others have independently recognized the significance of this reference for dating the document. See also Alan Kirk, "Examining Priorities:

Another Look at the *GP*'s Relationship to the New Testament Gospels," *New Testament Studies* 40 (1994): 593.N. T. Wright, *The Resurrection of the Son of God*, Christian Origins and the Question of God, vol. 3 (Minneapolis: Fortress Press; London: SPCK, 2003), 594, lists this expression, along with seven other elements, as "conclusive evidence for the *GP* being later and more developed than the canonical parallels."

31. Crossan, *Historical Jesus*, 429, states that the Cross Gospel was composed by the 50s probably in Sepphoris of Galilee. Other scholars have pointed out additional historical problems in the *GP* (Brown, *Death of the Messiah*, 2:1232).

32. See Matthew 3:16 and Luke 3:21.

33. See Mark 1:11 and Luke 3:22.

34. See Quarles, "The Protevangelium of James as an Alleged Parallel to Creative Historiography in the Synoptic Birth Narratives" *Bulletin for Biblical Research* 8 (1988): 139–49, esp. 144–49, and Brown, *Death of the Messiah*, 2:1135.

35. *GP* 9:37. In the Greek text of the *GP*, this prepositional phrase appears first in the participial clause in a position of emphasis. This serves to express the author's astonishment at the mysterious movement of the stone.

36. *GP* 10:39-40.

37. Crossan (*Historical Jesus*, 389) describes the cross as a "huge cruciform procession" of individuals who were resurrected along with Jesus. See also Crossan, *Who Killed Jesus?* 197. Most scholars have not been convinced by Crossan's interpretation of the speaking cross. See Wright, *Resurrection*, 595.

38. *GP* 10:39-42.

39. I am indebted to doctoral student Bevin J. Creel for pointing out these second-century parallels to the *GP* first compiled in Vaganay, *L'Évangile de Pierre*, 300.

40. *Epist. Apost.* 16.

41. *Apoc. Pet.* 1.

42. Later, the author explained the details of his extensive allegory. *Shep. Herm.* 89.8 identifies the lofty figure as the Son of God. *Shep. Herm.* 90.1 identifies the tower as the church.

43. The bulk of 4 Ezra was written around 100 C.E. However, this text is part of a Christian introduction added in the middle or latter half of the third century. See B. M. Metzger, "The Fourth Book of Ezra," in *Old Testament Pseudepigrapha*, ed. James Charlesworth (New York: Doubleday, 1983), 1:520.

44. Petronius was a common Roman name. However, it seems more than a coincidence that the centurion has a name so similar to the putative author of the Gospel. See Brown, *Death of the Messiah*, 2:1294.

45. In Crossan's view, Matthew drew the reference to "the next day" (τῇ ἐπαύριον), which he used to indicate the time of the Jew's request for a guard from *GP* 9:34. Crossan commented: "This was not very wise, since the tomb was then unguarded one whole night" (*Four Other Gospels*, 151). "Not very wise"

is a definite understatement. Matthew clearly has apologetic concerns. To borrow the guard from the *GP* but then destroy the very purpose for its presence at the tomb by indiscriminately borrowing a temporal reference from later in his source portrays Matthew as terribly stupid. It is more reasonable to assume that Matthew's commitment to historicity guided his writing. His account left the tomb unguarded for several hours because the Jewish leaders' concern over the disappearance of Jesus' body was an afterthought. Matthew's account of the closing of the tomb better fits with Jewish burial customs. The *GP* has the tomb left open overnight and the corpse thus exposed to scavengers of all kinds. Alan Kirk notes that the chronology of events in the *GP* results in "the incongruous picture of Joseph carefully washing, wrapping, and laying the body in his own tomb, only to walk away leaving the entrance agape!" (Kirk, "Examining Priorities," 590).

46. See Vaganay, *L'Évangile de Pierre*, 275–78, for additional Petrine alterations to the Matthean narrative that were driven by apologetic concerns.

47. A similar conclusion was reached by Joel B. Green, "The Gospel of Peter: Source for a Pre-canonical Passion Narrative?" *Zeitschrift für die neutestamentliche Wissenschaft und die Kunde der älteren Kirche* 78 (1987): 293–301, esp. 300–301. However, Green suggests that, in Matthew, Pilate refused to give the Jews a guard. See also Christian Mauer, "The Gospel of Peter," in *Gospels and Related Writings*, vol. 1 of *New Testament Apocrypha*, ed. Wilhelm Schneemelcher (Philadelphia: Westminster, 1963), 181.

48. See Quarles, *Midrash Criticism*, 115–16.

49. Crossan, *Historical Jesus*, 392: "If, as I maintain, Jesus' followers had fled upon his arrest and knew nothing whatsoever about his fate beyond the fact of crucifixion itself, the horror was not only that he had been executed but that he might not even have been decently buried." Even without reliable Gospel testimony, Jewish legislation regarding the treatment of corpses, and evidence of Jewish burial practices from archaeology, Josephus and Philo create difficulties for the theory that Jesus was left unburied. However, Crossan is aware of these difficulties. See Crossan, *Who Killed Jesus? Exploring the Roots of Anti-Semitism in the Gospel Story of the Death of Jesus* (San Francisco: HarperSanFrancisco, 1995), 163–69.

50. Wright explored the possibility that the account of the guard at the tomb may have been made up by an early Christian, but he suggested that "it seems more likely that it goes back to some kind of well-rooted memory" (*The Resurrection of the Son of God*, 637). Wright later argues that the essential historicity of the account of the guards and the bribe is more plausible than alternative theories, particularly the complex development of the account suggested by Rudolph Bultmann (638–40).

7. The Resurrection: Faith or History

1. See Alan F. Segal, *Life after Death: A History of the Afterlife in Western Religion* (New York: Doubleday, 2004).

2. Alan F. Segal, *Paul the Convert: The Apostasy and Apostolate of Saul the Pharisee* (New Haven, Conn.: Yale University Press, 1997); and Alan F. Segal, *Rebecca's Children: Judaism and Christianity in the Roman World* (Cambridge, Mass.: Harvard University Press, 1986).

3. Defenses of a single-body hypothesis are legion. A very interesting article maintaining two bodies is to be found in Richard Carrier, "The Spiritual Body of Christ and the Legend of the Empty Tomb," in *The Empty Tomb: Jesus Beyond the Grave*, ed. Robert M. Price and Jeffery Jay Lowder (Amherst, N.Y.: Prometheus Books, 2005), 105–232. This is a long, programmatic article that deserves to be studied in great detail.

4. See my *Paul the Convert*.

5. Ralph P. Martin, *Carmen Christi: Philippians 2:5-11 in Recent Interpretation and in the Setting of Early Christian Worship*, rev. ed. (Grand Rapids, Mich.: Eerdmans, 1983), from the Cambridge University Press 1967 edition. See also James Sanders, "Dissent Tradition," *Journal of Biblical Literature*.

6. The other candidate, Peter's Pentecost discourse, in Acts 3 seems to me to have undergone much more editing before reaching written form. See J. A. T. Robinson, "The Most Primitive Christology of All," in *Twelve New Testament Studies* (London: SCM, 1962), reprinted from *Journal of Theological Studies* 7 (1956): 177–89; and Richard Zehnle, *Peter's Pentecost Discourse: Tradition and Lukan Reinterpretation in Peter's Speeches of Acts 2 and Three* (Nashville: Abingdon, 1971).

7. The bibliography on the Pauline and post-Pauline hymns in Philippians 2:6-11 and Colossians 1:15-20 appears endless. See E. Schillebeeckx, *Jesus: An Experiment in Christology* (New York: Seabury, 1979); M. Hengel, "Hymn and Christology," in E. A. Livingstone, ed., *Studia Biblica* 1972, 173–97, reprinted in Hengel, *Between Jesus and Paul* (Philadelphia: Fortress Press, 1983), 78–96; J. Murphy O'Connor, "Christological Anthropology in Phil. 2:6-11," in *Revue biblique* 83 (1976): 25–50; and D. Georgi, "Der vorpaulinische Hymnus Phil. 2:6-11," in *Zeit und Geschichte, Dankesgabe an Rudolf Bultmann*, ed. E. Dinkler (Tübingen: Mohr, 1964), 263–93, esp. 291 for bibliography. As David Balch reminds me, Käsemann emphasizes that Paul's metaphoric use of the body and its separate parts is characteristic of paraenetic sections, emphasizing the relationship between the believer and the risen Lord. See Eduard Schweitzer's discussion in *Theological Dictionary of the New Testament*, 7:1073.

8. See Segal, *Paul the Convert*.

9. See my *Two Powers in Heaven: Early Rabbinic Reports about Christianity and Gnosticism*, 2nd. ed. (Boston: Brill, 2002), 33–158, esp. 68–73, and now L. W. Hurtado, *One God, One Lord: Early Christian Devotion and Ancient Jewish Monotheism* (Philadelphia: Fortress Press, 1988), 377–91.

10. Scholars like Kim who want to ground all of Paul's thought in a single ecstatic conversion experience, which they identify with Luke's accounts of Paul's conversion, are reticent to accept this passage as a fragment from Christian liturgy because to do so would destroy its value as Paul's personal revelatory experience.

But there is no need to decide whether the passage is originally Paul's (hence, received directly through the "Damascus revelation") since ecstatic language normally is derived from traditions current within the religious group. Christian mystics use Christian language, Muslim mystics use the languages developed for mysticism in Islam, and no mystic is ever confused by another religion's mysticism unless it is the conscious and explicit intent of the mystic's vision to do so. See R. C. Zaehner, *Hinduism and Muslim Mysticism* (New York: Schocken, 1969); see also Steven Katz, "Language, Epistemology, and Mysticism," in *Mysticism and Philosophical Analysis*, ed. Steven Katz (Oxford: Oxford University Press, 1978). In this case, the language is not even primarily Christian. The basic language is from Jewish mysticism, although the subsequent exegesis about the identification of the Christ with the figure on the throne is Christian; the vision of God enthroned is the goal of Jewish mystical speculation.

11. Nils A. Dahl, *The Crucified Messiah* (Minneapolis: Augsburg, 1974); James D. G. Dunn, *Baptism in the Holy Spirit: A Re-examination of the New Testament Teaching on the Gift of the Spirit in Relation to Pentecostalism Today* (Philadelphia: Westminster, 1977).

12. Jonah Steinberg is finding evidence that the rabbis sought transformation too and thought of themselves as angels on earth.

13. A. J. M. Wedderburn, "The Problem of the Denial of the Resurrection in 1 Corinthians XV," *Novum Testamentum* 23 (1981): 229–41.

14. The quotation may extend to the word *other.*

15. Like me, Peter Lampe suggests that Paul is arguing against Greek notions of immortality and replacing them with his own. See Peter Lampe, "Paul's Concept of a Spiritual Body," in *Resurrection: Theological and Scientific Assessments*, ed. Ted Peters, Robert John Russell, and Michael Welker (Grand Rapids, Mich.: Eerdmans, 2002), 103–14.

16. Gk., "fallen asleep."

17. Rudolf Bultmann, "The New Testament and Mythology," in *New Testament and Mythology and Other Basic Writings*, selected, edited, and translated by Schubert M. Ogden (Philadelphia: Fortress, 1984), 40 (German original 1941).

8. The Historicity of the Resurrection

1. N. T. Wright, *The Resurrection of the Son of God*, Christian Origins and the Question of God, vol. 3 (Minneapolis: Fortress Press; London: SPCK, 2003), 685.

2. Ibid., 687.

3. Ibid., 694.

4. Ibid., 695.

5. Kirsopp Lake, *The Historical Evidence for the Resurrection of Jesus* (London: Williams and Norgate, 1907), 29–33.

6. Ibid., 708. See William Lane Craig, *Assessing the New Testament Evidence for the Historicity of the Resurrection of Jesus*, 3rd ed., Studies in the Bible and Early Christianity 16 (Toronto: Edwin Mellen, 2004), ch. 5 and appendix B.

7. Wright, *The Resurrection of the Son of God*, ch. 13, sec. 3.

8. Ibid., 612.

9. Craig, *Assessing*, 256–60.

10. Wright, *The Resurrection of the Son of God*, 695.

11. On cognitive dissonance, see ibid., 697–801; on grace, see ibid., 701–6.

12. Ibid., 707.

13. Ibid., 710.

14. Ibid., 716.

15. Ibid., 717.

16. Ibid., 710–16.

17. Ibid., 718.

9. The Future of the Resurrection

1. Mark Ralls, "Reclaiming Heaven," *Christian Century* 121, no. 25 (December 14, 2004): 34.

2. Carl E. Braaten, *The Future of God* (New York: Harper, 1969), 75.

3. John Dominic Crossan, *Jesus: A Revolutionary Biography* (San Francisco: Harper, 1994), xi.

4. Ibid., 199.

5. Ibid., xi–xii. In a subsequent book, Crossan writes: "My new *method* is an interdisciplinary combination of anthropological, historical, archeological, and literary disciplines." John Dominic Crossan, *The Birth of Christianity* (San Francisco: Harper, 1998), x.

6. Crossan, *Jesus*, xiii, 83, 145.

7. Ibid., 198 (emphasis in original); see John Dominic Crossan, *The Historical Jesus: The Life of a Mediterranean Jewish Peasant* (San Francisco: HarperSanFrancisco, 1991), 421.

8. Crossan, *Jesus*, 69.

9. Ibid., 71.

10. Ibid., 85.

11. Ibid., 82.

12. Crossan, *The Historical Jesus*, 341.

13. Crossan, *Jesus*, 95.

14. Crossan, *The Historical Jesus*, 404.

15. Ibid., 399.

16. Crossan, *The Birth of Christianity*, 524 (emphasis in original).

17. Ibid., xi.

18. N. T. Wright, *The Resurrection of the Son of God*, Christian Origins and the Question of God, vol. 3 (Minneapolis: Fortress Press; London: SPCK, 2003), 8 (emphasis in original).

19. Ibid., 696 (emphasis in original).

20. For this portion of my analysis, I am dependent on Robert H. Smith, "(W)right Thinking on the Resurrection?" *Dialog* 43, no. 3 (Fall 2004): 244–51.

21. Ibid., 612.

22. Ibid., 19.

23. Ibid., 712 (emphasis in original).

24. Ibid., 18. For a thorough critique of the Troeltschian overuse of the principle of analogy in historical research, see Wolfhart Pannenberg, *Basic Questions in Theology* (Minneapolis: Fortress Press, 1970–1971), 1:38–53.

25. Wright, *The Resurrection of the Son of God*, 737.

26. Ibid., 210.

27. Ibid., 336.

28. Smith, "(W)right Thinking," 250.

29. Wright, *The Resurrection of the Son of God*, 733.

30. Crossan, *The Birth of Christianity*, xxi. Robert W. Funk similarly argues that the early church distorted Jesus and that orthodox Christianity is a perversion that only the historian can set right. A scholarly "reconstruction" of Jesus will liberate "the gospel of Jesus" from "the Jesus of the gospels," and then "Jesus rather than the Bible or the creeds becomes the norm by which other views and practices are to be measured." Robert W. Funk, *Honest to Jesus: Jesus for a New Millennium* (San Francisco: Harper, 1996), 19, 300–301. If for orthodox Christianity the scriptural Jesus is traditionally and currently normative, one wonders just how a descripturized Jesus reconstructed by a historian could become the norm for anybody. Yet the descripturized Jesus appeals to Jesus Seminar proponents because he is more realistic and more egalitarian than the fantastic Christ of the orthodox church, who endorses hierarchy.

31. Wright, *The Resurrection of the Son of God*, 718.

32. Crossan, *Birth of Christianity*, xxx (emphasis in original).

33. Ibid., xxx–xi.

34. Margaret R. Miles, *The Word Made Flesh: A History of Christian Thought* (Oxford: Blackwell, 2005), 26–27. Helmer Ringgren examines ancient claims of dying and rising gods, such as Baal, Tammuz, Adonis, and Osiris. He finds their myths associated with the agricultural cycle and not connected in any way to what would become the distinctively Christian understanding of resurrection. Similar ideas did not pervade and may not even have existed in other religions. Helmer Ringgren, "Resurrection," in *Encyclopedia of Religion*, 2d ed.

35. Arland J. Hultgren, *The Rise of Normative Christianity* (Minneapolis: Fortress Press, 1994), 112.

36. Günther Bornkam, *Jesus of Nazareth* (New York: Harper, 1960), 183.

37. Luke Timothy Johnson, *The Real Jesus: The Misguided Quest for the Historical Jesus and the Truth of the Traditional Gospels* (San Francisco: Harper, 1996), 50.

38. Crossan's definition of *eschatology*, in *Birth of Christianity*, 282, is adequate: "Eschatology is divine radicality. It is a fundamental negation of the present world's normalcy based on some transcendental mandate." When applied to ethics, eschatology stands in critical judgment of oppressive systems. Crossan

writes: "*Ethical eschatology* (or ethicism) negates the world by actively protesting and nonviolently resisting a system judged to be evil, unjust and violent." *Birth*, 284 (emphasis in original). So far, so good. Yet, for some reason, Crossan identifies eschatology in its apocalyptic form with a "genocidal heart" and, at least to this reader, unnecessarily de-eschatologizes the resurrection destiny of Jesus. If Jesus' person has no eschatological grounding, then neither does his ethics.

39. N. T. Wright, *Jesus and the Victory of God*, Christian Origins and the Question of God, vol. 2 (Minneapolis: Fortress Press; London: SPCK, 1996), 50–51. Apocalyptic is "*not* the 'darkening scenario of an imminent end to the world' but the radical subversion of the present world order" (57).

40. "When now the Christians preached that God *had* raised Jesus from the dead, this meant that God in the case of this One unique person had already accomplished the resurrection process expected at the end of time." Ulrich Wilckens, *Resurrection*, trans. A. M. Stewart (Louisville, Ky.: Westminster John Knox, 1978), 20 (emphasis in original). In Jesus' resurrection, "God has inaugurated eschatological existence," writes Reginald H. Fuller in *The Formation of the Resurrection Narratives* (1971; reprint, Minneapolis: Fortress Press, 1980), 181. Eschatology itself transcends history, so it cannot fully be history. Yet, history can anticipate it. Fuller continues: "What can happen within this age is a certain event which is perfectly explicable as a historical event, yet is a disclosure of the transcendent and eschatological to the eye of faith."

41. Wolfhart Pannenberg, "Focal Essay: The Revelation of God in Jesus of Nazareth," in *Theology as History*, vol. 3 of *New Frontiers in Theology*, ed. James M. Robinson and John B. Cobb Jr. (New York: Harper, 1967), 112–13 (emphasis in original).

42. Ibid., 114 (emphasis in original).

43. Ibid., 126–27.

44. Ibid., 128. Not everyone ties faith to history so closely. Luke Timothy Johnson, for example, holds that "the resurrection experience, then, is not simply something that happened to Jesus but is equally something that happened to Jesus' followers. The sharing in Jesus' new life through the power of the Holy Spirit is an essential dimension of the resurrection." *Real Jesus*, 134. This explains the birth of the church. Yet Johnson has reasons to deny an essential role to history: "By definition the resurrection elevates Jesus beyond the merely human; he is no longer defined by time and space. . . . The Christian claim concerning the resurrection in the strong sense is simply not 'historical'. The problem in this case is, however, not with the reality of the resurrection. The problem lies in history's limited mode of knowing." *Real Jesus*, 136.

45. Gary R. Habermas, *The Risen Jesus and Future Hope* (New York: Rowan & Littlefield, 2003), viii.

46. Wolfhart Pannenberg, *Theology and the Philosophy of Science*, trans. Francis McDonagh (Louisville, Ky.: Westminster John Knox, 1976), 310. Pannenberg writes: "The truth of the Christian tradition can function only as a hypothesis in

any theology which proceeds scientifically." *Theology,* 261. On the provisionality of dogma, see Pannenberg, "What Is a Dogmatic Statement?" in *Basic Questions,* 1:181–210.

47. Wolfhart Pannenberg, *Jesus—God and Man,* trans. Lewis L. Wilkins and Duane A. Priebe, 2nd ed. (Louisville, Ky.: Westminster John Knox, 1977), 66–73.

48. Wolfhart Pannenberg, *Systematic Theology,* trans. Geoffrey W. Bromily (Grand Rapids, Mich.: Eerdmans, 1991–1998), 3:627. See Ted Peters, "Clarity of the Part versus Meaning of the Whole," in *Beginning with the End: God, Science, and Wolfhart Pannenberg,* ed. Carol Rausch Albright and Joel Haugen (Chicago: Open Court, 1997), 289–302.

49. Robert John Russell, "Bodily Resurrection, Eschatology, and Scientific Cosmology," in *Resurrection: Theological and Scientific Assessments,* ed. Ted Peters, Robert John Russell, and Michael Welker (Grand Rapids, Mich.: Eerdmans, 2002), 3–30.

50. John Polkinghorne, 1993–1994 Gifford Lectures, in John Polkinghorne, *The Faith of a Physicist* (Princeton, N.J.: Princeton University Press, 1994), or John Polkinghorne, *Science and Christian Belief* (London: SPCK, 1994), 167.

Appendix: Bodily-Resurrection Faith

1. John Dominic Crossan, "The Parables of Jesus," *Interpretation* (2002): 247–59.

2. John Dominic Crossan, *Jesus: A Revolutionary Biography* (San Francisco: HarperSanFrancisco, 1994), 197.

3. I was already thinking along those same lines in the opening lecture, "The Resurrection of Jesus in Its Jewish Context," to the Annual Meeting of the New Testament Society of South Africa at Potchefstroom, South Africa, on Tuesday, April 9, 2002. It was later published in *Neotestamentica* 37/1 (2003): 29–57.

4. This first part presumes, summarizes, and reorganizes earlier responses to Tom's book (N. T. Wright, *The Resurrection of the Son of God,* Christian Origins and the Question of God, vol. 3 [Minneapolis: Fortress Press; London: SPCK, 2003]) at the Annual Meetings of the Evangelical Philosophical Society, Atlanta, Saturday, November 11, 2003, and the Evangelical Theological Society, San Antonio, TX, Friday, November 19, 2004.

5. Wright, *The Resurrection of the Son of God,* 477, 612.

6. Ibid., 109–10.

7. Ibid., 150.

8. Wright calls it "a mutation from within the worldview of the second-Temple Jews" (225) or "mutations within the Jewish worldview" (372). He describes this Christian "mutation" as "sudden and dramatic" (9), "extraordinary" (175), "new" (206), "fresh and unique" (472–73), "dramatic" (476), "striking and consistent" (686).

9. See, for examples, ibid., 8, 10 or 696, 706.

10. See, for examples, ibid., 372, 395, 415, 448, 473, 568, 681.

11. See ibid., 360, and also, for a few other examples, 240, 271, 273, 310, 320, 360, 373, 436–37, 439, 448, 450, 475, 478, 522, 547.

12. See the discussion of this theology in John Dominic Crossan and Jonathan L. Reed, *In Search of Paul: How Jesus's Apostle Opposed Rome's Empire with God's Kingdom* (San Francisco: HarperSanFrancisco, 2004). See such earlier works as Simon R. F. Price, *Rituals and Power: The Roman Imperial Cult in Asia Minor* (Cambridge: Cambridge University Press, 1984); Paul Zanker, *The Power of Images in the Age of Augustus,* trans. Alan Shapiro, Jerome Lectures: Sixteenth Series (Ann Arbor: University of Michigan Press, 1990); Karl Galinsky, *Augustan Culture: An Interpretive Introduction* (Princeton, N.J.: Princeton University Press, 1996); and these volumes edited by Richard A. Horsley: *Paul and Empire: Religion and Power in Roman Imperial Society* (Harrisburg, Pa.: Trinity Press International, 1997); *Paul and Politics: Ekklesia, Israel, Imperium, Interpretation—Essays in Honor of Krister Stendahl* (Harrisburg, Pa.: Trinity Press International, 2000); *Paul and the Roman Imperial Order* (Harrisburg, Pa.: Trinity Press International, 2004).

13. Ramsay MacMullen, *Romanization in the Time of Augustus* (New Haven, Conn.: Yale University Press, 2003), ix–x, 134: "Roman civilization eventually appeared everywhere, as one single thing, so far as it was ever achieved. The degree of achievement, however imperfect, remains a thing of wonder, familiar to everyone. . . . Never, however, was there greater progress made toward one single way of life, a thing to be fairly called 'Roman civilization of the Empire,' than in that lifetime of Augustus. . . . The natives would be taught, if it was not plain enough on its face, that they could better rise into the ranks of the master race by reforming themselves—by talking, dressing, looking, and in every way resembling Romans. They would and did respond as ambition directed. They pulled Roman civilization to them—to their homes, their families, their world."

14. See, for example, these statements from *The Resurrection of the Son of God*: "Resurrection was from the beginning a revolutionary doctrine" (138); "Jesus as *kyrios* [is] the implicit contrast with Caesar" (568); "The resurrection always was a highly political doctrine" (243). I also agree with Tom on his understanding of Paul's epistle to the Philippians as an "overtly counter-imperial theology: Jesus is lord and saviour, and by strong implication, easily audible to residents in a Roman colony, Caesar is not" (225); and again, "In Philippians 2.6-11, what is said of Jesus echoes remarkably what was being said, in the imperial ideology of the time, about Caesar" (569). Finally, I agree with him that "we must not confuse *derivation* with *confrontation*" for that common entitlement (729).

– Index –

Index